STOLEN FIGS

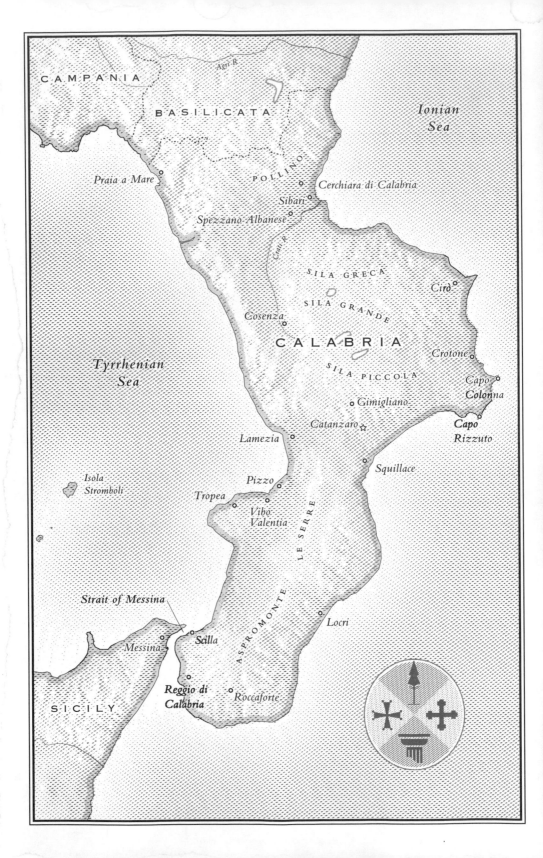

CAMPANIA

BASILICATA

Agri R.

*Ionian
Sea*

POLLINO

Praia a Mare

Cerchiara di Calabria

Sibari

Spezzano-Albanese

Cau R.

SILA GRECA

Cirò

SILA GRANDE

Cosenza

C A L A B R I A

Crotone

SILA PICCOLA

Capo
Colonna

*Tyrrhenian
Sea*

Gimigliano

Catanzaro ☆

**Capo
Rizzuto**

Lamezia

Squillace

*Isola
Stromboli*

Pizzo

LE SERRE

Tropea

*Vibo
Valentia*

Strait of Messina

Locri

Scilla

ASPROMONTE

Messina

**Reggio di
Calabria**

Roccaforte

S I C I L Y

STOLEN FIGS

AND OTHER ADVENTURES

IN CALABRIA

MARK ROTELLA

North Point Press

A division of Farrar, Straus and Giroux

North Point Press
A division of Farrar, Straus and Giroux
19 Union Square West, New York 10003

Copyright © 2003 by Mark Rotella
Distributed in Canada by Douglas & McIntyre Ltd.
Printed in the United States of America
First edition, 2003

Photographs of Calabria reprinted with the kind permission of G. Chiarella (chiarella.g@libero.it)
Map of Calabria by Steven Arcella

Library of Congress Cataloging-in-Publication Data
Rotella, Mark
    Stolen figs, and other adventures in Calabria / by Mark Rotella.— 1st ed.
    p.   cm.
    Includes bibliographical references.
    ISBN 0-86547-627-6 (alk. paper)
    1. Calabria (Italy)—Description and travel.   2. Rotella, Mark,
1967—Journeys—Italy—Calabria.   I. Title.

DG975.C15R64 2003
914.5'780493—dc21

                                                2003042052

Designed by Abby Kagan

www.fsgbooks.com

1   3   5   7   9   10   8   6   4   2

For Martha

CONTENTS

PART I: GIMIGLIANO

PART II: NORTH TO THE EDGE OF THE WORLD

PART III: GIMIGLIANO

❧

PART IV: A JOURNEY SOUTH

❧

PART V: GIMIGLIANO

Part I

GIMIGLIANO

THE ROAD TO GIMIGLIANO

THE DOORS of the train opened at Naples. Shrill announcements twittered over the station PA system, babies cried, people argued, and beyond the tracks cars honked amid the din of Vespas and motorcycles. The passengers getting off the train squeezed their way past those trying to get on. Train workers, passengers, and merchants communicated with one another as if yelling across bleachers at a football game. The smell of fried *zeppole* and calzone filled the station. Vendors selling ice cream, water, and wine appeared and roamed the aisles, knocking on the doors of first-class air-conditioned compartments. When no one looked up, they opened the Plexiglas doors themselves. They were followed by Gypsy women begging for change, musicians playing guitars and accordions, and packs of children—many with piercing green eyes.

My father and I, who had boarded in Rome, watched as the mob of people squeezed their way down the aisles, looking for seats. We were finally on our way to Gimigliano, in Calabria, the homeland of my grandparents.

I had been staying with my father in Perugia, where he was

sculpting stone, during the month of July. I had heard so many stories about Calabria, where his parents had been poor farmers. I suggested that we visit their village, but he shrugged off the idea. "That
was decades ago," he said. "Why go back to the past?"

"Why not?" I asked. "Anyway, what's so bad about the past?"

"Nothing," he said dismissively. Going back, I knew, would remind him of his mother, who had died the year before, and his father, who had died eight years earlier. My father pushed a hand
through his full head of hair, a soft mixture of jet black and silver. "I
don't even know if we have family there anymore. They've probably
all died—or moved to Torino or Milan."

"Well, why not find out? What's it gonna hurt?" I had already
decided to go even if he didn't, but I knew the trip would be better—would feel more appropriate—if we went together. "I know
you're at least a little curious. Anyway, look at it as the one time
you'll be able to take this trip with your son."

My father laughed. "Jesus, you're such a romantic." He, too, is a
romantic, but he wouldn't give in just then. He wouldn't admit that
he might enjoy it. He fits the Calabrese stereotype of being stubborn, or having a *testa dura*—a hard head. My parents had taken my
sister and me to Italy several times before, but this would be the first
trip we had made south of Rome.

He looked at his watch. I knew what he was thinking. Our
stomachs were on the same schedule.

"C'mon, let's get some dinner," he said. And with that, we
walked to the trattoria up the street from the apartment we were
renting.

At fifty-five, my father was fit and strong. Although he's a head
shorter than I am, everything about him is grand: his nose, his eyes,
his smile. And he eats with purpose and intensity.

By the time we finished dinner and a liter of wine, he had agreed
to take a two-day trip south, returning to Perugia on Sunday. Two
days seemed like no time. But it didn't really matter how long we
stayed: I would finally see Calabria, and I would see it with my father.

The compartments filled. New passengers greeted the old ones and, like next-door neighbors, fell into conversations about the weather—hot even for July—and the recent strike of railroad concession workers. I unbuttoned my shirt and leaned out the window, trying to find a breeze. A man in a light brown suit claimed a seat across from us and joined me at the open window. He turned and greeted me with an exhausted smile, his thick mustache glistening with sweat. The train coasted out of the station. The thunk of windows sliding open sounded throughout the car. Passengers flocked to the windows, letting their shirts fill with air.

As the train, an express, left old Naples, the yellow and pink seventeenth-century buildings of the historic center gave way to shoddy, colorless Mussolini-era tenements, which then yielded to the cinder-block Soviet-style structures of the 1970s, whose facades crumbled beneath their sagging balconies, then to suburbs, the Bay of Naples opening up on the west. Blue-and-white fishing skiffs lined the shore, their nets spread out to dry. To the east, Vesuvius's gaping crater broke through the smog.

This was Campania, and as the train continued south, I saw how the sirocco winds from Africa had dried the soil and left the bushes and trees scrubby and desiccated. Olive trees, fig trees, and grapevines—the only vegetation that can thrive there—lined the hills. The train passed villages and peasant farms, each smaller than the last. All the buildings were simple structures, painted pale yellow, olive green, or burnt red. All the shutters were closed, shading interiors that were most likely, in true Italian form, immaculately clean and organized.

This was the gateway to the south, the passage to Calabria.

Already I saw the difference. Campania's hills are not the rolling hills of Tuscany. Absent are wide-eyed pink travelers with their sulking kids. Absent are streets congested with souvenir shops. Absent are packed tour buses. Absent are crowded museums with their endless lines. Absent are English ex-pats and their summer villas. Absent are bilingual waiters and shop ladies. Absent are tourist menus in fourteen languages.

Within the train compartments and along the hallways, conversations grew comfortably loud; gestures became grander, more ebullient. An older woman (from Cosenza, Calabria, I found out) offered up nuts and fruits. A dapper Neapolitan pensioner talked local politics in a harsh dialect. The mustachioed man in the brown suit stood up to demonstrate the size of the fig trees in his backyard, his hands forming around each imaginary branch. The woman smiled and held up a white fig that she had picked from her sister's garden.

"My God," my father said as if to himself, "I've been all along here. I remember this." He eased back in his seat and stared out the window, mouth open. The right corner of his mouth turned up in a smile.

I went to the *carrozza ristorante*, the dining car, to get us some bottled water. Outside the open windows, the train hugged the ocean, the slate-blue water crashing against the rocks and boulders. Occasionally the jagged coast receded to an alcove of sandy shores. The sunbathers on these secluded beaches, reachable only by boat, didn't even register the train speeding above, but only stared out to sea, past their anchored motorboats rocking gently on the waves.

"The water is so blue, so light that it appears gray," someone said to me in Sicilian.

I turned to a deeply tanned man who shot me a smile almost as wide as his panama hat. The Sicilian version of a well-off, relaxed Florida retiree, he had unbuttoned his brightly patterned yellow-and-red batik shirt, exposing a bare chest the color of a ripe tomato; two thick gold chains, one with a pendant of a saint, broke the wall of red.

"So does the sky," I responded in Italian.

"The sky *is* gray," he said, turning to me with an indignant glare. "It's the factories." He waved with one hand; on each finger was a large gold ring, embedded with colored stones that sparkled in the light. His hand floated through the air, then sailed downward like an unfolded tissue.

"The factories?" I knew that there was little industry for hundreds of miles south of Naples; Calabria's economy was especially depressed.

"Yes," he said, squinting as if about to impart a secret. "Up in the north. Those Milanese destroy everything, they're almost like the Germans.

"Did you come from Naples?" he went on.

I told him I planned to stop there on the way back. He rested his large, gentle hand on my shoulder. *"È una bella città,"* he said—it's a beautiful city—and told me that whenever he passes through Naples, if only for a few hours, he ducks into a restaurant called Mimi alle Ferrovie, a block away from the train station. He had just been there, in fact: grilled calamari, mussels in a marinara sauce, and white wine—wine so distinct, he insisted, that you can taste the ashy soil of Vesuvius, where the grapes are grown.

"Ma, io sono Palermitano," he said, making sure that I understood that as a Sicilian from Palermo, he knew what he was talking about. "The marinara could have been a bit spicier, but the mozzarella di bufala . . . nowhere else can you find it so fresh!"

He explained what he did in his spare time, which was mostly what he was doing now, traveling and talking with strangers.

As the pensioner spoke, his *sh*'s and *ch*'s clicked between his tongue and teeth in the distinct, forceful Sicilian dialect, barely understandable to any Italian off the great island, much less anyone living north of Naples—let alone me, who had learned Italian growing up in Connecticut and Florida and going to college in New York. Confident that people would work to understand him, he made no effort to slow or regulate his speech.

He glanced at his chunky gold watch and, as if he'd almost missed an appointment, announced, *"Allora,* it's time for a *caffè."* We walked back to the bar—he for his coffee, I for bottled water.

Four hours out of Naples, our train crept through a desolate station—no one waiting alongside the tracks, not a single station door open or a window cracked. A blue sign at the edge of the platform read TORTORA. We had entered Calabria. For the next two hours I gazed out the window, the sea to my right, and to my left, far on the horizon, the deep green foothills of Calabria's Sila massif, locally known as the Black Forest.

The heat was suffocating, and I started feeling sleepy. As I was about to doze off, I caught sight of something I had seen in many old pictures of Calabria: ambling down a dirt path was a man riding a mule. Somehow, it fit right in with the landscape. I thought of the writer Carlo Levi, who in the 1930s described the south as a region that had evolved very slowly.

Carlo Levi was a doctor and writer from Piedmont, in the north-west of Italy. A vocal anti-Fascist, he was arrested in 1935 and sent as a prisoner to the province of Lucania. This poor, almost completely landlocked region, now called Basilicata, borders Calabria to the north; the train had passed through it during my conversation with the Sicilian pensioner.

For two years Levi was forbidden to leave the village of Gagliano. Italy had just invaded Ethiopia in the Abyssinian War; Mussolini's army had drafted many of the south's doctors (and its able-bodied men generally) and sent them to Africa. Levi offered his medical services in Gagliano, and did so openly, until the mayor, Don Luigi, feeling the political prisoner was becoming too popular, forbade people to visit him.

Thereafter Levi performed his work at night and in secret. During the day he painted pictures of the landscape and wrote about the villagers and southern life. His memoir, *Christ Stopped at Eboli*, was the first modern book to describe the people of the south, who, it seemed to him, still lived in the Middle Ages, practicing a blend of Christianity and pre-Christian paganism and fearing dragons, gnomes, and spirits that lurked in the forests.

According to Levi, the peasants with ancient Italic features, the natives of Basilicata, thought they were worthless people from a god-forsaken place. They were not Christians, not even humans, but beasts. "Christ never came this far," Levi wrote, "nor did time, nor the individual soul, nor hope, nor the relation of cause to effect, nor reason nor history."

Levi famously characterized Basilicata and Calabria as "that other world, hedged in by custom and sorrow . . . where the peasant lives out his motionless civilization on barren ground in remote poverty, and in the presence of death." To this day, many northerners see these regions this way: bereft of culture and economy, a burden to the rest of Italy.

In any case, the harshness of life in the south led many Calabresi to emigrate, especially to the United States. In 1936, the year Carlo Levi's sentence ended and he was allowed to leave Gagliano for Piedmont, my grandmother, at the age of nineteen, left Calabria for America.

Now the train approached the toe of the "boot" that is Italy. Out the window, I could see one, two, three more sets of tracks in each direction. Some tracks simply ended in mounds of dirt. We passed a freight train of two engines and seven boxcars, their open doors revealing their emptiness. There were several World War II–vintage locomotives and boxcars rusted to the rails.

This was Lamezia. Here train passengers can continue south to Reggio, where the entire train is pulled onto a ferry that continues the journey to Sicily, or they can take a train that cuts eastward across the peninsula, the narrowest point in all of Italy, to Calabria's capital, Catanzaro, and the Ionian Sea. And it was here where the train and the Sicilian pensioner continued to Palermo, while my father and I disembarked and boarded a small diesel train to Catanzaro. We stuffed our knapsacks on the narrow wooden racks above the window and passed a bottle of water between us.

Because it's located on one of the few plains in all of Calabria, Lamezia supports the region's largest airport. A half mile from the train station, small houses and condos lined the crowded coast of the Tyrrhenian Sea.

"I can't believe you've dragged me all the way down here," my dad said.

"You had a choice," I said. "I was happy to come by myself."

He rolled his eyes, but I knew he, too, was happy he had come.

The train veered across hilly, mostly barren land, past factories, tracts of plain new houses, foundations in cleared land. In time the hills grew to mountains. The train slowed to a walking pace. To one side, a field of orange trees bore rotting fruit that had not been picked; to the other, a Gypsy camp pushed up against the track bed: shacks made of wood and corrugated metal, with smoke from working fires rising from within.

A thud on the window bounced my head up; the juice from an orange trickled down the dust-covered glass. I looked out expecting to find kids running and ducking behind a tree, but I saw nothing except the sunlit grove of orange trees.

Finally, the train passed through a long mountain tunnel and emerged at Catanzaro. The station was at the bottom of a cliff. The walled city of Catanzaro crowned its top like a daunting fortress. We stepped off into the open-air station. It was four in the afternoon, almost the end of the siesta; outside a shuttered trattoria hung a sign that read CHIUSO, closed. An adjoining bar's door had been wedged open, and the entrance to the lightless room was covered only by a curtain of multicolored beads.

We still had one more train to take. We walked over to the local station to check the schedule of the Calabro–Lucano train to Gimigliano.

In Calabria and Basilicata there are two rail systems: one is the Ferrovie dello Stato, or the state railroad, which cuts through the low-lying valleys and skirts the coast; the other is the Calabro–Lucano Railroad, which traverses the mountain ridges, connecting the cliffside villages.

The train official at the ticket window motioned that he would come out from behind the window and talk to us. A short man who reached me just at chest level (and I'm an average five feet ten), he spoke in a voice both booming and raspy. He seemed to be missing every other tooth.

He explained that there were two more trains to Gimigliano, but that we would probably miss the last train back to Catanzaro and that we should stay in Catanzaro and visit the next day. We would have only a single afternoon to explore Gimigliano. In a display of what I would come to recognize as Calabrese hospitality, he walked us back to the state train station, where three cabdrivers stood talking by their cars under the shade of a portico. We took one of the cabs up to the city.

Catanzaro and its maze of streets are set on a plateau between two mountain gorges. The city can be reached from only two directions: one a narrow, spiraling ridge, the other a four-lane suspended highway, built in the 1960s. The cab cut alongside the mountain, climbed up a bit, then took the highway, which protruded from the cliff. I felt as if we were taking off in flight; the land dropped below us, the sea loomed ahead. At one point we stopped at an intersection—seemingly in midair over one of the gorges—to let other cars cross. With a final loop, we descended to a narrow cliffside road, where the buildings were packed tightly together in a discordant architectural mix of the nineteenth century and the 1970s.

We took a room at the Albergo Grand Hotel, a three-star establishment and one of Catanzaro's four hotels. It had been built in the seventies, and to judge by the dark brown furniture, it hadn't changed a bit since then. In my room, I opened the heavy dark green curtains to a breathtaking view of the gorge below me. Toward the right, the clear blue waters of the Gulf of Squillace spread out to the horizon.

Early the next morning, my father and I walked to a railroad station closer to the hotel. I would soon walk the streets of my grandparents' village. Now even my father anxiously awaited the sight of Gimigliano. The cogwheel train pulled us up the mountain, then crawled along the ridges of cliffs. Below, veins of nearly dried-up streams lined the valleys. Dust and smoke from the diesel engine funneled in through the open windows. We passed in and out of tunnels cut through the mountains, and each burst of sunlight as we exited a tunnel offered an endless view of mountaintops along the horizon. After twenty minutes, the train veered closely around a mountainside, its sheer cliff dropping off to the left, and I spotted a tiny village on a peak even farther above. It was a cluster of yellow and cream-colored houses with red terra-cotta roofs. It looked like the tiny archetypal village in the distant background of a fresco.

"That's it," my father said. "That's Gimigliano. Jesus, it's exactly as I remember it."

And I was sure that it hadn't changed since his father left in 1913.

The train came to a gradual stop at a clean single-story stuccoed railroad station the color of mustard. I stepped onto the platform and craned my neck to see the village still high above us.

The train pulled away, blowing up a swirling cloud of dust. The sun beat down on us. We were left with a sound I had rarely heard and one that I would come to associate with Gimigliano—the constant, lonely scratching of cicadas. We had only three or four hours to explore the village.

To our left, jutting out on a cliff, was Gimigliano Inferiore; Gimigliano Superiore was above us, a steep walk. "As I remember, there wasn't much in Inferiore," my father said. "We should go to Superiore."

A man wearing the official railway uniform of dark blue pants and a sky-blue short-sleeved shirt emerged from the station, and my father asked, "How do we get to up to Superiore?"

The man's thin cotton shirt was unbuttoned to mid-chest, exposing a gold Virgin pendant on a chain.

"By car, five minutes up that road," he said, pointing to a single-lane road that rose, then disappeared on the other side of the mountain.

"We don't have a car."

He pointed to the mountain. "Half hour up those steps." He patted me on the back and went on.

The steps, hundreds of them, were irregularly set—a few short steps followed by several long ones. Weeds sprouted through cracks, and bushes grew over the sides. Olive and fig trees grew wild; any space in between them had been filled with short rows of grapevines.

"Mark, look at this," my father said, pointing to a *fico d'india*, a prickly pear cactus. "To pick the fruit, they wear thick leather gloves; then they roll it in their hands to break off the spines." He touched one of the spines with his finger. "It's a lot of work, but the fruit is juicy and sweet." We were drenched in sweat; I was thirsty enough to want to squeeze out the juice then and there.

After twenty minutes—almost to the top—we were greeted by an old man in a wool sport coat with a large smile.

He was deaf and mute, it turned out, but this didn't stop him from conversing with my father. Their exchange took place entirely in hand gestures. A point to a tree; a cupping of the hand; a twist in the cheek with a single finger; a clasp of the hands, followed by a sigh. The man was at least seventy and seemed to be unaffected by the heat. After a few minutes my father turned to me and said matter-of-factly that the old man had recommended a café on the main street that served frozen *orzata*, a drink made of shaved ice, sugar, and crushed almonds.

"How the hell did you understand that?"

"Mark, weren't you watching? Pay attention to the hands. It's all in the hands."

On our way, we stopped at the first shop we saw. The proprietor was my father's height and was hefty in the middle. In his late forties, he had wavy white hair and a thick black mustache. His shirt was drenched from sweating out the powerful July heat. Recognizing my father's dialect as that of the village, he introduced himself, Giuseppe Chiarella.

"Rotella," my father said. "Giuseppe Rotella."

Giuseppe frowned quizzically, then asked for his mother's maiden name, since "the women always keep in touch with family."

"Critelli," my father answered, then explained sheepishly that he had not been in touch with our relatives, didn't even know if they still lived here.

Giuseppe stepped away from the cash register. "Today we will find them."

In his car, a new Fiat with air conditioning, Giuseppe told us that he was a photographer. As the car squeezed through tiny alleys of two-story eighteenth-century houses, he explained that he traveled all over Calabria, taking pictures of the region. He transferred the film to slides, sent them out to be made into postcards and posters with southern Italian greetings—"and then I go back on the road again." This time he would tour the province and sell his postcards and posters to all the novelty stores, train stations, cafés, and resorts.

Giuseppe stepped out of the car and called up to a balcony. An older woman leaned over and nodded shyly. "My aunt," he said, and told her my grandmother's name.

"You know their family," she said right away. "They live just down Via delle Grazie."

He turned to us and announced: "Your relative is Angela Critelli! I dated her when I was a teenager!"

We knocked on the heavy oak door of 27 Via delle Grazie. A woman stepped out, and I saw my grandmother's round face and warm eyes.

"Angela," Giuseppe said, "your cousin Giuseppe Rotella has returned from America." With a grand wave of his arm, Giuseppe presented us to one another and stepped back.

For a moment Angela looked as if she had been expecting us all along. Then she placed her hands on her waist and playfully scolded my father: "Thirty years and you don't write!" We kissed and embraced. Angela cried. Tears welled in my father's eyes, but he wiped them away as soon as they touched his cheek.

Angela showed us inside her house. Sitting under the low ceiling in the vestibule was an old woman dressed all in black, her gray hair pulled tightly in a bun. This was Zia Maria, Angela said, the widow of one of my grandmother's brothers. Zia Maria, my father's aunt, offered her hand and said between tight lips, "Last night I had a dream that a gift was coming from America."

As we walked upstairs and through the kitchen, my father and I both breathed in the sweet and pungent smell of tomato sauce. My father glanced at a pot on the stove. "I bet that's a rabbit ragù," he whispered to me. "That was my favorite meal."

My father apologized to Angela that we had to catch the train back to Perugia in a couple of hours; it was now just before noon. Wasting no time, Angela rushed to the bedroom window and called out to the next apartment, then darted to the living room window and alerted what seemed to us to be passersby that *i parenti sono arrivati d'America*, relatives had come from America. Within minutes ten Calabresi were sitting at a huge table. They were our extended family—Angela's daughters, Luisa and Sabrina, with their husbands, Tommaso and Masino, and their two children.

Angela's husband, Domenico Cantafio, brought out two jugs of chilled red wine. He was well tanned, a deep red really, and his jet-black hair framed a friendly face.

"I made this," he proudly exclaimed, filling our glasses. We toasted. His hands were large and thick and enveloped his glass. The wine had a fizzy bite on the tongue but went down smoothly.

Angela set out cheese—from their goats, she said—and hot peppers and fried zucchini flowers grown in their garden. At the same time, she brought out bottles of Coca-Cola and a box of crackers, perhaps unsure of what would appeal to our American appetites.

"Are you crazy?" my father said. "What do you think Mama cooked for us?"

Everyone laughed, and Angela reappeared with the rabbit *ragù*, which she then served with perfectly cooked ziti. While we were eating, she brought out photos of aunts, uncles, cousins, many still living in the village. The whole family huddled around us. Tommaso and Masino looked on in disbelief.

For dessert, Angela brought out a bowl of purple fruit. At first I thought they were oblong plums. But when my father reeled back in awe, I knew they were something special. "I haven't had these in such a long time," my father said. "My father had a tree in our backyard."

He reached in, pulled out a plump purple fruit, and handed it to me. "Fresh figs!" he exclaimed. "You can't buy them this ripe in the States."

It seems impossible to me now, but I'd never before eaten a fresh fig. I bit through the loose skin and sank my teeth into the juicy flesh. Angela, Domenico, and Giuseppe looked on in amazement at the rate my father was devouring the figs, as if they were manna from heaven. Why had he never introduced me to them?

In our rapture, we hadn't noticed another woman arrive. She was in her seventies, but her short hair was still a nice blend of black and gray.

"Zia Caterina!" Sabrina and Luisa called out in unison. They guided her over to my father and me. She gave both of us a full, strong kiss on each cheek.

"You were always up to no good here," she told my father, and pinched his cheeks. Then she grabbed my hand in both of hers. "After your grandmother died, I thought I'd never again hear from America."

"She's your grandmother's niece," Angela explained. "But she knew her better than anyone else."

"She was a sister to me." Caterina sighed, and she, Angela, and my father fell into animated conversation in a dialect I had trouble following.

Because I had taken Italian classes in college, I had been correcting my father's Italian throughout our trip. But here, in Gimigliano, it became clear to me that he hadn't been speaking incorrectly; he had been speaking the dialect of the village.

But even here his dialect stood out slightly. The children listened, fascinated. Just as television has smoothed the regional accents across the United States, so it is gradually eliminating the dialects throughout Italy. While the Calabrese language has evolved, my father was speaking the way his mother had spoken when she left in 1936. His speech, learned in Connecticut, was a relic of the Gimigliano of the early twentieth century.

Angela turned to me and took my hand. "*Allora*, so how is your sister?" she asked.

"How did you know I had a sister?" I said. Surely my father hadn't mentioned her already.

Angela reached into the bookcase behind her and pulled out an intricately hand-embroidered photo album. Inside, the pages were filled with pictures my grandmother had sent: my sister and me sitting on our grandfather's lap under his grape arbor in Danbury; the two of us sitting at her kitchen table. The Critellis had watched me grow from birth through college, while I had had no idea they existed.

Giuseppe tapped my father on the shoulder. "We should go. You still have another cousin to visit."

Everyone fell silent, not knowing how to say farewell when we'd only just arrived.

"*Io ritorno,*" I said, promising to return with my wife, Martha.

"*Ed io aspetto,*" Angela said—and I will wait—and waved to us as we walked up the alley.

Saveria Critelli stepped out of her house unfastening her kitchen apron. Her dark hair was pulled back. With a shy smile offering a glimpse of silver teeth, she walked out with her arms open; her husband, Cecco Trapasso, tall and thin with a serious face, walked behind her. Saveria was Angela's sister. Giuseppe had phoned her, and she had been expecting us.

"Please, you must join us for dinner," Cecco said.

"We can't," my father said. "We are going back north."

Giuseppe slapped his head and laughed to Saveria and Cecco. "Their train back to Catanzaro leaves in about half an hour."

"Today?" Saveria said. "Today?"

My father and I nodded our heads, embarrassed, as if in the never-ending struggle between Italy's north and south, we were on the wrong side.

"Why don't you just go back tomorrow?"

"I've got to get back to Perugia," my father said.

"For what?" Saveria said wryly.

"I have to go back to the studio," my father said. I knew he was wishing his excuse were more dire.

"Aah." Saveria rapped her knuckles on her head. "Typical Calabrese—*testa dura!*"

We talked for a few minutes about Grandma and about Dad's first visit, many years before. As we made to leave, Saveria brought out two long, thick pieces of *soppressata,* spicy Calabrese sausage.

"No, you shouldn't," my father said, but his gesture—he brought them to his nose and breathed in—said otherwise. We would return to the north with some good southern *soppressata.*

As Giuseppe drove to the station, my father asked if he could stop to make a donation to the church to which my grandmother had been sending money since she left the village fifty years before.

"You must mean the Madonna di Porto," Giuseppe said, conveniently producing a postcard of the sun-bleached white church from the glove box.

"Yes, that's it!"

"The church is a little ways away, and you probably wouldn't have time to make it before your train." Giuseppe said. "But you can make the donation at the church in Superiore, where the annual festival begins."

Five minutes later we were there. Three arches spanned the entrance to the yellow stone church. A half dozen men sat talking on the steps. As we walked by, they fell silent and stared. The doors, opened only during mass, were locked shut. Giuseppe directed us to the side door, introduced us to the priest, a dark-haired, soft-spoken man in a white collar, and explained our visit.

My father took out a combination of lire and U.S. dollars and gave it to the priest. "For my mother, Angelina Critelli."

"I can say a mass for her tomorrow afternoon."

"We're leaving today."

"But this money . . . it's for a mass, yes?"

Grandma had sent money in part because she believed in the power of the Virgin. My father was no longer a practicing Catholic and thought it hypocritical to act otherwise, but in his mother's village, his stance softened.

"Yes," he said. "It would make her happy to know that money was given in her name."

Giuseppe's store was across the street. There he brought out a handful of his postcards, flashing them before our eyes like a dealer at a casino. Each one offered a glimpse of Calabria—tiny cliff villages, ancient Greek temples, the beaches of Tropea, the clear blue waters of Taranto, and the deep, snow-covered forests of the Sila mountain range.

I pulled out from his stack a postcard with the name SCILLA blazoned across the top. A church crowned what looked to be a huge island boulder, white waves crashing against it. I could almost see the pass between Scilla and Charybdis, the coast where Odysseus faced the six-headed monster.

Another postcard showed the ancient trading city of Crotone, where Pythagoras, once exiled from Greece, formed his school of followers. I imagined leaning against the Greek ruins. The Calabria I'd read about was a harsh, dry terrain where cities had been devastated by earthquakes and where people, like my great-grandmother, had died by the thousands from malaria. Now, in Giuseppe's postcards, I saw that the region from which my grandparents had emigrated held its own treasures. The portals of rustic houses hadn't yet been fitted with modern windows; clotheslines still joined buildings across alleys. This is what Florence must have looked like when E. M. Forster set *A Room with a View* there. Calabria *is* old Italy; Calabria conforms to our idea of what Italy is.

Giuseppe had brought my father and me together with our Italian family. Now he offered a glimpse of a world where families stayed together and lived in the same town, perhaps on the same street. Giuseppe showed me a life I wanted access to, a life I wanted, in some sense, to live. I knew I had to travel deeper into Calabria.

Giuseppe must have registered my excitement, for he spoke the words I wanted to hear: "Come back, I'll take you around. I'll show you Calabria."

And I did. After that first trip I returned regularly for the next decade, usually every other year, or as Giuseppe would say, *come l'ulivo*, like the olive, which bears fruit only once every two years. It is with the olive in mind that the Calabrese gauge the passing of time: ten years become five, four years become two, and two years become one.

Meanwhile, I became obsessed with watering my Calabrese roots, with strengthening the strands between myself and the land that my grandparents had left. I began the process of getting my Italian citizenship. I asked my cousin Luisa in Gimigliano to send me my grandparents' birth and marriage certificates while I sent away for their death certificates in Connecticut.

I had always known I was Italian, but it wasn't until my first year of Catholic high school in St. Petersburg, Florida, that I learned that I was Calabrese—or that Italians identified themselves first by their region, then by their country. A boy who recognized my Italian-sounding name asked me where my family was from and proudly announced that his came from Sicily. I answered with a shrug.

That afternoon I asked my father, "Are we Sicilian?"

My father glared at me. "Hell, no. We're Calabrese! We're from the toe of the boot, the part that's kicking the shit out of Sicily." I had never seen him get his hackles raised over his nationality. From then on, my father (drawing on hearsay) would identify fellow Calabresi.

"Tony Bennett," he would announce, "he's Calabrese." The list grew: the singer Lou Monte; the Yankee great Phil Rizzuto; the actors Kaye Ballard and Stanley Tucci.

My father no doubt was always proud to be Calabrese. But after that first trip he became more vocal in his expressions of his Calabrese heritage. On Dean Martin ("an arrogant Napoletan' "); Sinatra ("a great artist, but he's a Sicilian' ").

I was driven to learn more about Calabria. I browsed the travel sections of bookstores. Rome, Venice, Florence, and Tuscany generally dominated the shelves. There was nothing on Calabria—and almost nothing on the south, although it appeared that Sicily had gained a toehold. At the public library, the database listed three books on Calabria, three for the entire twentieth century.

I sought out *Old Calabria*, written by a Scot named Norman Douglas and published in 1915. Douglas, legend says, came to know Calabria better than almost any other foreign traveler.

One afternoon I called Giuseppe from New York City, and just as my aunt Angela appeared to have been expecting my father and me all those years ago, Giuseppe answered as if he had been waiting for a call from me taking him up on his offer: "Ah, Marco. *Come va?*" And with this, I set out for my grandparents' village once again.

LA STORIA DELLA CALABRIA

THERE IS NOTHING ROMANTIC ABOUT THE NAME. Calabria. It sounds like a threat, a curse. The hard *c* dances on the sharp *l* before smacking you with its rolling one-two punch of the *b* and *r*. The name lacks the worldliness of Roma, the sophistication of Firenze, the medieval grace of Bologna, the fluidity of Emilia-Romana, the complexity of Venezia.

Calabria. It sounds like the name of a hard-lived whore, a prostitute in a Fellini film who has given everything she has except her protective, tough shell.

Calabria. The Byzantine Greeks named her—from the hyphenated term *kalos-bruo*, which means "fertile earth." Fecund she is, but her history is long and unglorified. The Italic tribe native to Calabria, the Bruttians, warmed to the benevolent Greeks when they arrived and began colonizing her in the eighth century B.C. The Greeks founded the cities of Locri, Sibari, Crotone, and Reggio. They brought with them figs, olives, grapes, and written laws.

It was around the fifth century B.C., with the rise of the Roman Empire, that Calabria's love affair with the Greeks came to an end.

The Romans, growing stronger, pushed the Etruscan and Samnite tribes from Tuscany and Campania farther south. The Samnites invaded the Greek colonies. The Romans, eyeing Calabria for her land and potential trade routes, followed the Samnites, engaging them in a series of wars that began around 343 B.C. and lasted about fifty years, ending in a Roman victory—with Calabria as a nice piece of ass. The Greeks had given the Bruttians and Bruttium, or Calabria, a taste of sweetness, a sense of glory that they would not feel again for the next two thousand years. Calabria would be known as that hunk of land between Naples and Sicily, a land grab for all who entered her.

Calabria, surrounded by ocean on three sides and mountains on the fourth, was isolated and in need of company. She opened her arms to Hannibal and his Carthaginians, who fled from Campania to Calabria after the Romans defeated them in the Second Punic War, which lasted from 218 to 201 B.C. The Romans chased Hannibal out of Calabria's bed, while she, in turn, embraced the Romans once again. Rome flourished, and Calabria offered up her fruit, vegetables, and forests, which fed, fueled, and fortified the Roman Empire.

But in time Rome's contentment led to its decline, and by the sixth century A.D. southern Italy had fallen under Byzantine rule. Calabria once again succumbed to the powers of these new Greeks, and during this time many of her cities, such as Rossano and Stilo, grew wealthy. But within four hundred years the romance would end when she was invaded by the Saracens, or Arabs, who had already taken Sicily. They ravaged Calabria and, in payment, tossed at her feet eggplants and peppers.

During these Arab invasions, the Calabresi—a people in which Bruttian, Greek, and Roman blood now mingled—retreated to the mountains for protection from invaders. The Byzantines and Saracens fought over Calabria, taking advantage of her at every step, until the Normans, led by Robert Guiscard and his nephew Roger II, conquered it in A.D. 1053. Hoping to centralize power—and tame the wild and fickle Calabria—they introduced the feudal system. Under the Normans, the Kingdom of Sicily—which stretched from Naples and the Abruzzi south through present-day Apulia, Basilicata, and Calabria to Sicily—was formed, and the Arabic, Greek, Bruttian, and Roman cultures were brought under one, so to speak, roof.

Frederick of Swabia gained rule in 1197, and while he tried bringing law and order to his kingdom during his reign, he also levied heavy taxes to pay for this extra attention. From 1261, beginning with Charles of Anjou, until 1442, the time of the High Renaissance in Rome and Florence, the Angevins ruled.

While art and thought flourished in northern Italy, the south—under the rule of the House of Aragon and later Ferdinand I—dug deeper in the fields. Calabria was kept down by fist and at knife-point.

For the next three centuries, the French, Spanish, and Austrians battled for a piece of her, knowing with taxes they could make a quick buck off her. Most of the rulers were fly-by-night noblemen, wanting just a taste of honey—a dip of the wick—not even thinking to leave bills by the nightstand. These barons and padrone, having to offer their king increasingly more, became Calabria's pimps. They took advantage of the feudal system and imposed even heavier taxes. Writhing naked on her dirt floor, Calabria would never feel lower. When she opened her eyes and looked out the window, the sight of oranges, grapes, olives, and the ubiquitous figs, which bear fruit twice a year, kept her going.

In 1713 the Austrians emerged victorious and, indulging their territorial fantasies, changed her name to the Kingdom of Naples (which also included Sicily) and later to the Kingdom of the Two Sicilies.

Two decades later the Spanish Bourbons, under Charles of Bourbon and later Ferdinand IV, took control and ruled the kingdom for the next century. Bourbon rule was interrupted in 1808, when Napoleon gained control and placed in the throne his brother-in-law Joachim Murat, who imposed legal order by installing the French Civil Code. That ended in 1815 with Murat's execution and a combined British-Spanish victory over the French.

During Spanish rule the now-hardened Calabria realized she needed to regain her strength. She built up her own internal de-

fenses, creating her own secret laws enforced by bandits and brigands, the precursors to the mafia.

In 1861 the Bourbon kingdom fell when Giuseppe Garibaldi and
his army of Red Shirts united Italy under the Sardinian House of
Savoy, ruled by King Vittorio Emmanuele II. But Garibaldi's plan
for a stronger south was thwarted as the new monarchy continued to
take advantage of the south with high taxation. In time, many Calabresi came to believe that the Italian monarch was just another
form of foreign rule that would continue to exploit them. Though
victorious, Garibaldi felt defeated, knowing that his ideal of a truly
united Italy would never be realized. The Risorgimento marked the
beginning of the mass exodus to America.

For the next hundred years impoverished Calabria struggled on.

The 1940s saw riots and peasant uprisings as the farmers tried
claiming land that had been owned by absentee landlords, good fertile land that had been wasting for centuries. In the 1960s the central
government boosted Calabria's economy with funds called the Cassa
per il Mezzogiorno, billions of lire for roads and public works. It
helped set Calabria on her way. While Calabria benefited from this
purse, the factories promised by the government—the employers
that would have enabled Calabria to survive on her own—never
came. Many Italians (both northern and southern) believe that the
cassa has helped only superficially, a larger purse for an expensive call
girl.

Today southern Italy suffers one of the highest unemployment
rates in Western Europe. Drought, earthquakes, sandy soil, antiquated farming methods, corruption, and a distant national government have all played a part in Calabria's economic suffering.
Northern Italians seem to enjoy debating the problem of the Mezzogiorno, any point on the Italian peninsula south of Rome. Can
the south be brought up to the efficient standards of the fair-skinned
young men in the cafés of Milan, Florence, and Bologna? Northerners believe southerners remain poor because of their own laziness
and dependency on a powerful mafia. Meanwhile, Calabria, desperate to bring more money into her home, has awaited the govern-

ment's transfer of industry to the south. But the government's promises are corrupted by its suspicion that she will sneak in her apron pocket any federal cash that it sends. So far the only market Calabria has found is for her produce. She exports a large share of olives, olive oil, and figs but sees very little monetary return.

Calabria has other problems. The mafia, which had its roots in defending her from foreign exploitation, is still strong. In Naples the government has been able to rein in the criminal Camorra; in Sicily the most extensively and reliably networked organization, the Cosa Nostra, has come under increasingly intense government fire in the past decade. The Sicilians, many of whom broke from their tradition of silence, paid a price for speaking out against the mafia: in the early 1990s, two major crime-fighting judges were assassinated. The people of Calabria, on the other hand, don't acknowledge their own criminal element, the 'ndrangheta. They prefer to speak about their gardens. They still keep their omertà, their code of silence.

Kalos-bruo is indeed fertile. She has given her peppers, olives, oranges, and figs. But more than food, she has offered her heart and soul, giving the world her sons and daughters. Since the 1880s millions of Calabresi have left the region in hopes of finding work—in the United States, Canada, Argentina, Australia, anywhere.

Few people in North America realize that after Campania and Sicily, the largest group of Italian-Americans trace their lineage to Calabria. Perhaps it is because of the quiet nature of the Calabresi, who are overshadowed by the Siciliani and Napoletani, that little is known about them.

In America, as in Italy, each region of southern Italy has its own reputation, however clichéd. The Napoletani: loud and gruff and love to sing. The Siciliani: secret, guarded, and arrogant. The Calabresi: hardheaded but kindhearted. The mere mention of the region causes people to knock their knuckles on their heads and say testa dura, hardheaded. Because the Calabresi are quieter than their southern Italian neighbors, they tend to blend into their environment.

Americans tracing their ancestry brought Calabria into contemporary consciousness in the late twentieth century. Gay Talese wrote his Calabrese family history in *Unto the Sons*; Barbara Grizzuti Harrison stopped off in her ancestral Calabrese village while writing *Italian Days*.

In the last few decades, as the Italian economy has strengthened, Calabria has come to life with the beginnings of her own tourist industry. Now the aged province in Italy, wizened in her experience, may be ready to share her stories.

RITORNO ALLA CALABRIA

IN THE HAZE, I couldn't tell where Calabria ended and the mountains of Sicily began. We had taken off from Rome, and now the plane's landing gear was being lowered. I was used to approaching Calabria from the ground, by way of a daylong train trip from Rome or Naples. This trip took less than an hour. For the first time, I saw Calabria's jagged coast from the air. The mountains ended; then a larger set of mountains towered above them.

"Is that Sicily?" I asked the man sitting next to me. He turned to me; his face was stern, but his eyes were warm. He wore a dark blue suit and was obviously returning home from business.

"No, it's Calabria."

"So far away?"

"It's not so far." He looked out the window again and began pointing out towns. "There's Pizzo. On the other side of that peninsula is Tropea, and farther is Palmi." When he turned to smile, he seemed immediately familiar, someone I'd known all my life but saw rarely.

"These are the mountains of Le Serre; those," he said, pointing to the tall dark range, "are the Aspromonte. Sicily is beyond, far beyond."

We had descended through the haze, and I could now clearly see where the blue water met the beaches. I spotted villages that filled gorges and crevices in the mountains.

"Is this your first time in Calabria?"

"No, I've been here several times, but never arrived by air."

"Are you from Rome?"

"No, I'm American. I'm visiting relatives in a little village outside Catanzaro."

"Oh, really? Which village?"

"Gimigliano."

He looked at me, shocked. "That's where I'm from. Excuse me, what's your name?"

"Rotella."

"That's my wife's name. My name's Ventura . . . Tonino."

His tight mouth softened, and he searched my face, I was sure, for a hint of something familiar. I did the same, and thought I saw a family resemblance. Although he was short and thin, he had the sad eyes and downturned mouth of my uncle Tom, my father's youngest brother, who still lives in Danbury.

He asked if he could give me a lift from the airport. I thanked him and told him that someone was picking me up.

"Then we'll see each other in Gimigliano."

Ours was the only plane on the tarmac. We faced the rust-colored airport. A dozen circular windows on top faced the sea. I imagined that the architects who had designed the building had intended for the airport to reflect the seaside setting, a ship with portals. It reminded me, though, of a building in a 1960s Jacques Tati film called *Mon Oncle*, in which a house had two large, circular windows that looked like eyes. I felt as if the eyes of Calabria were peering at me.

My bags were among the last to come off the conveyor belt. As I walked out of the baggage claim to the central terminal, I searched the terminal for Giuseppe. And just as I spotted him, he caught sight of me. He took a last sip of his *caffè*, left money on the bar, and casually walked over as if it had been two days, not two years, since we'd last seen each other. As he greeted me with Italian double-cheek kisses, he took my bags, directed me to the bar, and ordered two more cups of *caffè*, demitasses of espresso.

"Have you been well?"

"Yes, thanks. And your family?"

"Non c'è male," he said—not bad. It was a way that Calabresi answer; even if all is going well, you don't want to jinx what is good in life.

"I hear you met Tonino," Giuseppe said, smiling.

"How did you know?" I sipped the coffee; even here, in a tiny airport, it tasted better than anything in New York.

"I saw him on the way out. I think he's a distant relative of yours," he said, then asked: "Your father . . . when will he come again?"

"In two months," I said. "I'll bring Martha and my folks back for the festival."

Giuseppe registered approval with a nod and a low, chesty *"Bene."* To Giuseppe—and all my relatives—my father was the Calabrese son, returning from America. He held a fascination for them. I was simply the son of the prodigal son—more American than Calabrese, a blood relation but little more.

Giuseppe stopped at the newsstand to make sure that the owner had stocked enough of his postcards—and to pick up his monthly payment. On his way out he noticed an illustrated map of Calabria.

"No," he said to himself. He turned to the owner and said, "Mimmo, this one is crude; look at the one I made." He opened his briefcase and pulled out a map on heavyweight glossy paper, with illustrations of tourist attractions over the name of each city.

The proprietor looked at it, pursed his mouth approvingly, then shrugged his shoulders. They discussed price and quantity, and the store owner agreed to stock them when the ones he had ran out.

Puffs of cumulous clouds dotted Calabria's great blue skies. We walked out the automatic doors, and the cool air hit us. I got goose bumps.

"Fa freddo oggi," I said to Giuseppe.

"Sì, the cold air came in last night. It's been warm here for months."

"Is it usually this cold?" I asked.

"No, we should have had this cold last month when it was so hot. But in April you never know."

I had decided to come to Calabria in April so as to be present during Easter, one of Italy's biggest holidays, when everyone would be with family. While I knew that I wouldn't feel the intense summer heat, I had assumed that spring would have begun to settle in, and I hoped that this cold was just passing.

Outside, I almost didn't recognize Giuseppe's dark gray sedan: the paint had dulled, the wheel covers were missing, and a large scrape ran along the driver's side back door to the front door.

"What happened here?"

"A drunk driver hit me . . . about a month ago."

Still, the Fiat's heft and composition set it apart from the other smaller, cheaply built Fiat models in the parking lot.

"I want to show you something," Giuseppe said, calling me around to the trunk. He lifted the lid and took out two cardboard envelopes, each about a foot long and six inches high. He opened the first and showed me galley proofs of a book he'd been working on, a book on Calabria. Each page displayed one of Giuseppe's photos, with a description in Italian, German, French, and English below. There were about sixty pages of beaches, Norman towers, excavations of Greek cities, Byzantine villages.

"It's fortunate you came today because I have to send them back this afternoon. A day later, and you wouldn't have seen them."

He slid the proof pages back into their cardboard casing—the same one that had been sent to him—taped it shut, scratched out his address, then readdressed the package to the publisher in Milan.

He opened another cardboard box about the same size and pulled out more proofs, photos of small lifelike figures carved from clay. Each figure, dressed in nineteenth-century costume, represented an artisan working an individual craft. There were wine makers, farmers, weavers, and cobblers, each one set against a detailed backdrop. One image was of a woman kneading dough; behind her was a brick oven in a field of olive trees.

"This was life here last century . . . and even the beginning of this century," Giuseppe said. "And tomorrow we are going to the country to do this," he said, pointing to the image of the bread maker.

He turned to the center of the book to a heading that read "The Museum of Science and Industry." There was a photo of a three-foot model ship enclosed in a glass case. "All of this was designed and built by a man who lives in Tropea, but his family is from Gimigliano," Giuseppe said.

"Can we visit him?"

Giuseppe flashed a smile. "We will."

Lamezia Terme is a coastal plain that begins at the Tyrrhenian Sea and stretches between the foothills of two mountain ranges, the Sila and the Aspromonte. Three villages make up the region: Nicastro, with thirty-five thousand people; Sambiase, with nineteen thousand; and Sant'Eufemia Lamezia, a village of about four thousand. It is on the shores of Lamezia that many believe Odysseus washed up and was greeted by Nausicaa, a mesmerizing girl from a village where Tiriolo, the sister city of Gimigliano, now stands.

We drove up a small hill, into the tiniest village, Sant'Eufemia Lamezia, which has a few hotels and the region's two most important hubs of transportation—the airport and train station. Apartment buildings constructed in the 1970s lined the streets. These newer buildings looked older, more worn than the few older ones scattered throughout the village. Tiny stores filled the first floors of these buildings. Lining the gently sloping street below us, the buildings parted and the sea opened up.

"Do you mind if I stop off at two places for work?" Giuseppe asked me.

I said I didn't, and Giuseppe stopped the car and went into a store. Through the window I could see toys displayed, as well as a couple of racks of postcards. A small hotel abutted the card store. Within a few minutes, Giuseppe returned. The half smile on his face belied anger, but in typical Calabrese fashion, he said nothing. I remember my father once telling me, "Never let them know what you're thinking. Never let them know what you're feeling." It was sound advice, but I was always too emotional to follow it.

Giuseppe got in the car, closed his door lightly, and started his engine. He put his car into gear, paused, turned to me, and said, "They never have enough money. They sell the postcards but claim to have already spent the money, that they have made no profits."

"How often does this happen?" I asked.

"More often than not. You have to come the right time of month."

We drove to what seemed to be the outskirts of Sant'Eufemia, along a strip of garages and storefronts with their metal gates pulled down. Giuseppe pulled off the side of the road across the street from a store whose front windows had been papered over.

"Last year two people were killed here in Lamezia," Giuseppe said. "And it was Christmas."

"Who's doing the killing?"

"Mostly the mafia. They kill themselves."

Inside, two young men in their twenties sat at a desk; one guy set down his cell phone, the other stopped clicking on an old computer, as Giuseppe announced himself.

"I told Signore Biamonte to meet me here at two."

The man at the computer, annoyed to have been walked in on, shrugged his shoulders. "He's in the other warehouse."

"Please call him and tell him I'm here."

The man reached out to the other man for the phone.

The narrow room went deep. Boxes were stacked up on shelves along the walls, and two hydraulic hand trucks, left in mid-job, were parked in the center of the room. It was a shipping warehouse for toys and gifts and, I assumed, postcards.

"He'll be here in ten minutes," the young man said.

Giuseppe nodded and crossed his arms. I did likewise. There we stood, halfway between the desk and front door, looking around the room in silence.

"Are those your postcards?" I asked him, pointing to a stack of cards on the table next to the phone.

Giuseppe shook his head. I took his cue that we were to stand impassively.

Cheap gifts filled the shelves of the front room. There were stuffed bears wearing the colors of Juventus and AC Milan soccer teams; shrink-wrapped bow and arrow sets—complete with the suction cup and cheap string of the kind any American kid who grew up in the sixties would remember—covered the shelf. New York street-cop sets lay in neat rows on another shelf; each set included a badge, handcuffs, a flashlight, and a black plastic gun, the kind that's illegal in New York because it's often been mistaken for a real one. On the cardboard packaging was a cheap color drawing of a New York cop in action—though it looked more like a character from *Adam 12*.

My first day back in Calabria, and I was acting as muscle for Giuseppe. When he said business, I had envisioned a congenial swap of postcards for a check.

Giuseppe cleared his throat. "Excuse me, boys, but it has now been fifteen minutes."

The two young men looked at the phone on the counter and turned to Giuseppe. "He said he would be here, but he's with another client."

"Yes, but the client with whom he had an appointment twenty minutes ago is here now."

The white-shirted man lifted his palms and glanced around the room as if searching for answers. The other man looked down at his feet as his toe tapped from side to side.

"Tell him I came by and that I will stop by again tomorrow."

As we walked out, Giuseppe rolled his eyes. "Nothing, nothing I do will make them come out of hiding. No one has money to pay me for my postcards! . . . Are you hungry?" he asked.

I nodded.

"Good, let's get something to eat!"

In Calabria, your expectations are never met head-on. You can't expect to just fly into Calabria and settle into your hotel. Something is bound to interrupt the flow; something will catch you off guard.

I decided then to simply let Giuseppe show me his Calabria.

AN OLD TALE

MY GRANDFATHER SHOT A MAN over my grandmother. My father told me the story on that first
trip together to Calabria. He and I have always been
close, but that trip brought back to my father a rush of memories
that he felt compelled to share.

The evening we spent in Catanzaro, the day before we took the
train to Gimigliano, he and I had walked the *passeggiata* along Corso
Mazzini, which ends as the road skirts the edge of the cliff. A railing
was the only thing that separated you from the sheer drop to the valley.

My father and I got gelato cones, sat on a bench, and looked out
over the Ionian Sea.

"I gotta tell you," he said. "Days would go by when there was
absolutely nothing to do. No movies, no streets to cruise—hardly
any cars. I remember one day I got so bored that I joined a few
guys—they were about my age, twenty-one or even younger—on a
walk, and we ended up raiding some farmers' fields.

"Of course we didn't destroy anything, and we took only what we could eat. But at the end of the afternoon we sat down in the woods, opened a bottle of wine, and ate fresh figs and the sweetest peas."

Swallows flew above us as we crunched into our cones.

"I never told you the story about Grandpa, did I?" my father asked.

He didn't need a response because he knew he had never told me.

"It was in 1958, I guess," my father began. "I had just met your mother, but my mother was going back to Italy and insisted that I come along as her escort."

He was twenty-one; it was Grandma's first visit back since she had emigrated in 1936. Upon their arrival by steamer in Naples, they realized some of their luggage had been misplaced. They were told the luggage would be forwarded to Catanzaro in a week; then they took the train—probably along the same tracks that my grandmother traveled when she first left Calabria—down through Campania, Basilicata, and Lamezia, where they changed again for Catanzaro and finally Gimigliano.

The entire family greeted them at the station and brought them to Gimigliano Inferiore; they would spend the next three months with my grandmother's older sister, Caterina, whose house rested on the highest point of Inferiore's plateau, just before the mountain rose farther to Superiore. The steep mule path that connected Inferiore with Superiore cut directly in front of their doorway.

They were given the top floor of the house, with a patio overlooking the rest of Inferiore as well as the valley below and the mountains directly across. My father stood on the edge and breathed in the cool mountain air. He had just been discharged from the navy, where he served almost five years on a battleship. He was lucky to have missed the Korean War. His military haircut had grown out into a pompadour, but his arms still displayed their tight sinews of muscle. He had just met an eighteen-year-old girl named Murielle La Fontaine working at a five-and-dime in Danbury and was eager to find his first job out of the service. He looked out at the view, at the village below him. He saw fields of grapes, olives, and figs. His first thought was, What the hell am I doing here?

It occurred to me, as he was telling the story, that I had brought him to Calabria for my own reasons, just as Grandma had done, and that he had come along more out of obligation than desire.

Shortly after they arrived, Caterina, who had been cooking all of the day before and most of the morning, began placing a banquet on the table. It seemed as if the entire village squeezed its way around the dining room table, all shouting questions at Grandma and my father. The women cupped my grandmother's cheeks and grabbed her arms; they were all amazed at how large Angelina had become. Her face had always been smooth and beautiful, but twenty years of Americanized Italian food had rounded her jowls.

She smiled and began to speak. From a person who could barely speak a word of English, her first words to her relatives were "So, howa issa evvabody?"

The room went silent. Her brothers and sisters all stared at her.

"Ma," my father said, "what's wrong? *Parla italiano!*"

"Joey, I'ma sorry, but I forgotta alla my Italian." After twenty years of living in the United States—and missing Gimigliano every day—she wanted to show off her English.

After the siesta my father and Grandma took a walk through the village's tiny piazza.

"Ma, what are you doing?" my father asked. "Why didn't you speak Italian? You write to them every month in Italian, but suddenly you don't remember it?"

"It just comes and goes," my grandma responded in Italian.

"You're back for the first time since you left and you're not going to speak in Italian?"

My grandma changed the subject. "Well, tomorrow we are going to have dinner with—"

"Angelina, is that you?" a voice to the side of them called out. A man who must have been in his late seventies stood up from the bench he was sitting on. "How are you, Angelina?"

"Non c'è male," my grandmother said—not bad. "How are you, Pino?"

"You know, the same," Pino answered, looking at a point just above my father and his mother.

"We'll see you later, Pino," my grandmother said.

"*Sì, sì.*"

My father realized that the man, looking now beyond them, was blind and had recognized my grandmother by her voice.

The next day, when my father and his mother came down to Caterina's kitchen for lunch, four people they had never seen before sat along one side of the dining table: two middle-aged adults, a young man my father's age, and a girl of sixteen, who was blushing. The two men rose to shake my father's hand, and one introduced my father to his daughter, Maria.

The family had brought cakes and nuts, bowls of figs and strawberries, and bottles of homemade wine. Caterina served dinner—chicken, which was saved for special occasions. Throughout the meal Maria kept looking at my father and turned away whenever he looked at her. At the end of the meal they all agreed to take a walk through the village.

It didn't take long for my father to realize that he and Maria were walking about twenty feet ahead of everyone else. He turned back to see that the dinner group had swelled to about two dozen people; old ladies all mumbled intently to one another as Grandma smiled knowingly.

My father decided to break the ice—and to give the old ladies some excitement.

"Where do you live?" my father asked.

"Not too far away," Maria answered. "Over on the other side of the mountain, in Tiriolo."

"Do you like music?" he asked.

She nodded a tentative yes.

"What kind of music? Rock and roll?"

She lightly shrugged her shoulders.

At the end of the night, when Maria and her family had gone home, my father walked into his mother's room as she was getting ready for bed.

"Ma, what are you doing?"

"Whatta you mean, Joey? I no doohah nothin. They justa show up."

Every night for the next week a new family would arrive, bringing food and yet another daughter. And every night my father, not wanting to appear rude, played along. Besides stealing fruit with his young cousins (which my father explained they did almost every afternoon while everyone else was taking a siesta), these late-afternoon strolls were my father's only diversion in the tiny medieval village.

Then, one late afternoon, a man showed up in a three-wheeled APE—a cross between a motorcycle and a small pickup truck—to drive my father to Catanzaro to retrieve the lost baggage. His face was thick with creases and covered with two-day-old bristles; without breaking a smile, he motioned for my father to get in. My father squeezed in and closed the flimsy door. The man reached in front of my father and took the handlebar, in effect locking my father in place.

They drove for two hours, up through the mountains and down to the coast. With every turn and bump the man's elbow ground into my father's chest. Wondering why the man didn't use his other hand to steer, my father glanced at his left arm and saw that he, in fact, had no left arm.

They reached Catanzaro in silence, loaded the baggage onto the bed of the truck, and set back out to Gimigliano as the sun dropped behind the mountains. The sky darkened; my father often lost sight of the edge of the road.

"We'll pull over to eat," the man said, some of the first words he spoke.

He slowed the APE as they crested a hill and pulled over to a wide section of the shoulder. It had become cold. He made a fire and sat down to watch the embers burn. The light from the fire cast shadows on his rough face, exaggerating the crevices.

"Do you know what happened to my arm?"

"No," my father said. "Was it in the war? A farming accident?"

"No," the man said, his eyes narrowing. "Your father shot me."

My father froze. This is it, he thought. The vendetta.

"It was back before the Second World War, well before the war," the man explained. "Most Italian boys were in Ethiopia."

From hunting together in the woods in Connecticut, my father knew how perfect Grandpa's aim was. And he knew that Grandpa, not wanting to kill this man, had undoubtedly intentionally shot him in the arm. "What happened? Did you go to the police?"

The man grinned. "No, no. It was my fault. I knew that your mother was engaged to someone back in *l'America*. But I loved your mother, and I thought she loved me.

"I was wrong . . . and your father had no choice. He had to save face," the man went on, shrugging as if my grandfather's response were the most logical action. He looked back down at the flames, then offered my father a sandwich of hard sheep's cheese, onion, and tomato.

And so they ate and talked about the Calabria of long ago.

My earliest impression of old Calabria is a memory of a time before I was born. It is a memory of my father's, told to me so often and so vividly that it has become my own.

On Sundays my father would awaken to the aroma of garlic, olive oil, and tomatoes. His mother would send him and his four brothers and sisters off to church, while she would prepare dinner. Most of the time when they returned, the table would be set for just my father and his parents and siblings. Sometimes my grandmother would set a buffet for relatives and friends.

There would be an antipasto platter of cheeses from the milk of sheep and cows, *soppressata*, *capicola*, and salami. Grandma would then serve homemade fettuccine and *ragù* (which she called "*maccheroni* and gravy") simmered with pepperoni and her version of *braciole* (which she pronounced *rah-zhol'*), oblong meatballs infused with herbs and cheese. The men would pour themselves wine that Grandpa had made.

For the next course, Grandma would pull out of the oven a

roasted chicken or rabbit on a bed of sliced potatoes. Bowls of sautéed spinach, dandelion greens, broccoli rabe, or zucchini would follow. She would place in the center of the table a dish of hot Italian peppers, which only she and my grandfather would eat, along with any other Calabrese adults who were present. They would either slice them onto the *maccheroni* and gravy or nibble on them between bites. (My grandmother once told my father that when she was pregnant with him, she craved hot peppers.)

This was a typical Calabrese dinner—eaten in Danbury, Connecticut.

After those dinners with the extended family members, people would migrate outside to the picnic table under the grape arbor. Grandpa would bring out his concertina and play folk songs as the older relatives joined in singing.

My grandfather, Filippo Rotella, was almost a quarter century older than my grandmother and had lived in America from the time he was eighteen. He was quiet, and he worked hard; although he spoke several languages, English was the one he knew least.

I knew Grandpa as a retired Stetson milliner who had once worked as a gravedigger and stonemason. The community records in Gimigliano seemed to end with him. His mother had died when he was two; his sister had married young and moved north to Milan. His father had moved to America and, many years later, died in Danbury. But almost everything else remains a mystery to me. Even when I went back to Gimigliano, no one could recall him or his family. He had outlived all his friends and relatives in Danbury, leaving only one person, my father's uncle Frank Critelli (a nephew of Grandma's, who was nevertheless older than she), who was old enough to remember Grandpa as a young man. As my father was growing up, Frank Critelli would narrate pieces of the life of my dad's father.

After emigrating, my grandfather first lived in Niagara Falls, where, at twenty-two years old, he enlisted in the army during World War I. During his twenties and into the Depression, he was a rumrunner who, working for the Irish mob, supplied cities from Buffalo down to New York with booze. We have pictures of my grandfather dressed in well-tailored suits and nicely polished shoes, a fedora on his head mischievously tilted to one side. I remember my father often saying, "The only difference between my old man and John Kennedy's was that his was a more successful bootlegger." Story has it that at one point my grandfather was chased by police coming out of Canada. He wrecked his car off the side of the road, crawled out, and found his way to a Seneca Indian reservation, where he hid out for several months.

My grandfather taught my father how to grow tomatoes and vegetables, cultivate grapes and make wine, raise rabbits and chickens. My father learned how to slaughter pigs, as well as the rabbits and chickens he had raised. Whatever he learned, his father had taught him the old Calabrese way.

My father was eleven years old the first time he killed a rabbit for Sunday dinner. He had seen his father do it many times before. Suspending the rabbit by the hind legs, his father would give a single swift chop to the back of the neck. A clean kill. With his father standing by, my father picked up a rabbit by the hind legs. At first the rabbit was still, but sensing my father's nervousness, it began to squirm. After my father gave it a hesitant blow to the back of the neck, the rabbit squealed like a baby. My father hit the rabbit again. It continued to squeal and writhe. His own father looked on patiently.

Flustered, my father let go of the rabbit, which fell to the ground in a shocked lump. He reached for the thing closest to him, a shovel leaning against the garage, and whacked the rabbit over the head. The deed was done; my father's heart sank at having just killed the rabbit he had raised.

After Sunday dinner under the grape arbor, the music from my grandfather's concertina got everyone talking, singing, dancing. With a pipe in his mouth, hat cocked to the side, my grandfather would start off with a fast tarantella. By dusk the exhausted guests would relax, stretching out on the grass, or settling into their chairs under the grape arbor. The music slowed to a lament. As Grandpa caressed the buttons and depressed the bellows, he would hum along, his pipe poking out of the side of his mouth. The music became softer, the conversation quieter. At some point my grandfather would fall asleep. One of his daughters would take his hat off and ease the concertina out of his hands. But the pipe would remain clenched between his teeth.

My father and his siblings were the last people in the family to experience old Calabria.

HOMECOMING

THE ROAD FROM LAMEZIA cut through the mountains.

"Marco," Giuseppe said, "I'll take you to your aunt Angela's first; then tomorrow we'll plan our trip."

"Are you sure you can take the time?" I asked.

"I've got clients everywhere. It's no problem."

The narrow roads folded on top of one another, each curve cut closely to the edge, leaving only a few inches of shoulder. The side that hugged the mountain was overgrown with scrub brush and prickly pear. I rolled down the car window and tried to find the horizon so as to stave off motion sickness. This road, I realized, was the one that my grandfather had taken when he left here—and probably on a mule.

We cut through the main street of Tiriolo, Gimigliano's wealthier sister village, on the local road that connects the Tyrrhenian Sea with the Ionian. The village is known for its handwoven silk shawls and table settings, distinguished by a triangular weave; each of the surrounding villages has its own distinct pattern.

Tiriolo was bustling. Villagers strolled the sidewalks, and a few shopkeepers locked their doors and pulled down their gates. The noon "rush hour" would soon begin. While the big cities of northern Italy have adopted a nine-to-five workday in the desire for prosperity, Calabria has preserved the familial afternoon meal and siesta, which last from noon until three or four.

We left the village and circled the mountain. Directly across the valley to the right, a gap in between chestnut trees framed the village of Gimigliano. I could see the streets of red-roofed yellow houses perfectly and could almost make out the square adjacent to my aunt's house.

By the time we got to Gimigliano, the streets were deserted. Giuseppe parked in the tiny, quiet piazza in Gimigliano Inferiore and helped me carry my bags down the stepped alley of Via delle Grazie. Halfway down, just as the alley curved to the right, I saw my cousin Sabrina waving to me from Zia Angela's window. Her four-year-old daughter, Marisa, stood on her tiptoes to see who was coming. Down below, the door opened up, and Luisa, Angela, and Tommaso walked up the stairs, waving.

Finally, after several years of my visiting my grandmother's hometown, it almost felt like my own. Seeing my aunts, uncles, and cousins every other year, I felt that I was getting to know them.

Just then I knew how the month would play out. I would take a couple of days to explore Gimigliano—to acclimate myself to Calabria—and to spend time with my relatives. Soon after, I would set out on the road with Giuseppe. I remembered asking Angela whether a month was too long to stay. Of course, I assured her, I would be traveling for most of that time. I looked forward to an Italian welcoming.

Uncle Domenico—Mimmo—picked up the bags with his dark, thick hands and brought them in and left them by the doorway. His face radiated with his customary bright smile.

Angela brought out a plate of cheese and *soppressata*. Mimmo poured us all an overflowing glass of a light red wine.

"The grapes this year were very good," Mimmo said.

Disappointed that my father couldn't come, Mimmo asked me about my family. Angela then set down on the table a plate of fried turkey breasts and a large bowl of spaghetti, tossed with olive oil, garlic, and parsley.

She then handed out Italian hot peppers to everyone—small, green, but potent. These peppers are a defining element of Calabrese cooking. I accepted a pepper, but Giuseppe passed with a shake of his hand and a smile.

"So, where are you going to travel?" Mimmo asked me.

"All the way north to the edge of Basilicata, to where they speak Albanian. Then I want to go south to Reggio, and travel through the Aspromonte Mountains."

Mimmo shook his hand as if waving a towel, signifying that it was a long journey. "È pericoloso, Marco." It's dangerous.

Giuseppe and Mimmo began explaining the problems they'd had and stories they'd heard. They warned me of all the kidnappings that had taken place throughout the 1980s and 1990s.

"Just a few years ago they found a boy who had been held for over a year, eating only every other day!" Giuseppe said.

"Why every other day?" I asked.

"The shepherds would only come by every other day. Maybe they didn't have enough food. Maybe it was too far away to make the trip every day."

Mimmo kept our glasses full to the top. Having traveled from the United States that day, all I could think of was of putting my head down on a pillow.

Giuseppe and Mimmo said something to each other in dialect. My aunt and cousins fell silent. Angela then walked to the kitchen. My cousins headed into the guest bedroom, where I had stayed before. A six-foot-long wooden plank connected the bedroom to the living room window of Luisa's house on the next alley. Rather than walk around the corner, my cousins and their kids entered the house through this bedroom window.

"Ah . . . Marco . . . how long are you staying?" Mimmo asked.

"About a month," I asked.

Pause.

"So you are welcome to eat dinner here whenever you want," Mimmo said.

"Thank you," I responded.

There was another pause. Mimmo looked at Giuseppe, who nodded and looked down at his plate.

"Ah . . . Marco . . . where are you staying?" Mimmo asked.

I realized that I wouldn't be able to lie down anytime soon.

"Here, I thought," I answered. At that moment I heard my father's voice: "Remember, guests are like fish, after three days. . . ."

Mimmo looked at me, startled; he looked at Giuseppe, who glanced down at his plate.

"We thought you would only be staying three days. I'm so sorry, but we have no room here. Angela's mother has moved up from her apartment down below." He pointed to the bedroom with the plank. "She can't move around so much . . ."

"Don't worry, I can stay in Catanzaro, in a hotel there," I blurted, not bothering to disguise my shock. I had no money for a month in a hotel; my wife and I had just bought a house, and because I had taken a leave of absence from my job, I wouldn't be receiving any paychecks for the next month.

I thought, how could they put me out, a relative? But I didn't feel like a relative; I felt like a visitor.

Giuseppe offered his place, but I didn't want to inconvenience him. I was already indebted to him for his generous offer to take me around Calabria.

Angela came out of the kitchen and pointed to the floor. Mimmo smiled shyly, then looked to my aunt for approval. "There's always Angela's mother's place downstairs. She hasn't lived there in a year. There's no heat, but I think the electricity is still on."

Angela nervously awaited my response, covering her mouth with her hand. This seemed to me to be a wonderful option, but perhaps they felt they could not offer accommodations that were less than optimal to a family member.

"Perfect," I said.

Angela, Luisa, and Sabrina smiled, then went downstairs to begin cleaning.

Domenico brought out another liter of wine and topped off our glasses.

As we drank, I thought about having guests stay with me back in New York. A month is a long time for anyone, family or not.

THE BREAD OF LIFE

Growing up, my sister and I were never allowed to eat the soft, doughy bread that all our friends ate. My father would constantly remind us that our grandfather had all his teeth—well, almost all—until he died at the age of ninety-eight. "And it's because he ate bread with a good, thick crust." And now Giuseppe, on my second day in Calabria, would take me to see bread made, Calabrese style.

The bedroom in which I was staying narrowed toward the front of the house, where it ended at a window framed and divided into panes with heavy wood. A curtain danced lightly about it.

I got up, walked to the bathroom, washed my face in cold water. The shower was a square plastic basin with a ring of shower curtain that did not entirely enclose it. On the wall, a frayed wire ran from the light switch to a naked bulb dangling above the shower. Someone had attached a piece of thin aluminum foil at the socket to reflect the light. The gallon-size hot-water heater hung above the sink; my showers would be short.

Out the window, an old man wearing a tweed coat and snap-brim hat let his cane lead him down the alley. A distinct chill had settled in Calabria. Having never traveled to the south in spring, I couldn't have anticipated the drastic temperature changes in the mountains. I dug through my bag for a sweater, until I remembered setting it aside at the last minute before I left for the airport, opting for yet another short-sleeved shirt.

Giuseppe knocked at the door at seven-thirty exactly. I would come to realize that Giuseppe did not play into the Italian stereotype of always being fashionably late—or any other stereotype, Italian or Calabrese.

"Un momento," I called out. The toilet was missing the flush handle, and I realized that the only way to flush it was to fill it with water from a bucket that had been placed next to the toilet.

Giuseppe's wife, Elena, got out of the car and kissed me on both cheeks. I crawled into the back, where Alessio, their eleven-year-old son, curled up against the door half asleep. He offered a pouty "Ciao," then closed his eyes again.

We eased out of the sleepy piazza, following narrow streets, through Gimigliano on our way to the village of Simeri Crichi. As the car wound down the mountainside, we passed the local plots of farmland and, just beyond, the village's cemetery. Here, as throughout Italy, the buried bodies are dug up after the last member of the immediate family dies and are replaced by the newly dead. In a country that has been densely populated since antiquity, and one whose religion forbids cremation and the scattering of ashes, this is the only way to preserve land for farming.

Alessio opened one eye, hesitating. I smiled and reached into my backpack. His eyes followed, and when I pulled out a Pokémon toy, he leaped up suddenly awake and opened the box.

"Grazie," Alessio said. "How do you say 'Jessie' in English?"

"I think that is English," I said.

"Do you know Digimon?"

"No."

"Why not?"

"Alessio," Giuseppe said, "leave him alone," turning almost entirely around, careless of the hairpin-curved road ahead of us.

Eventually, he turned the car onto an even narrower road, his eyes still on me. "Marco, now we will take a *scorciatoia*. This way we don't have to go through Catanzaro."

"If there's a shortcut, he'll take it," Elena said, rolling her eyes. Her young face, framed by dark hair, was warm and friendly.

"Of course, because not everyone else knows the shortcuts. This will cut twenty minutes out of our trip. Just think of all that traffic we would miss in Catanzaro!"

In Catanzaro, buildings are constructed along a sinewy, slender mountain ridge, meaning all the streets going in are extremely congested. Giuseppe switched the subject. "You've never made bread before, have you?"

"No, but a lot of people in the States now have small bread ovens," I explained, miming a box shape with my hands.

"But Americans have never had it like this," Giuseppe scoffed. "Fresh yeast, brick oven, the *profumo* of burning olive branches."

At eight in the morning the streets of Simeri Crichi were empty. Giuseppe pulled up in a small piazza, got out of the car, and walked up a staircase to someone's house, where he disappeared around a balcony to the other side of the building. He returned five minutes later. "She must be at the farm already." And we got on the road again.

"How's your family?" Elena asked.

"Good."

"Martha?"

"Great. She wishes she were here." Martha, who was of Dutch and English descent, was far from being Italian, yet was immediately accepted as family. She found our new family more exciting than my sister, Michelle, did. I knew she would have loved this trip.

"It's too bad you couldn't have brought her," Elena said.

Alessio returned to naming the characters of Pokémon, pointing out each one on the back of the box.

As soon as we left the last building of the village, a beautiful mountain range appeared before us. The sun was already bright, quickly burning away the clouds from the previous night. Alessio had moved closer to me and snuggled up against my side like a puppy.

Fifteen minutes later we reached the gate of the farm, which was little more than a newly built cinder-block house with a garage attached, the same size as the house. A Siberian husky lurched from behind the bed of a red pickup truck and ran toward our car, barking more of a greeting than a threat. Two abandoned, wheelless Fiats seemed to sprout from the ground: a dark gray one missing its side panels and doors and a larger blue wagon sitting without its front end, stripped of its seats. Low-lying green pine brush hid yet another car frame, bellied on a green patch of weeds and grass, surrounded by rich red soil that appeared to have been recently plowed. If the ground had been covered by Chevys or Fords, and the mountains a deep forest of green, I could have been in the Appalachians.

Giuseppe pulled up the large aluminum garage door. I had expected to see a couple of cars or, at least, some spare engine parts. Instead there was a wall-length brick oven. The cinder-block walls behind it were only partially cemented over, as if the builder had run out of compound halfway through.

On the far side of the oven hung a hefty red winch with a solid chain and a thick hook. "That's to hang the pig after it's slaughtered," Giuseppe said, pointing to a drain directly below. There wasn't a spot of blood on the floor.

Giuseppe directed me to a door that led to a kitchen. There was a simple dining room set with eight chairs, a counter and cabinets from the 1950s, and in the middle of the floor, the centerpiece for this day's activity, a giant blender of sorts, with blades as long as my forearms dipped into a knee-high trough.

Giuseppe's eyes bulged, and he took a step back.

A woman's voice bellowed, "*Allora*, now you see how easy it will be this time."

"Ciao, Rosetta," Giuseppe said, still staring at the bread contraption. He introduced me to a woman who reminded me of my aunt Rose, my father's sister who had died several years before. Her face seemed to rest in a smile.

"Before, we did this all by hand," Rosetta said.

"Before? How about just last year! My arms would be tired for days," Giuseppe said as his arms kneaded the air into dough. He looked back at the bread machine. I could tell he was disappointed, that he wouldn't be able to show me how to make bread the way he had made it.

The room next to the kitchen was cool and dry and smelled of concrete and red pepper. The walls were corrugated metal, and on shelves in front of me were five-gallon jugs of wine like the ones I remembered seeing in my grandfather's garage in Connecticut. From the ceiling dangled what I recognized as pieces of pig.

The most obvious, and largest, was the prosciutto, the pig's hind leg. There was *capicola*, hung in a net, the neck section stemming from just below the head (*capo*) down along the spine (*cola*). A squarish piece of meat bound with string was the pancetta, the fatty stomach area just below the ribs. A wide slab of ribs, called *costata*, lined the far wall. Coarse grains of salt and pepper blanketed the pipe organ–like set of ribs. Two long pieces of *salsicia*, or shoulder meat, dangled close to the prosciutto. Hanging in the center was a piece of meat that any Calabrese would know—*soppressata*, ground pork that's been infused with red pepper and stuffed inside intestine lining. Wrapped in a mesh of string, the *soppressata* widens to about four inches at its thickest point in the middle and tapers at both ends.

By the time I was old enough to participate in the meat-drying process, my grandfather was too old to slaughter his own pig and smoke the meat, but my father told me stories from his childhood in Connecticut. Every October my grandfather would trade wine with a Portuguese friend for a pig.

Right there in downtown Danbury, my grandfather would slaughter the pig in his driveway and hang it to drain in front of the garage. Once the pig was bled, he would carve it up and hang the cuts of meat in his smokehouse, which was built onto the back of the garage. Decades later and living in Florida with two young kids, my father would proudly point out all the cuts of meat hanging in St. Petersburg's only Italian deli.

Here in Calabria I could taste freshly cured meats. I could taste the only flavors that my grandparents had known.

Finally—Giuseppe told me—there is the *magularu*, dialect for all the stuff that's left over, from the fat to the ground gristle, ears, and snout. It's boiled in a large pot and mixed with hot pepper, as every meat in Calabria is, then refrigerated. The spicy paste is then mixed with ground roasted peppers, salt, and olive oil. This is called *'nduja*, and it is spread on *panini*, on homemade pizzas, or mixed with a marinara to heighten the intensity.

Giuseppe pulled me over to two large wood barrels covered with a fringed tablecloth. He rolled up the tablecloth and slid the thin wood cover to the side. A mixing spoon appeared in his hands, and he dipped it into the barrel, then carefully handed it to me, motioning for me to put the entire thing in my mouth, which I did. The flavor of nuts and butter burst in my mouth as I gulped the olive oil.

"Each barrel is four hundred liters," Giuseppe told me. "The olive trees are down the hill. They bring it to a press once a year, paying them in olive oil."

We went back to the kitchen, where Elena handed me a cup of espresso, already mixed with a spoonful of sugar, then walked out to the garage.

Alessio appeared in front of me, daisies stuck out of his ears and one each from his nostril. His short cropped hair framed his large hazel eyes and thick eyebrows. He rolled his eyes back in his head and fluttered his eyelids. *"Sono morto,"* he groaned—I'm dead.

"Marco, let's see the pigs," he commanded, leaving the daisies in his face. He led me to the far side of the garage to a large doorway with a wood fence, four feet high. He reached his head through the opening of the pen and began calling out to the pigs. Five black-and-white pigs grunted and snorted, huddling together in the soft, moist dirt.

Now Giuseppe brought in dried olive branches and began snapping them into foot-long segments; each still had smaller leafy branches coming out of it. "You heat the house with the stumps . . . and bake with the branches," he said. Because olive branches burn slowly and produce surprisingly little smoke, olive wood is perfect for baking and for warming houses. Giuseppe pointed to the red bricks lining the circular oven walls, explaining that the lighter the bricks became, the hotter the oven was getting.

An old woman walked down the rocky driveway toward the garage. She seemed to have appeared out of nowhere. She was stooped over, her eyes fixed directly on us. Giuseppe waved. She smiled back. A dark blue *fazzoletto*, handkerchief, covered her head. Wisps of gray hair poked out. She wore a dark blue skirt and a dark gray sweater.

She was Rosetta's ninety-three-year-old mother, Giuseppina. As Rosetta introduced us, Giuseppina grasped my hands with both of hers and held them tightly as she looked into my eyes with a nearly toothless grin. She spoke to me in a dialect very similar to Gimiglianese. "He speaks only Italian, Giuseppina," Giuseppe said, as if Italian were Urdu. She pulled me into the kitchen. There she plunged both hands inside the metal basin and pulled out two masses of dough and plopped them on the counter. She tossed a couple of pinches of grain flour on long sheets of wood, then lightly patted the palms of her hands in the flour so they wouldn't stick to the dough. She set the balls of dough on the wood planks and began to roll them, first one, then the other. With a solid, forceful push she rolled out the dough with her fingers, then gently returned the dough to her palms with the outside of her thumbs. Push, roll back; push, roll back; push, roll back. Alessio sat on my lap; both of us were transfixed by the balanced, rhythmic motion of her hands.

Like my grandmother, Giuseppina followed no recipes, just techniques handed down for centuries. This day she rolled three types of bread: the typical large round loaf, or simply *pane*; an oblong roll called a *filone*; and finally, with the smaller, leftover dough, several flat, thin pieces called *pitte*.

Meanwhile, the oven was heating up; once the bricks had turned white, Giuseppe spread the ashes evenly along the bottom. Elena stuck a half dozen red, yellow, and green peppers in the center to roast. We all carried out to the oven long planks of rolled bread. We balanced them between chairs.

Now Elena took out the peppers, their skins blackened; in the kitchen she peeled off the skin and mixed them with sausages and olive oil.

Giuseppina pulled out a serrated knife, and with five quick strokes, she sliced the top of a large round loaf into a pentagon. She stuck the knife in her mouth pirate style—clenching with her molars—and put the bread on a flat paddle with a long handle for Giuseppe to slide it into the oven. She repeated these cuts with each loaf, each quickly executed, each exact; Giuseppe followed her.

After he had placed all fourteen loaves in the oven, he scattered olive branches in between them. The leaves would absorb the heat so the bread wouldn't burn.

As the bread baked, we all stood nibbling on the roasted peppers. "I remember your grandmother," Elena offered. "I was very young, of course."

"What was she like?"

"She was very young then, too." Elena said. "She was large. She was always laughing."

By now it was time for lunch. In the meat room, Rosetta climbed onto a footstool and with a serrated table knife cut a few of the ribs from the *costata*, putting them on a plate. Rosetta's husband, Nicola, was home, having just finished the night shift as an orderly at the hospital, and his red eyelids showed his fatigue.

"Looks good, huh?" he asked me, extending his hand toward the hanging meats.

"Yes, I can't wait to try some."

"This will last another seven months."

We walked outside into the pigpen. He pointed to the largest pig, fat and pink with a few black spots on his back. "We'll slaughter that one this fall," he said. "You cut his throat and let him bleed to death. Then hang him by his heels, and with an ax, you cut him in half, evenly, from anus to snout." He made short, precise hacks with his hands, demonstrating the motion of the ax.

Nicola tried to open the door to the kitchen, but the metal latch wouldn't slide. Giuseppe spotted a liter spring water bottle filled with olive oil. He poured a few drops on his fingers, then rubbed the latch.

"Olive oil fixes everything," he said.

I found it was true. From door latches to getting rings off fingers or getting rid of a squeak, olive oil was the multipurpose salve. I remembered my father asking me if I knew why Grandma's face was so smooth and soft: "It's because whenever she got olive oil on her hands, instead of washing it off, she would rub in into her skin."

We settled around the table. Nicola poured me a glass of his wine, which was actually a chilled, bubbly rosé. I finished the glass, and he poured me another. And then another.

Elena and Rosetta first served Giuseppina's homemade *bucatini*, long, thick hollow tubes of pasta, with a tomato sauce called *sugo*. We each grated our own pecorino, or sheep cheese, onto our plates. The pancetta was passed around, as were bowls of pickled porcini and eggplant, and anchovy in oil. The assorted peppers that Elena had cooked in the oven were served with drizzled olive oil.

Then came the bread, which Giuseppina had taken from the oven. Giuseppe cut off a triangle of bread for me, sliced it open, slathered olive oil on the inside, sprinkled salt and red pepper on it—he looked at me to make sure I could handle the spice—and then, with a big smile, sprinkled on some more. As I bit into it, olive oil dribbled down the corner of my mouth. The bread was light, soft, and airy. I could taste the salt, then the welcome bite of the red pepper. My teeth rested in the crust. It was substantial, without being too thick; it crunched, but it wasn't too crisp. "It's all about the crust," my father always said. "You can tell the quality of the bread with your first bite into the crust."

The meat course followed: sliced hard sausage, freshly cut from the meat room and simmered in the *sugo*.

Everyone talked about this year's peppers and tomatoes. How the greens were doing. And the beans—the fava beans had gotten even bigger this year. And of course a little about how dry the spring was and how *pazzo*, crazy, the temperature had been. Eighty degrees in March, and now, April, they expected a cold front to come in.

The chewing spread the flavors around my mouth. My belly

warmed. The sound of their dialect—an Arabic mixture of hard *h*'s and words ending with *u*—mixed with the peppers, tomatoes, and wine.

Late in the afternoon we loaded Giuseppe's car with four long loaves of bread and said goodbye. I felt good and full. Alessio fell asleep against the door, and I closed my eyes, breathing in the comforting smell of the freshly baked bread, emanating all the way from the trunk.

I took one last look across the valley. Not a single electrical wire broke my view. Only in the distance, on top of the tallest peak, stood a lone telephone tower.

"Gimigliano is on the other side of that mountain," Giuseppe said.

That evening, as I was about to fall asleep, I smelled fresh-baked bread again. Surely no one was baking bread at midnight! I sniffed until I realized that the scent was coming from my clothes, gathered on a chair next to the bed. I was struck by how fitting it was that one of the first things Giuseppe had shown me was how to make bread—in Italy, life's basic necessity.

PALM SUNDAY

THE COLDEST WINTER I have ever experienced was that spring in southern Italy. I slept fully clothed. I would walk into the bathroom and run the hot tap so as to breathe a cloud of warm moisture. The chilly wind would whistle between the buildings and through the gaps in the window frame, which had been set in six inches of concrete.

On Palm Sunday—typically a brilliant spring day in New York— I bundled myself in scarf and leather jacket and set out to explore my grandmother's village, Gimigliano Inferiore. I was on my way to Palm Sunday services at Santa Maria Assunta, the church of Gimigliano Inferiore, where my grandparents had been married, and where my grandmother's brothers and sisters had been married, and where her own parents had been married. When my grandmother died in 1994, her service happened to fall on Ash Wednesday. Every Ash Wednesday I think of her, and since then—whether it's guilt, a desire to remember, or for myself—I've never missed an Ash Wednesday, Palm Sunday, or Easter service.

From my doorstep at the bottom of the alley, forty-five steps, long and irregular, led up to the top and opened out onto the piazza. If I extended my arms, I could almost touch the houses on each side of the steps. A few feet away was a wall of rough-cut rock; several of the houses had been built directly into the mountainside. A balcony jutted out from nearly every house. Pots of pink and yellow flowers colored the balconies, and clotheslines zigzagged above, connecting each of the balconies—each of the owners' lives.

Fog rolled in, dipping deeper into the village. Stray cats poked their skinny heads out of doorways and from under stairwells. A calico darted in front of me, paused, then crept past. As I continued up the steps I heard a fluffing of feathers and a couple of chirps. Below all the doorways were storage closets, some of which had been converted into chicken coops. They weren't large, and they housed at most two chickens apiece.

With decades of emigration to the north and foreign countries, sons, daughters, and eventually entire families had left the village. But for whatever reason—nostalgia, desire to return one day—many of them never sold their houses. Now the houses lay abandoned.

"There are only ten families living on this street," my aunt Angela once told me.

The abandoned houses were discernible only by their lack of potted plants on the balcony or clotheslines from the front door. Southern Italians seem to connect with the earth, with the land. They let the exteriors of their houses erode just like the mountains.

As I reached the top of the stairs and walked out onto the piazza, the mountains broke through the clouds, and the valley dropped below. The fog grew thicker, and with it came a chill. I expected to hear the clop of a mule's hooves, the grinding roll of wooden wagon wheels, a voice calling for the dead.

I walked into the only bar on the piazza at about eight-thirty. A woman stood behind the bar; two men leaned against it; several others were playing a card game at the table on the opposite side of the room. Everyone turned to face me. The woman, who was probably in her late forties with long dark hair, smiled at me and shyly averted her eyes.

"Un cappuccino," I requested.

"*Cappuccino . . . sì,*" she said, and walked to the refrigerator in the back of the room for milk.

All the men were in their fifties or sixties and wore the heavy tweed coats and sport caps that I had always associated with Ireland. Even the weather made me feel as if I were in the North Atlantic.

"Visiting family?" a man asked. He was the youngest of the men and was missing a couple of teeth. Brown spots darkened the bottom row of teeth.

"Yes. Angelina Critelli."

"Critelli . . . Angelina . . . ?" he thought aloud. I couldn't believe that in a village the size of a high school in the United States, a name didn't automatically conjure associations. My idea of village life must have been formed by Italian movies or, more so, by tight Italian communities in the States, one of the many differences between Italians and Italian-Americans. In the United States, relationships became stronger in order for people to adapt and survive in a new country; for those living in small southern Italian villages, people needed to cultivate a sense of anonymity.

"My cousin is Luisa Cantafio," I said, knowing that everyone would know Gimigliano's former alderperson.

"Ah, yes, of course. Her father is Domenico," another man piped in.

"Her husband is Tommaso," an older man said. He put on his tweed cap and started for the door. "He's my nephew," he said with a smile. "See you around."

The bartender set my cappuccino in front of me and courteously opened the silver sugar tray, ubiquitous throughout Italian cafés. "Where do you live? Torino?"

"No, I live in New York," I said, putting in two spoonfuls of sugar.

"Aah, Niagara? I have cousins who live in Niagara."

"No, New York City."

"What's your name?"

"Marco Rotella."

"Rotella? I'm Rotella . . . Maria." Her face lit up with excitement.

After going through our family lineage, we realized that we weren't directly related. And she had never heard of Filippo Rotella, or his family, from Superiore, just minutes away.

Mass was at nine-thirty, and it didn't seem that anyone else intended to go. Maria walked from around the bar and led me to the door, giving me directions to the church as if this foreigner were too limited to make his way around the village the size of a football field. Two men, eager to help out, joined us.

"First, you go across the piazza to the little chapel, there to the right. Stay to the right or you'll miss it. That's where you get your palm leaves. There's a door there. Go in. Then after you get your palms, go straight down the alley, Via Assunta, to Chiesa Maria Assunta. And mass will be there."

I paid the fifteen hundred lire for my coffee, just under seventy-five cents, and left a small tip.

"Your change," Maria called after me.

The men all looked up at me.

I said to Maria in a low voice, "It's a tip."

She knitted her eyebrows and looked at me in confusion. "No, no," she said, and handed me the change.

Five minutes later I was lost. I walked in and out of the little alleyways (of which there were four). I turned back to the bar, where the patrons nodded at me, as if to say, "Yes, it is confusing, but try again." Then I saw Maria's hand direct me to take that first right. I gave her a look that said, "Of course, there it is." Then I dashed into the first alleyway, hoping to spot someone handing out palms.

At the church, a small pink stone building with heavy chestnut doors, not a person was in sight though the bells rang loudly, tunneling through the alleys of the village and echoing throughout the mountains. I remembered that Luisa had told me to stop by before going to mass.

She answered the door in her nightgown and invited me in for coffee. I remarked on the time. "I heard the church bells," I said.

"Oh, that's just a warning. The one that counts rings at nine forty-five. It's like hitting the snooze button on alarm clocks."

She sat me next to the heater and poured me a *caffè*, my second of the morning, while everyone got ready for church. When the next bell rang, Luisa and her ten-year-old son, Francesco, bounced down the stairs, and we walked the hundred feet to the church. The women and children started filing in, while the men and older kids lingered behind. Luisa led me by the arm to a front pew. Mass had begun.

So this was the church in which my grandparents had been married. It was smaller than I had imagined—with only about ten short rows of pews—and less majestic. Bright frescoes had been painted on the pink-and-rose-colored walls, and a brightly colored statue crowned the altar. The Virgin Mary, dressed in robes of white, red, and blue, looked to heaven with outstretched hands. The gold trim of her sleeves and the starburst halo sparkled above her head. She was floating on a white cloud—ascending to heaven—as angels hovered around her. A saccharine sunburst had been painted on the wall behind her, probably added within the last decade. A comfortable soft light filled the church.

I was sitting among the mothers, children, and old ladies. All the men were standing behind the pews; the teenage boys slumped against the walls. Only two men were sitting anywhere around me: an older man who had obviously assisted his wife to the front, and a conspicuously pious man in his twenties sitting in the pew across from me, his arm looped around a very pregnant woman sitting next to him. Neither wore a ring.

After communion, the doors opened behind us, and the priest led the congregation, in the traditional Palm Sunday procession, outside and up the hill to the main road that wound around the mountain from Inferiore up to Superiore. Although it was drizzling, we stopped at a ten-foot-wide shrine of five icons set in stucco. Christ was in the middle, flanked on the immediate left by the Madonna di Porto, the patron saint of Gimigliano, and on the immediate right by a saint I didn't recognize. My cousin told me that it was Maria Assunta, for whom the church was named. When someone behind her asked her to repeat what I had said, she sighed. "I'm just explaining Christian symbols to my cousin. He's from America," she said, raising her lip as if to say, "He's limited, you know."

Realizing that I couldn't do any more harm or look any more like a Philistine, I pointed to the one on Christ's far right. "And who's that?"

"That's Matthew. No, wait, that's . . . You know, I don't remember."

Back at Zia Angela's, we all warmed ourselves by the fire in the kitchen. From time to time, Angela would open the potbellied wood-burning stove and toss some trash in—napkins, paper, even plastic disposable plates—to keep the fire going.

We all sat for a quick meal of pasta and lentil soup, tripe stew, and an onion-and-pepper frittata, while drinking wine that Masino's father had made. Calabresi very rarely eat desserts; they prefer to end their meals with fruit and nuts. But at the end of this meal, Luisa brought out fresh pastries that she had bought in Catanzaro—cream puffs, rum babas, and *torta crema chjina*, which is sponge cake filled with ricotta.

Everyone retreated to home and bedroom for a nap. Not wanting to go back to my cold room, I took a walk around the empty village. Spying another bar—the only other one in Inferiore, it turned out—I walked through the beaded curtain. Boys and teenagers in heavy coats crushed around a video game. A boy with his arm in a cast walked by me and nodded, curling the corner of his mouth in a smirk. On his cast was written, in bold marker, "Rotella."

In the back, six rough-looking men my age smoked and drank. They started a card game. I ordered a glass of wine. The bartender, in his mid-twenties with blue eyes and light brown hair, opened a bottle of homemade wine, discernible by its reusable glass bottle.

"You're Luisa's cousin?"

I nodded.

"I'm her husband Tommaso's cousin."

I extended my hand. I was so happy that someone recognized me.

"I'm also Luisa's father's nephew. We're almost related." He told me his name was Carmine.

I finished my wine and reached for change.

"No, it's on the house. I'll see you around."

A MEDIEVAL VILLAGE

SOMETIME AROUND A.D. 800, villagers along the Ionian Sea began migrating to the interior, the area that is now Gimigliano. Individual family settlements opened up to extended family members, until they grew to *frazioni*, or hamlets. These hamlets bordered others, each with its own church. From there, thirty such *frazioni* came together to form Gimigliano, a village of just over thirty-five hundred people.

Each hamlet had its own family head and even ethnic origin. One of the first, Villaggio Rejina, was settled by Greeks. In Villaggio Casale, Greeks lived with Jewish settlers. Villaggio San Biaggo was founded by a Domenico Chiarella, who could very well have been one of Giuseppe's ancestors.

Shortly after I arrived in Gimigliano, Sabrina's husband, Masino, presented me with a thin book on the history of Gimigliano (many villages, I would learn, have printed their own history books).

The origin of the name Gimigliano is not known. The book suggests that the name comes from the Latin *oppidum geminianum* or the Greek *gimilon*, both of which refer to its fertile land. Some say that the village is named after Saint Geminiano, from Modena. Others, considering the two most populated parts of the town—Inferiore and Superiore—say the name may come from the word *gemelli*, or twins.

Eventually, people in the outlying villages moved to the mountaintops, where they were protected from invading Carthaginians, Saracens, and Normans and from malaria-carrying lowland mosquitoes. From a distance the town must have seemed impregnable. Its connected buildings formed uniform rings and its terra-cotta-roofed houses were stacked one on top of another, built on the mountains' farthest outcroppings, with no visible means of reaching them.

This was Gimigliano Superiore (*susu* in dialect), where my grandfather was born and where Giuseppe keeps his store. Superiore contains about two-thirds of the village's population, and even now they consider themselves better and more sophisticated than the people of Gimigliano Inferiore (*jusu* in dialect), where my grandmother was born. Historically, the villagers of Superiore were better prepared against enemies and were farther away from disease-carrying streams (they tossed their waste and garbage downhill).

Situated within Superiore's walls are the church and the narrow rectangular piazza, where every other Friday vendors from all over the province set up their booths. The main street that leads off the piazza is Corso America, one of the only streets in the center of Superiore where there's enough room for a car. Alleyways leading down the mountain from Corso America are lined with eighteenth-century houses.

A quarter mile of mule path, loosely paved with irregular cuts of stone, connects Superiore and Inferiore. Halfway down, there is a dilapidated one-room chapel. The roof has collapsed, and the windows have long been without glass or frames. The yellow stuccoed walls have faded in centuries of sunlight. The path descends along the back of a building, then cuts between two more buildings, family homes, and ends at the tiny open piazza of Inferiore. Through the beaded doorways of the houses, you can almost detect movement within. Human voices compete with sounds from the radio or TV. The aroma of sautéed garlic and peppers wafts onto the street.

My father always told me that Grandma and Grandpa were poor farmers—peasants—and that all our relatives before them were farmers, too. Growing up in Florida, I imagined them living in a single farmhouse, working acres of tomatoes or groves of oranges. I never would have pictured farmers clumped on top of one another in one village. But they were. Before the sun rose, men, women, and children would walk two or three miles to their fields—actually, slopes where mules can't even work. On these slopes they cultivated figs, oranges, and olives and grew tomatoes, grapes, and eggplant. At the end of the day, just as the sun was setting, they wearily made the same journey home.

But for the people of Gimigliano, their village reaches beyond the medieval walls, beyond their farming fields; their village extends to the Chiesa della Madonna di Porto. The Gimiglianese revere this church, even those who have long since emigrated.

Even to me Gimigliano was a single painting. Copies of it hung throughout my grandparents' house: a pursed-lipped, Anglo-faced Madonna covered in a blue robe, with two hovering angels placing a crown over her haloed head. The baby Jesus, also with a crown and halo, sits on her lap grasping the Virgin's breast exposed through an opening in her red blouse. Gazing out, they share a similar contented expression. She is an Italian woman breast-feeding in public.

Christ may have stopped at Eboli, but for Italians, Mary is with them at birth, all through life, and more important, Mother Dolorosa is present at death. My grandmother prayed to the Virgin and took comfort in the images of the nursing Madonna throughout her house. In my grandmother's village, the townspeople honor Mary once a year by forming a candlelit procession and carrying a statue of her from the countryside church of the Madonna di Porto to Gimigliano a few miles away. Some make the journey barefoot, some on their knees. Three days of celebration follow.

Nearly every year my grandmother sent money to the Madonna di Porto. When people came to her door—salesmen, plumbers, Jehovah's Witnesses—she would ask in broken English if they could make a contribution to the church, her sad eyes refusing a "no." She was the one who kept the ties to Italy through her siblings and through the Virgin Mary. She was devoted to this distant place, the country and the village she and my grandfather had come from.

The more I spent time with my aunt Angela, the more she reminded me of my grandmother, who was also named Angela. She has a round face like my grandmother, and the same smooth skin that defied wrinkles. Maybe she, too, rubbed excess olive oil into her skin while standing over the stove.

In her kitchen, above the refrigerator, was the same portrait of the Virgin Mary that hung in my grandmother's house. I knew Zia Angela could show me something about this painting of the Virgin Mary I wouldn't forget.

When Martha and I visited in the summer of our first anniversary, Angela and Mimmo took us to the Madonna di Porto. Leaving the house, we walked through the steep and narrow streets of Gimigliano Inferiore. Angela stopped by her mother-in-law's house to show us the local costume worn since the eighteenth century. Well into her eighties, her mother-in-law stepped out of her apartment, proudly displaying the thick ankle-length black wool dress with a hint of white trim and a white cotton blouse underneath, all of which she had made herself. Angela lifted the bottom to show us the intricate stitching, pulled at the seams to prove how strong the material was. "No one wears them anymore," she said, "except widowed grandmothers."

Driving along the gently winding road, we passed several white stone arches. In each of these three-foot-high roofed arches was the painting of a saint. Angela explained that these were prayer temples for travelers. This is the road the procession follows from the Madonna di Porto to Gimigliano, and it's at these sites that the devotees stop to pray along the way. Flanking one display of five saints, two upturned ends of sewer pipes acted as flower planters.

We arrived at the Madonna di Porto, where the original painting of my grandmother's Madonna hangs. The church, constructed a few miles from Gimigliano, seemed almost intentionally hidden from the main roadway. It was built precisely where Mary appeared to a lost youth, Pietro Gatto, who in 1753 had found refuge from the cold in a cave. Mary helped Pietro find his way home. Every Pentecost the local townspeople celebrate the miracle.

Angela took us into a tiny chapel connected to the church apse. Inside the chapel, the Madonna icon rested on a stand. We walked around it on an elevated wooden pathway, below which flowed a small stream. Beyond the stream the altar loomed in the nave. On the apse behind the altar, in place of the crucifix, was the large painting of the Madonna and the nursing Jesus. The painting dwarfed the small, freestanding gold crucifix that was placed, seemingly as an afterthought, to the right of the altar.

A few older ladies prayed there, and a family about three pews back, talking slightly above a whisper, sprawled as if lounging on a living room couch. Intricate designs covered the tile floors, and the marble gleamed in the rays of sunshine filtering through the stained-glass windows. It was to this church that my grandmother had sent her money; it was probably to the memory of this church that my grandmother had prayed.

Angela handed me a camera and insisted that I take a picture to bring back to my family. I hesitated, concerned about the flash. She tossed up her hands. "This is a family church, no?" She smiled and turned me back toward the altar. I took one last look at the painting before focusing the camera and noticed that this original painting was different from the replicas everyone had in her house. Though both Mary and Jesus had golden-brown hair, their skin was sallow, and their faces looked weary and sad. They had the faces of southern Italians. I realized that Mary, too, was a peasant.

A VIEW OF HOME

GIUSEPPE STOOD AT THE DOOR wearing a down jacket. I invited him in. He looked inside and shrugged his shoulders.

"No, no, no. Elena and Alessio are waiting outside in the car. Come, let's go for a little drive." He looked over his shoulder as if he didn't want anyone to see him. "Get a jacket. It's cold." He smiled, showing his two silver teeth, and turned to walk up the alley to the car. I put on my leather jacket, but as I stepped outside and saw clouds of breath form under my nose, I told myself that I would buy a sweater in Catanzaro.

Elena rolled down her window to greet me with a kiss. *"Fa freddo,"* she said; she wrapped her arms around herself and gave off a shiver. No sooner had I climbed in than we took off out of the small piazza that was Gimigliano Inferiore as if we were undercover.

Giuseppe drove up steep, winding mule roads, barely one car wide. Fifteen or twenty minutes beyond Gimigliano, we entered a dense wood of chestnut trees, large and gray with bare branches that wouldn't bud for yet another month.

Now Giuseppe pulled over, seemingly at a random point; we got out of the car and walked along a dirt path farther up a hill. Giuseppe looked at the sky above us. It was still misting. Giuseppe and Elena bent down every once in a while to pick up chicory. These flat herbs that reached out to cover the ground would roll up into a ball when cut from their stems.

I was reminded of a folktale retold by Italo Calvino, "The Three Chicory Gatherers," in which three poor Calabrese sisters meet their fate while picking chicory. When the eldest sister, separated in the fields from her other siblings, tugs at a chicory plant, she unearths a hole. Staring up at her is a dragon, who pulls her down and makes her an offer she can't refuse. He proffers a human hand and says, "You can either eat this hand and marry me, or I will lop off your head and eat you."

Then the dragon goes off to hunt, leaving the girl to dine alone. In his absence, she throws the hand into a washbasin. When the dragon returns, she tells him that she ate it. To be sure, the dragon calls out to the hand asking where it is. The hand replies, "I'm in the washbasin." The dragon takes her to a room of headless corpses and cuts her head off.

After the second sister fails the same test and meets her sister's fate, the youngest girl, Mariuzza, sets out in search of the other two. She, too, picks up a chicory plant and greets the dragon eye to eye. The dragon presents her with a foot and offers the same deal. The dragon leaves, and Mariuzza, desperately trying to cover up the foot, wraps it in the front of her dress. The dragon returns and calls out to the foot, asking its whereabouts. The foot replies, "On Mariuzza's stomach." The dragon, believing that the foot is "in" her stomach, marries Mariuzza. In celebration the dragon gets drunk and reveals the secret of his power.

Mariuzza offers the dragon more wine and follows his secret instructions. She cuts off the head of a canary, where she finds an egg, which she cracks over the dragon's head, killing him. Instantly her sisters joyously return to life, as do all the other people, who turn out to be kings, princes, and noblemen.

Each of the sisters marries royally, and from that point on, they are no longer poor. They never have to pick chicory again.

We passed small stone buildings, which had to be at least two hundred years old. The sides were standing, but all the roofs had collapsed. In these chestnut houses, or *caselle*, which were made of stone and marble, cemented with clay, families smoked chestnuts in the fall and winter. Each family built one deep in the woods. Now Giuseppe climbed on top of one and explained how such a house functioned. He pointed out the holes in the stone walls, where slats once formed the floor of the second story. The fire burned below, and the smoke seeped through the slats and roasted the chestnuts. The terra-cotta roofs contained the smoke and heat within the entire structure. The family would roast the chestnuts for about twenty days, then pick through them. The large chestnuts would be eaten or turned into farina; the smaller ones would be fed to the pigs.

"That is why the pork is so flavorful here," Giuseppe said.

I'm sure if he had had the space—and if chestnuts hadn't been killed by disease in the eastern United States—my grandfather would have built a cabin to roast chestnuts. In his small urban backyard, he had a garden, a rabbit hutch, and a smokehouse. It was the food and the connection to the land that my grandfather brought to America.

From him and my father I learned the art of picking mushrooms. We picked our way through woods in Danbury. My grandfather would test for poisonous mushrooms by putting each one in a sack with a silver dollar or a clove of garlic. If either the garlic or the coin turned color, he knew the mushroom was poisonous. Several times my father would catch Grandpa eating those same mushrooms we had been warned against.

I would later ask my father how Grandpa was able to eat the poisonous mushrooms.

"It's his Calabrese body," my father said.

Along with his knowledge of nature, my grandfather also brought to America his Calabrese skepticism toward modern medicine. My father remembers as a child hearing groans coming from the smokehouse in the back late one night. He peered out of his bedroom window and saw that the smokehouse light was on. He walked out barefoot and peeked in the window to see his father sitting on a chair with a bottle of whiskey in front of him. His father had wrapped a piece of leather around a tooth way in the back of his mouth and was clenching it with a pair of pliers. My grandfather saw my father in the window.

"*Vai via, Giusepp'!*" my grandfather roared. Get out of here!

My father ducked back into the night. Halfway back to the house, he heard a bloodcurdling howl. He ran back to see the pliers lying on the table, still holding on to the molar. His father tossed back the whiskey, swished it around in his mouth, then spat out a long stream of dark blood. He took another swig to kill the pain. He then bit off the nub of his cigar and pressed it against the pocket in his gum to cauterize the wound. My father ran off in tears.

Giuseppe eyed the sky again and urged Elena, Alessio, and me onward. We passed through a field of chestnut trees that had been cut down. From within the stumps, new trees had begun to shoot up. The higher we went, the fewer trees there were. I could tell we were getting close to the top. Giuseppe stopped, studied the sky one last time, and smiled at me. "Close your eyes," he said.

I closed them. He grabbed one arm, and Elena grabbed the other while Alessio darted in and out of my legs. With each step my foot fell on harder ground, from clay to rock. The wet wind whipped my face. Slowly they led me several feet forward, then stopped.

"Open your eyes," Giuseppe said.

I did so. I stood on a piece of rock jutting out of the edge of the cliff. My knees buckled. Before me the valley opened wide. Below me the terra-cotta rooftops of Gimigliano clung to the ledges. The water on the rooftops glistened when a ray of sun poked through the clouds and shot to the mountains across from us.

Dark green mountains undulated and rolled into the horizon, to Reggio, to Sicily, to America. Beyond the mountains was another world, but down below was a world you could understand. The view was small enough to keep a photographic image in your mind, an image you could take with you. I wondered if my grandfather had ever come up here to take one last look at his village.

Walking back to the car, we collected handfuls of chicory. Holding the herbs close to my nose, I breathed in the damp, woody smell.

Back at his house that night after dinner, Giuseppe and I spread out a map and planned our tour of Calabria. I circled all the cities I wanted to visit. Because Calabria is long and narrow, the most efficient way to see her, Giuseppe announced, was to explore her in quarters—and, by doing so, divide Calabria pretty much by regional capitals.

"We'll start with the north Ionian, the area around Crotone," Giuseppe said as he brought his finger down the center of Calabria through her spine. "Then we'll do the south Ionian, Catanzaro and south."

I looked at the west coast, the Tyrrhenian Sea. The distances between places weren't great, but I knew that a map, in this mountainous region, could be deceptive. "We'll do Cosenza and north," Giuseppe said. He took a deep breath and continued. "And by the end of your trip, we'll go down to Reggio." I was ready to venture beyond the only Calabria my grandparents ever knew.

Part II

NORTH TO THE EDGE OF THE WORLD

MATTIA PRETI'S VILLAGE

CALABRIA runs about 150 miles from north to south, and she is only 25 miles wide at her narrowest point. Looking at Calabria on a map, you search for the bold letters that indicate a city of moderate size. You see masses of brown and green in the center. Your eyes immediately scan the east coast. The first city you see is Catanzaro, Calabria's capital. Just above lies Crotone. Your eyes move southwest across the peninsula to Vibo Valentia, then down to Reggio di Calabria. With one last glance to the north, your eyes settle on Cosenza, which is buried in the mountains. That's it: five cities. The rest of the map is spotted with villages marked in fine print. You get the feeling that in the ages that Calabria could have been settled, there was little to draw people—that Calabria has remained the same since the landmasses formed.

I would love to get high enough to see an aerial view of Calabria. Maybe the mountain range would resemble the spiny back of a long-extinct creature; Gimigliano would lie just about in the middle and just to the east.

Two mountain ranges fall south of Gimigliano: the Le Serre

Mountains and, at the land's end, the Aspromonte range. North of Gimigliano are the Sila massif and the Pollino mountain range, which separates Calabria from its neighbor, Basilicata, and from the rest of Italy.

The Sila massif is divided into three sections and is one of Italy's largest, least-settled areas. Most of the Sila has now been designated a national preserve. Gimigliano clings to the southernmost section of the range, the Sila Piccola. Beyond, and much more remote, lie the Sila Grande and the Sila Greca, named for its many Greek Orthodox Albanian communities.

In the center of the Sila Piccola, deep in its folds and crevices, lies Taverna, known throughout Calabria as the birthplace of her most famous artist, seventeenth-century painter Mattia Preti.

Although it is just twenty miles from Catanzaro and fifteen from Gimigliano, Taverna is reached only after an hourlong drive along nauseatingly winding roads—especially when Giuseppe takes his *scorciatoia*. "You see, the average driver would drive to Catanzaro, then take the newly built autostrada to Taverna, but from Gimigliano, that adds another half hour," Giuseppe said, explaining his shortcut. "I've traveled these roads since I was a kid; they aren't on any map."

Recollecting, he went on: "When I was about twenty years old, I had an old Fiat. A friend and I were driving fast on these roads . . . right about here," he said, pointing to a curve, where the road fell off thirty feet or so.

"Back then, not many people had cars, and these roads were originally cut out of the mountainside for mules and two-wheeled carriages. And, Marco, I went off the road, we rolled and rolled, then suddenly the car stopped. A big olive tree had stopped us from a sheer drop. We both crawled out and walked the rest of the way home," Giuseppe said.

We had come to a plateau, where half-finished buildings dotted the ridge: light brown walls, four or five stories high, protruding from the deforested land.

"This was going to be a hotel," Giuseppe said. "Ten years ago they were going to develop a resort. But the owner took the money and left."

"Mafia?" I asked.

"Who knows? Everything's mafia, but in this case, I think it was the promise of damming one of the rivers and building a lake resort."

Along the way patches of cleared land broke the otherwise dense forest. On a few of these patches of land stood more abandoned construction; the state had given the owners money to build here, pledging to create a tourist site to attract business.

"But nothing has ever happened," Giuseppe said. "They live with the promise of construction, but money is slow in coming, and progress is slow here, as it is throughout Italy."

To me, these were like the empty promises from the north, where industrialists pledged to open car and gun factories throughout Calabria to boost employment.

Once we passed the decaying hotel along the ridge, we could see the valley crevice within the trees and folds of the dark green mountain. Within a deep valley lies Taverna, which is like schist; the hard, unassuming outside hides its center crystals.

The road gradually narrowed until we came to the village of Sorbo, where the houses crept right up to the road, making it too tight for more than one car to go through. The road, and village, dropped precipitously, and it seemed that the unwritten code was that cars heading up had the right-of-way. With each car that approached, Giuseppe pulled his Fiat up on the sidewalk or squeezed into any nook or cut in the buildings that was available.

The rules changed at a hairpin curve, after which the road plummeted even farther into the valley. As far as I could tell, whoever approached this point first had the right-of-way, meaning that the car in the opposite direction—as well as every car behind it—had to back up. I'm sure that it wasn't mere coincidence that the town's only café stood at this point. The Italian lover of spectacle would find an endless source of entertainment here, watching—and wagering, I imagined—which car would make it through first and which would be forced to back off. Wool-capped and tweed-jacketed men took their front-row seats, sipping their anisette-enhanced coffee.

Once in Taverna, Giuseppe parked directly in front of a store similar to his, and we went in. The walls were stacked with toys, and behind the counter were shelves of stationery—and a photocopy machine.

"Pino!" the owner exclaimed, using Giuseppe's nickname. *"Come va?"* He was about six feet tall, with neatly trimmed thinning hair. He wore a tailored tweed jacket and a fashionably wide silk tie. He was light-complexioned, with a prominent nose.

Giuseppe introduced us—his name was Walter d'Aquino—and told him that I was writing a book about Calabria.

"Ah, very good," the man said. "And I can see that you hurried to Taverna, I'm sure, to see the birthplace of Mattia Preti."

We hadn't gotten there yet, but I nodded, realizing how pleased and surprised he was to have a visitor to the village.

D'Aquino disappeared behind the counter, then emerged with brochures and two paperback books about Mattia Preti, about the church where his work is hung and the modern museum that, because of Preti, has drawn funding to show the work of living artists.

"So your name is Rotella?" d'Aquino asked. "Any relation to the artist Mimmo Rotella? We held an exhibit of his work here in 1990."

I told him I wasn't, but I knew of the artist who had made his name in the politically tumultuous 1960s with collages made of torn posters. Mimmo Rotella grew up in Catanzaro, then moved to Rome, where he still lives. He was part of the New Realist movement whose artists incorporated the time's icons and pop culture themes into their work.

After a while Giuseppe turned the conversation to business. Walter, impressed by Giuseppe's postcards, agreed to carry more. Walter looked at his watch and suggested we rush to the church before it closed to see Mattia Preti's paintings.

All the while I had been curious how my guide had got such a German-sounding first name. Now I asked him: was his family from the north?

He smiled. "No, no, we are from here originally, but during the war my father, who was stationed near Naples, met an American soldier. They became close friends, and he gave me his friend's name."

The twelfth-century Chiesa di San Domenico dead-ends a street. Alongside it is a row of eighteenth-century buildings, the baron's palazzo. The windows face the promenade, offering a glorious view of the rest of the village of three thousand people, the valley, and the Ionian Sea in the distance.

At one time Taverna was located on the sea, halfway between the settlements of Squillace and Crotone, but the village was destroyed by Saracen invaders in the tenth century. Like many other seaside villages, it was rebuilt inland. By the fifteenth century Taverna was thriving again, this time as a stopover for merchant travelers between the Ionian and Tyrrhenian seas.

D'Aquino directed Giuseppe and me inside the church. The interior was light yellow stucco, with white-and-gold trim. I first noticed a statue to the right, the Madonna Addolorata holding the dead Christ on her knees. The Madonna gazes at her dead son's hand. Hers is not a beatific expression, but that of a defeated Calabrese mother who has not yet accepted her son's death. Looking at the hole where the nails had been driven, she seems to say, "How could they have done this to my boy?"

The left side of the church was lined with Mattia Preti paintings. Because it was Easter week, the lights had been turned off the paintings to draw the focus to a statue above the altar of the crucified Christ. There was just enough sunlight filtering through the stained glass to get a good look at Preti's paintings.

Painting in the latter part of the 1600s, Preti, known as the Cavaliere Calabrese, the Calabrese knight, was part of the Neapolitan school, and the almost impossible realism of his work is reminiscent of Caravaggio. The largest painting, *Cristo Fulminante*, pictures an angry Christ against a blaze of orange throwing down lightning bolts from gray clouds; the Virgin Mary is next to him, almost pleading with him to stop. The next painting shows the sermon of John the Baptist, who, set against dark cave walls, has a burnt red robe draped over him. Preti has painted himself at the bottom, ironically smirking back at the observer. Perhaps the most famous of his paintings is displayed in the Uffizi Gallery in Florence. It's a portrait of himself wearing the costume of a Knight of Malta; he lived and worked for many years on the island of Malta, where he died in 1699.

On the way out of the church, Giuseppe ran into yet another business associate, a tall, soft-featured man named Rinaldo Veraldi, the owner of one of the card stores that lined the main street, two blocks down from Walter.

"Do you get many tourists?" I asked.

"Yes," he said, then muttered, "but they are mostly schoolkids from Calabria and Sicily."

I asked him if he was from Taverna originally. He nodded and pointed to the palazzo behind us. "This is my family's. My distant grandfather, Cesare, who was at one time the baron, bought this in 1771. We are descended from the Normans. And this place has been in our family since then. Would you like to see?"

"I'd love to," I said, and looked at Giuseppe, who was clearly eager to talk business.

"I've never been in," Giuseppe said, giving up on the business prospect. "It would be a pleasure to see inside."

We faced two garage-size doors made of chestnut. A small door, just tall enough for a single person to duck through, was built into one of the larger doors. Rinaldo directed us through it and into a cavernous stone carriage house, then through a back door to a garden. The decrepit palazzo walls surrounded us.

"I apologize about the state of the place," Rinaldo said, pausing before we ascended the wide marble stairs. "But restoration costs so much money, especially if you want to do it right."

He walked us through bedrooms and living rooms that hadn't seen a paintbrush in at least two centuries.

"This was my grandmother's room, until she died a few years ago." The bedroom had twelve-foot ceilings and was as wide as a village block. The room dwarfed its contents: a bed, a painting of the Virgin Mary above it, a nightstand, a chest of drawers, and a prie-dieu. Frescoes on the ceiling, damaged by water and humidity, had peeled off and hung in strips.

"My wife and our children live in the next part of the palazzo. It's completely redone with modern fixtures," Rinaldo explained, pointing to a door beyond which I could hear a television and smell peppers sautéing.

He led us back outside. The bottom corner housed a very modern store, with bright lights and neatly stocked shelves.

"Oh, yes," Rinaldo said, noticing where I was looking. "That's my other store. It's for baby supplies as well as for geriatrics. The new and the old."

THE LAND OF TUFO

WHEN MY WIFE, MARTHA, AND I VISITED Calabria for our first anniversary, Zia Saveria took us to the beach at Soverato, just south of Catanzaro on the Ionian Sea. Zia Saveria, Zia Angela's sister, is the crazy aunt, the relative guaranteed to show you a great, if unpredictable, time. By the time we reached the ocean, we were exhausted from Saveria's wild shortcuts and fast driving in her Suzuki Samurai and were anxious to jump in.

Heads turned to Martha and me as we cut a path across the white sand to the water. I should say, they all stared at my wife, who has light hair and light skin. We laid out our blankets on the sand. A woman sitting a few feet away hurried up to Martha and offered La Bianca an umbrella; another woman trotted up to Martha proffering a straw hat. Zia Saveria helped Martha rub number forty-five sunblock over her shoulders.

Myself, I decided to forgo sunblock, explaining to Martha that being Italian with a Mediterranean complexion and having grown up in Florida, I of course would only tan. But I had underestimated the Calabrese sun—and the paling effect of seven years in New York City. My skin turned pink in minutes.

To cool off, I waded into the water, which was colder than I had expected it to be. Then I dived in. As I was surfacing, I felt my wedding ring slip off my finger. I opened my eyes and watched as it twirled down. I tried swimming after it but lost it in the sand.

I came up looking very upset. A small kid swimming next to me asked, *"Che è successo?"* When I told him what had happened, he summoned all his friends with their snorkels and masks—seven in all—and they went exploring.

"What happened?" asked Martha, who looked like a mummy all rolled in white cotton—with stray smears of cream around her face.

I took a deep breath. "My wedding ring . . . it slipped off my finger."

"On our anniversary?" Martha said, and, realizing the irony, began to laugh. "Oh, no," she said, feeling worse for me than for the lost ring.

I told Zia Saveria. She stood up and exclaimed, "That's good luck. Now you will have to return!" Then she walked over to Martha and grabbed her finger. "Now you will throw yours in so they can be joined forever!" Zia Saveria laughed and kissed her on the cheek.

Now Giuseppe and I left Catanzaro along the same route that Zia Saveria had taken to the beach, then headed north along the two-lane coastal road.

Ten minutes in, Giuseppe brought the car to a screeching stop— from about sixty-five miles an hour. In front of us, an old woman dressed in black had stopped traffic in both lanes. She angrily looked at the drivers, then turned to the side of the road and gave the all-clear to what must have been her husband in a green three-wheeled APE. The man frowned at his wife, taxied out into the road, barely stopped to pick up his wife, and continued across.

For about forty-five minutes, we followed the coast north. To our left, or northwest, tiny ancient villages dotted the hills, surrounded by eucalyptus trees, and below them olive trees in neat rows. To our right, newer apartment buildings, restaurants, and the occasional strip of stores lined the ocean road.

"Everyone has moved from the mountains to the ocean, where they can make more money from tourists," Giuseppe told me in Botricello, turning left onto a road that led up to the mountains. While centuries ago villages like Taverna moved to the mountains for safety, now, in order to survive economically, they move to the ocean to cash in. They give their villages suffixes like Marina or Lido. Older folks remain in the mountain villages, while their sons and daughters settle along the sea.

We veered off along the foothills and coasted into a tiny part of the village just slightly up the cliff called Botricello Superiore. An eroded concrete sidewalk lined the sandy road, scarred with cracks and broken up by weeds. In this village, which once counted nine hundred inhabitants, there was not a single car. The shutters of all the houses had been nailed closed.

Cats peeked out of corners and crept toward Giuseppe's car: one, then three, then seven, all crouching, skinny and haggard, their fur poking out in rough tufts. Suddenly dogs appeared from every corner and overtook the cats, which scattered back to their holes, then paused in exactly the same places as the feline predators, their mouths hanging open.

In a courtyard I spotted a clothesline. "Someone must live here," I said to Giuseppe.

"There are only about four families who still do. Women and old men. They are the last; they still fight the flight to the coast. This is where they and their parents and grandparents all grew up," he explained.

Only a cat's mew could be heard, as the dust and debris blew along the alleys.

"They wait here now for their sons and daughters to return from the north," Giuseppe added. Like the more prosperous coastal villages, Botricello feels the footsteps and voices of its sons and daughters, smells the comforting spicy food only two months out of the year. By keeping their primary residences in the south, many are able to receive government subsidy grants. Some don't want to lose their ancestral homes, but most couldn't sell them if they tried.

Isola di Capo Rizzuto is not an island, but a village on a relatively flat peninsula on the ball of Italy's foot. This stretch of land and the valley of Lamezia Terme on the Tyrrhenian Sea offer Calabria's only notable flat surfaces. As you gaze off the coast, you see a spot of calm in the turbulent sea and picture the mythical island Ogygia, where Odysseus landed and for seven years lived with the "wily Calypso, of the fair braids, a dread goddess. With her no one has intercourse, either of gods or of mortal men." She's a Calabrese father's dream daughter.

This part of Calabria became a port for Greeks, Aragonese, and Normans; during the post–World War II land reclamation, it was inhabited mostly by *contadini*, or peasants. In the 1970s, when those same peasants realized that they could successfully tap into the Italian tourism industry, they gradually built hotels and restaurants.

On one outcropping of the peninsula lies the *frazione* of Le Castella, the only elevation in an otherwise flat, nearly treeless part of the peninsula. We entered the hamlet by way of a narrow two-lane road. Faded yellow nineteenth-century buildings abutted stores and houses built in the 1970s, which seemed to have deteriorated at a much faster pace, as if to match their older neighbors. They were stuccoed like the older ones, but where the stucco had chipped, you could see the reinforced concrete. Few people gathered outside.

The closer to the water we got, the larger the stores became; windows offered views of shelves packed with beach blankets, towels, umbrellas, and souvenirs. I spotted rows of carved wooden statues of nineteenth-century Calabrese *contadini*, men with muzzled rifles at their sides or pistols in their belts and "La Mafia" written at their feet.

Though it was April and the town was deserted, Le Castella reminded me of coastal villages in Florida, like Tarpon Springs and Panama City, which cater to tourists from south of the Mason-

Dixon Line. Likewise, in July and August the beaches are populated almost exclusively by Italians—some who come down from the mountains, but mostly those who have moved north for work and return home on holiday.

The road ends at a piazza, which faces the castle island for which the town, Le Castella, is named. The castle was built by the Aragonese between 1510 and 1545, but its main tower is purported to have been first constructed by Hannibal during the Second Punic War, which lasted from 218 to 201 B.C. Once a strong defense against intruders and pirates, the castle feels more like a tourist playground.

Here at this piazza were the first signs of life—workers who had started construction and cleaning for the tourist season. Bulldozers were widening the streets, stucco artisans were reworking store facades, and carpenters were putting additions onto remodeled restaurants. Just workers, no passersby, no ladies buying produce, no produce stands. Two roads led to the castle, which could then be reached only by a footbridge.

The air was cold, but the sky was clear blue—perfect lighting for the castle. Giuseppe took out his camera and tripod from the trunk and backed away in order to get a clear shot.

"This postcard will be beautiful," he called out to me.

At one time the entire towns, was villages by the walls of the fortress. Mounds of rubble and stone now mark the boundaries. Like North Florida coastal towns, these villages were scarcely inhabited as recently as thirty years ago. Now they have become alternative destinations, out of the way of the *conoscenti*, but a find for the locals and those looking for isolation. The village would swell for two months out of the year and then, like Panama City, would all but close.

Giuseppe needed to call on a client in the village of Capo Rizzuto, another outcropping on the peninsula. From here you can see Le Castella, but because Capo Rizzuto was farther from this tourist sight, if only about five miles, and empty of decent beaches, the region's namesake was small and slightly shabby.

"A man was gunned down here a couple of months ago," Giuseppe said. "It's dangerous, but only for locals."

Young men lingered on the edges of the piazza; whenever someone walked by, they looked up and with curious eyes followed the passerby, all the while keeping their conversation flowing. I wondered, had my grandparents never left—had I grown up here— would I have filled my days *passa tempo*, passing time?

The streets are wider here than in Le Castella; people actually live here. Farmers mostly, some fishermen; some make the half-hour drive to the textile factories and electrical companies, such as Montedison, near Crotone.

The smell of baking bread filled the village.

When Giuseppe was done, we walked along through an alleyway at the end of the piazza, which took us to the outskirts of the city. We passed by the village's church, which was constructed from light clay-colored stone. Brick size blocks of this stone were laid out in front of the church. Bricklayers were at work mending damaged parts of the wall.

Giuseppe got the foreman's attention. "May I pick one up?" he asked.

The foreman looked at Giuseppe and with a formality that lent a seriousness to the situation said, "Yes, of course."

Giuseppe picked up the stone and explained that this was tufa (*tufo* in Italian), a hard, though porous, rock that was the foundation of most coastal Calabrese villages. Tufa, which feels like coral but is almost as light as pumice, lines the entire coast and is sandwiched between layers of clay and rock; all the buildings, including Le Castella, were made of it. It's usually found just below several feet of earth, and its hardness makes it expensive to cut. The workers were following the centuries-old tradition of cementing each brick with clay.

A flutter of wings broke through the dull, rhythmic sound of mallets lightly tapping the tufa in place; pigeons and sparrows burst from the church belfry above to the roofs of the surrounding buildings.

AS SIMPLE AS A PANINO

CALABRIA'S NATURAL BEAUTY has been spoiled by drought and destroyed by earthquakes. Her riches have been stolen by barons and kings, borrowed by peasants. To appreciate Calabria, you have to imagine all she has been through. You have to build a narrative from an eighteenth-century doorway around which an entirely new house has been built; a stone wall that's sprouting weeds in its mortar and serves as the backdrop to a vegetable garden; a pile of rocks that at one point was a temple in one of the largest, most powerful cities in Magna Graecia.

On the north side of the Capo Rizzuto peninsula, and twenty-two miles south of Crotone, stands Capo Colonna. As you drive across desolate fields of weeds and scrub brush, cresting tiny hills, a monolithic figure comes in and out of view until suddenly it stands in front of you, holding strong to its ground right on the coast: a single Greek column rising about twenty-five feet from the ground. This column is the last remnant of the Greek city of Crotone (or, as the Greeks called it, Kroton). The last vestige of the great temple of Hera Lacinia, queen of the Olympian gods and the wife and sister of

Zeus, it is also older than the Parthenon. At one time forty-eight such columns supported the temple, which could be seen by passing sailors arriving from Greece or returning there.

I followed Giuseppe into the ruins. The grounds surrounding the temple had been recently excavated; we walked through the bases of onetime arches, which led to an oven. Simple honeycombed designs decorated the chest-high walls. Looking up from the sunken excavation, I saw red poppies dancing in the wind. Close to shore, a military tower blocked the view of the ocean.

Much has disappeared from the temple, which was probably leveled by an earthquake. Throughout the centuries, peasants had carried off pieces of rocks and tiny treasures.

"Even that military tower was built with the stones of the temple," Giuseppe said in disgust. "And that was built only a hundred years ago."

I noticed one other building, a small church near the coast. It was called the Santuario SS Madonna di Capo Colonna. Italians had taken Hera, the goddess of women and children, and co-opted her as their own, now Catholic, protectress.

As we walked out, Giuseppe stopped and picked up a piece of the temple rock. "Marco, *guarda*," he said. "What is this?"

I looked closely, thinking he wanted me to tell him which part of the temple it had come from.

"What is this?" he asked again. "You should know by now." Realizing I needed reminding, Giuseppe said, *"Tufo, Marco."* He looked around and held out his arms. *"Tutto in tufo!"*

You could stock a gourmet shop with what grows along the way north to Crotone. Flowering orange blossoms line one side of the narrow light gray road; growing on the other side are short, flat-topped peach trees and lines of drab green olive trees, some of them three hundred years old. One can see the round bushy almond trees, tucked in between, scattered throughout.

We passed a sign that read KROTON. The citizens of Crotone have reclaimed their Greek roots and changed the spelling, which from the eleventh century until 1929 was Cotrone (still used by some of the old-timers). Crotone was the first Greek colony in Italy, founded in 709 B.C. by Greeks who left their country to explore, in response to the oracle of Delphi, and landed on the south shore of Italy's toe. For the next several hundred years it flourished, as did other Greek settlements, Sibari, Locri, and Reggio. Calabria would never be a richer place.

Two hundred years after Crotone was founded, Pythagoras, leaving behind the conservative thinking of Greece, settled here, developed his theorem, and attracted a cultish following—until it was said that Pythagoreans could pass a person on the street and know instinctively whether or not he was a believer. Pythagoras was more than a mathematician and philosopher; he was a spiritual leader who believed in the unity of the community and who outlined its codes of behavior and even its diet, which, while vegetarian, did not allow the consumption of beans. After thirty years he was forced out of the city and fled farther north to Metaponto. It may be that the Calabresi tired of someone who looked down on beans, which in a region without broad fields or grazing lands were (and still are) a staple food.

These Greek colonies raided and pillaged one another. Locri, which is south of Catanzaro, attacked Crotone. In 510 B.C. the Crotonesi attacked the more powerful and richer Sibari; with the help of Milo, one of the greatest Olympian athletes, the Crotonesi leveled Sibari and changed the course of its rivers to flood the city. It wasn't until the 1940s that Sibari was recovered.

In 206 B.C., during the Second Punic War, Hannibal fled to Crotone. Having gotten used to the hospitality of the south, and the southerners' desire to get out from under the Roman yoke, Hannibal felt safe and settled in Crotone, but after a time the Crotonesi, who had long been loyal to the Romans, expelled him from the city.

After Hannibal came the Longobards, the Byzantines, and, in the middle of the sixth century, the Normans, who installed the feudal system, which governed Crotone and most of the south until the 1940s, when peasants revolted in order to claim latifondi, parcels of land owned by absentee barons. It was here that some of the most violent peasant uprisings took place.

In the neighboring village of Melissa in 1949, peasants occupied an abandoned estate. A man who claimed ancestral ties to the estate called in the military. Three peasants were killed, and a monument circled by stones now lies beneath olive trees.

Giuseppe and I followed the coastal main road to the center of Crotone. The open sea was to our right, and to our left rocky cliffs rose like a wave ready to pounce on the city. With a population now of sixty thousand inhabitants, Crotone is the only harbor between Taranto in Apulia and Reggio di Calabria at the tip of Calabria's toe.

We drove along Piazza Pitagora, named after Crotone's famous philosopher. All the buildings around the piazza, and many throughout Crotone, had porticoes over the sidewalk, which reminded me of the majestic porticoes in Bologna. Doric columns support the porticoes, which provide shelter from rain and sun. This day the sun was strong, but the ocean wind was cold; it seemed to tunnel through the porticoes and bounce off the mountains back into the city.

George Gissing, traveling in 1897, hated Crotone, lamenting in his memoir *By the Ionian Sea*, "What has become of Croton? This squalid little town of to-day has nothing left of its antiquity." But the city came alive in the last half of the twentieth century, thanks mostly to the Montedison electrical plant. Power plants and great cables and relay towers surround the city, sending electricity south to Sicily. The mafia still has a strong hold here. It's common to read in the papers about recent arrests of members of the *'ndrangheta*. Whereas ships used to bring food and spices from Asia and Africa, today Crotone's chief import is prostitutes from Russia and former Eastern bloc countries.

Gissing found the "common type of face at Crotóne [to be] coarse and bumpkinish," but I saw beautiful full-lipped women with strong cheekbones, noble noses, and thin, straight eyebrows.

Despite the mafia, money from the electricity plants has actually enriched the city of Crotone. The municipal archaeological museum, for example, is one of the most modern museums in Calabria.

It is housed inside a restored fifteenth-century Aragonese castle, and the docents are young and knowledgeable—a rarity in most of Italy. The museum offered a detailed history of the excavations of the region, including the discovery, during the rebuilding of the local soccer stadium in 1998, of another part of the Greek foundation of Crotone.

In general, throughout Italy, I found that museum attendants greeted you with a look of boredom that, after a few minutes, turned into one of annoyance as if you were the only thing that was preventing them from taking their next break. I found this to be less so in Calabria.

I asked one of the docents, a young women with long brown hair and green eyes, if there was any information available on the thirty years Pythagoras lived here—what the city was like then. She apologized, saying that all that remains is an oral history of his teachings.

"Are you staying here long?" she asked.

"No, we are just here for the afternoon," I said.

"It's too bad. You'll have to come back sometime. There are treasures throughout the city," she said, and offered a friendly smile.

She was one of the few women who would freely offer their knowledge. Many women in Calabria seem inhibited, as if they are afraid to talk to a man for fear of what people might think. But this woman and others like her seemed to view the job as a license to break tight-lipped social mores. In this way, the museum of Crotone's past was oddly forward-thinking.

On our way back to the car Giuseppe paid a visit to one of his clients, explaining that I was trying to find any information on Pythagoras. The man shrugged but then directed us to the historical society a few blocks away. There a pleasantly plump woman greeted us and took down several volumes of history about the construction of Crotone.

Giuseppe addressed her as *gentilissima*; as with many things, Giuseppe seemed to know more than the experts, and their conversation became his twenty-minute peroration on the development of

Crotone. The woman listened politely, gently correcting him on a couple of dates.

Giuseppe looked at his watch. He had one more client to visit later this afternoon. We hadn't even gotten to ask about Pythagoras.

"Of course we can come back," Giuseppe said. "We can come back next week. Crotone or Cotrone or Kroton, it will always be here."

It had taken us only an hour and a half to get to Crotone from Catanzaro. In the days of Gissing, who traveled on a slow train or by horse and wagon, it would have taken an entire day.

Gissing had fallen very ill here and had been bedridden for days, yearning to get back to Catanzaro, which, in his delirium, became paradise. As Gissing's appetite returned and he knew that he would soon be able to leave for Catanzaro, he was able to look at Crotone anew. He often awoke to musicians playing in the piazza beneath his hotel window: the beat of a drum, the drone of a street organ, the cry of the singer. "All the faults of the Italian people are whelmed in forgiveness as soon as their music sounds under the Italian sky . . . An immemorial woe sounds even through the lilting notes of Italian gaiety." Perhaps by facing his own temporary hardship, Gissing realized the hardship the Calabrese peasant continually endured. "Listen to a Calabrian peasant singing as he follows his oxen along the furrow, or as he shakes the branches of his olive tree. That wailing voice amid the ancient silence, that long lament solacing ill-rewarded toil, comes from the heart of Italy herself, and wakes in the memory of mankind."

It was the ill-rewarded toil that had driven my grandparents out of Calabria, although I imagine that this aspect of character, this ability to find solace in centuries of hardship, was what had allowed my grandparents to survive their first few years in America.

It's been my experience that you can't get a bad meal in Italy as long as you stay away from the tourist sites, and there are few such sites in

Calabria. Italians will simply not eat something that doesn't taste good—be it a dinner prepared at home or a quick sandwich at a road stop.

Along an undeveloped strip outside Crotone, we pulled up to a long roadside building with tables and benches out front. Half a dozen men were at a counter; the only woman was the bartender—a rarity in Calabria, where a masculine society still dominates—who had black hair pulled back, with a smooth light complexion and crooked teeth that would have been considered a blemish in the United States.

"What would you like?" Giuseppe asked me.

I looked up at the board of special sandwiches, each with its own name, unusual for Italy. The place reminded me of a New York deli.

I ordered a *panino* with salami, mozzarella, tomato, and *piccante*, something that I assumed was simply spicy red peppers.

Without smiling or even nodding the bartender just looked at Giuseppe, alerting him that it was his turn to order. After he had ordered, we turned to wait toward the back. Someone caught Giuseppe's eye. A man about my height and size with light brown hair and blue eyes had walked in and looked up at the menu.

Giuseppe smiled and continued to look at him. The man must have felt Giuseppe's stare, for he turned and acknowledged Giuseppe's look. Giuseppe held out his hands, and his chin jutted out in an expression that said, "Hey, you should know me."

The man walked over. "I'm sorry, but do I know you?"

"Maybe a few years ago. No, maybe eight years ago. You must have been twenty or so, and you were at your father's store in Cariati. I brought postcards to your father. . . ."

Something triggered in the young man. He finally remembered Giuseppe. But there was not the excited recognition that we Americans might have expressed. It was casual, almost an "Oh, you again."

Time is different for the Calabresi, who expect that people (for good reason) will run into one another from time to time. This means that the Italians' long sense of history notwithstanding, they are concerned almost exclusively with the present and are not terribly nostalgic; what has happened has happened. How different, I thought, from Italians in the United States, who long for an old country that may not miss them quite as much as they miss it.

I once heard a joke about a Calabrese returning to his village after a decade in America. All the while Luigi had missed his village, his country. What got him through was his belief that he would one day amass enough money to return to Calabria for a visit.

When that day came and Luigi arrived in Reggio, his eyes welled with tears. By the time he reached his village, he was sobbing. The village was exactly as he had remembered it. And as he walked through the piazza, Luigi spotted the bar where he used to hang out and play cards with Pasquale and Salvatore. He wondered, What are the chances that my friends are there right now?

He walked in the bar. Pasquale and Salvatore were playing cards at a table in the back. Luigi ran up to them, tears running down his cheeks, and dropped his bags and opened his arms in greeting.

"Pasquale, Salvatore . . . I'm back," he said.

His two friends looked up at him, cards still in their hands, and said, "Luigi, did you go somewhere?"

Back at the road stop, as Giuseppe and I carried our trays of food to the benches outside the bar, he said to the young man, "Tell your father I'll stop by his store when we make it up there again"— whether it was a week or a decade.

I buttoned my jacket with one hand and picked up half the *panino* with the other. Just as I brought the *panino* to my mouth, Giuseppe asked, "You must have had piccante before, right?" Somehow he knew that I never had.

The ingredients in *piccante*, he explained, can vary, but it's often made with a combination of dried tomatoes, red pepper, olive oil, and salt. Sometimes it's made with pork fat, but around Crotone it's made with *resca*, which is dialect for *lisca*, crushed anchovy or sardine bone. It is in the *piccante* that the Arab influence is evident in Calabrese cooking.

With the first bite I tasted the thin, chewy homemade salami along with tangy mozzarella, which melted on my tongue. Then came the punch. The spiciness of the *piccante* overwhelmed my mouth. Giuseppe kept his eyes on me, laughing to himself. I could taste the hot pepper and olive oil and then something subtle, though salty. The tomato and cheese tempered the spice.

"There's something salty in this, something rich," I muttered.

"It's the anchovy," Giuseppe answered. "Probably mixed with ground fish roe. They make it differently wherever you go."

Even here at this roadside café, I was bombarded with flavor in something as simple as a *panino*. The vegetarian Pythagoras would have moaned.

WINE FROM CALABRIA is only now flowing to the United States. And the rustic red wines from the vineyards of the Cirò area—Librandi, Duca San Felice, Ippolito—are making a name for themselves. From September to November workers pick the grapes and press them into high-test fruity nectar. Made from a combination of local Gaglioppo and Greco grapes blended with Trebbiano grapes from Tuscany, Cirò wines are hearty; at first sip you can almost taste the ancient grapevines rooted in the windbeaten Calabrese soil. Once those flavors settle, the taste of peaches and almonds soothes your tongue. The wines are more potent than most, containing about 14 or 15 percent alcohol.

Like most Calabrese coastal towns, Cirò is really two towns: Cirò Superiore and Cirò Inferiore, as the old-timers call them, or simply Cirò and Cirò Marina. Giuseppe and I drove through Cirò Marina, where the buildings, all new, radiate not from a town center but from the bay. A small port town, Cirò Marina has worked to get on the tourist circuit, though like Crotone, it has attracted more drug traffickers than tourists. Many believe that the newly emigrated Albanians are introducing drugs to the region. You can never tell if this is true or if Italian xenophobia is escalating with newer waves of *extracomunitari*, or non–European Union immigrants.

"A year ago a woman was kidnapped because her husband was a *pentito*," Giuseppe said, using the word that means someone who has ratted on the mafia. "And no one has found her yet."

From the coast we drove for a half hour up steep, winding roads to Cirò Superiore, leaving the coast and vineyards below us. Above us a fifteenth-century castle topped the village; as Giuseppe cut through the tight streets up to it, I saw that the village continued farther up, hidden from the ground below.

A few people strolled around the castle. Most of them were old men who stopped their stroll to gather in tiny piazzas or in crooks in the street, standing and smoking. Their hand gestures had slowed with age but were as emphatic as ever. They smiled at us as we walked by; we smiled back.

"Dove andate?" one of the men asked.

Giuseppe stopped. The men's eyes lit up when we approached them. Not much happens here, and the chance to speak to strangers seemed to delight them.

Giuseppe said, "We'd like to visit the castle."

As a group they looked at it and shrugged their shoulders. "It's closed," one said.

Now the youngest of the group, a man in his seventies, approached Giuseppe. His gray hair lay neatly on his head. "The castle is beautiful. It's a shame you can't see it now. Maybe we can get Salvatore to open it?" he said, suddenly turning to his friends. "He's the custodian, but he might be down in Marina."

Giuseppe introduced us—himself as a photographer and me as an American writer of Calabrese descent—and we joined them in their afternoon stroll.

"It was built in the sixteenth century and is still amazingly well preserved today," said the man with gray hair. He pointed up at the castle, which I realized had once formed a side of the village; weeds sprouted through the mortar between the gray stones. All the houses on that side had actually been built directly into the castle wall so that each house had only three sides with windows.

Giuseppe paused. "Are you sure that it's the sixteenth century?" I had begun to realize that Giuseppe had a way of respectfully correcting historical inaccuracies. "Because if you look at the way the stone is lined . . ."

I felt a tug at my arm. The oldest of the men, a character in an Italian postwar film, was looking up at me. He was hunched over and wore a black jacket and gray sweater. A cap covered a seemingly full head of hair. He wove his arm through mine and nudged me to continue walking.

"Where in America are you from?"

"New York," I told him.

"I have relatives in Toronto. Pino Garafolo, do you know him?" He looked at me, hoping for an affirmative answer. Gray bristle spotted his cheeks, a drop of his morning *caffè* stained the corner of his lip.

"No, that's in Canada; it's about a ten-hour drive."

He stopped to absorb this information, then continued. "I also have a cousin—well, really it's the husband of my wife's cousin—in Niagara Falls. He went over in 1936."

"That's when my grandmother came over," I said.

He patted me on the back. "The same year?" He thought to himself, perhaps hoping to make another connection. Perhaps his cousin had met my grandmother on the boat?

"What's her name?"

"Critelli, Angela." I, too, wanted to make the connection deeper, as unlikely as it was.

No, he didn't know it. "Well, they left the same year." He looked at me as if he were at a loss, then directed me farther up the narrow alley. Pigeons huddled above us in the crevice formed by the houses and the castle wall, the only refuge from the wind.

For the past two hours, since my *caffè* at the roadside stand, I had been needing to find a bathroom, and as we spiraled up the alley, I saw a three-walled metal urinal stand of a type, once ubiquitous, that has been disappearing throughout Italy since the Second World War. The metal wall of what's gruffly called a *pisciatioio* starts at knee level and reaches to just above the shoulders. A simple hole marks the bottom. I motioned for my companion to excuse me, and when the old man saw what I intended to do, he furrowed his eyebrows. "No, no. I'll take you someplace proper."

Was it because I was a guest, or did people simply not use them anymore? In any case, we walked into a building that had no sign— a store once—and stepped into a wide, long room. To my amazement, Roman spears, helmets, shields, and armor lined one wall. A teenage boy emerged from the back room. His hair was slick, obviously gelled, and was sticking up in a style that many Italian boys and teens were wearing at the time. He was also the first Italian I saw with a pierced lower lip.

"What is it?" the teenager said.

"Is the maestro here?" the old man asked.

"Yes, he just went around the corner."

"This is a journalist from New York. He needs to use your bathroom."

"It's not working here. And I think the café is closed now."

I turned to the old man. "Don't worry. I can just step outside. It's not a big deal . . ."

"No, no, no. We'll go someplace else," the old man insisted.

At this point the Roman costumes caught my attention. I could tell that each shield had been hand-molded, hand-painted, but out of what I didn't know. There were gold shields and helmets—some spiked, some with thick-bristled plumes—silver swords, shiny red capes.

A large man walked in. His meaty frame filled the doorway. He was about six feet two and had a full graying beard with curly white-and-black hair that fell halfway below his ears. He looked like Zeus to me. He wore a denim shirt and jeans, and a cigarette dangled from his mouth.

"Maestro, *buongiorno*," my companion greeted him. "This is Signore Rotella; he is a writer visiting from New York. He is writing a book about Calabria, and he needs to use a bathroom."

Zeus smiled knowingly, shook my hand, and introduced himself as Francesco Florielli. "I'm sorry, the toilet here doesn't work. But I can show you where—"

I stopped him. All I needed now was the entire village trying to find me a proper bathroom. I turned back to the costumes.

"It's for the Easter procession," Francesco offered. Ten armor breastplates rested on the backs of wooden chairs, which had been lined up against the wall. Dark gray shields with gold centers had been perfectly set on a long wood table.

"Are you the artist?"

"Yes," he said.

"Are you from here?"

"I'm originally from Crotone, but I moved here to construct these costumes."

"You made all these?" I asked. "How?"

He offered me a cigarette, which I declined, and led me to the pile of weapons. He held a shield, which was about two feet in diameter, then carried it over to a large garbage can and turned it over. That was it! The rings at the bottom of the garbage can matched the rings of the shield. But by heating the plastic, Francesco had pressed and molded an ornate pattern within those rings. Now he lugged the garbage can over to one of the chest plates and placed the plate along the side of it. From this flat, ribbed surface, Francesco had beautifully formed the breastplate on the armor as well as a ribbed stomach.

Now he reached for a sturdy silver helmet with a red plume sticking out the top and directed me to a worktable. He showed me how he had rounded the bottom of the bucket to make the helmet, gluing a broom brush on top for a plume. Once it was molded and cemented together and painted gold, it looked like it could have served in war, not just as decoration.

He stood proudly, smiling at the simplicity of it all, of knowing how to make something beautiful out of something ordinary. This is the art of Calabrese beauty.

"Cirò used to have this procession every year, but then they stopped. Maybe it was because everyone started moving to the shore

. . . But now I have made costumes for fifteen soldiers. And that does not include the costumes I've made for the disciples and mourners—for Pontius Pilate—and the cross for Jesus."

Giuseppe came in with his gray-haired friend and without a break in conversation, said, "I'm sorry, Marco, but if we're going to try to make it to Cerchiara, we'll have to start going."

"Aah, Cerchiara," the older men said almost in unison.

"Bellissima," my companion added.

On the way to the car I ran for the metal wall.

STOLEN FIGS

"I used to be an electrician," Giuseppe said, as if he hadn't thought about that time in his life in a while. "I almost went to Africa."

Leaving Cirò on our way to Corigliano Calabro, we drove beneath Montedison's high-tension wires, which electrify all of Calabria and Sicily.

This was the second day of our trip along the north Ionian coast, and it was the first time that Giuseppe had offered me something about himself. He had, for the most part, taken on the responsibility of professional tour guide, showing me the Calabria he knew.

"It was the late 1950s," Giuseppe began, "and I needed work."

He had a friend who, along with many others, had been hired by an Italian company that was laying electrical wire in East Africa. The pay was quadruple what anyone in postwar Calabria could make. Giuseppe took the train up to Naples, where he signed a contract that would bind him to Somalia for two years.

Later that same day, his father called to tell him that a friend of his working in Africa had just died of malaria. Giuseppe had no choice—the contract was signed—so the next day he lined up to board the ship for Naples. He walked up to the window and handed his contract to a man checking papers. The man hammered the paper with a rubber stamp. As Giuseppe was about to walk away, he saw that the stamp had missed the paper. It was invalid. He took it as a sign. With a quick catlike swipe, he reached his hand under the window and grabbed the papers; he ran and didn't stop until he was back in Calabria.

"So I came back to my job as an electrician. Then after a while I moved to Catanzaro, where I first repaired typewriters . . . which then turned into a sales job."

"My father used to be an electrician, too," I said.

"Really? Marco, tell me, what does your father do now?" Giuseppe had probably wanted to know but thought it rude to ask. I was happy he had.

"La sua passione è la sculture," I said. "But his work is sales."

"Ah." Giuseppe nodded. "And, Marco, what does he sell?"

"X-ray equipment. Not for medical use, but for industry— mostly large X-ray machines to detect flaws in things like plane fuselages, helicopter blades, engines."

"I like your father," Giuseppe said, not needing a response. "He's simpatico."

Giuseppe looked out the window and pointed to another Norman remnant, a wall. Trees burst out of the wall, so strong and healthy that the wall seemed to have been built around them.

"Fig trees, Marco," Giuseppe pointed out. Then he faced me squarely. His thick black mustache spread as he grinned. "I still remember your father eating all those figs when you two came here the first time."

"Yeah, and I never knew how much he liked them until then."

"Marco, do you remember that night in the fields?" Giuseppe asked, and I told him of course I did; it was a night I'll never forget.

On that first-year anniversary trip, when Martha and I had visited Calabria, Giuseppe spoke of my father's love of figs and recalled the look on my face when I bit into my first Calabrese *fico nero.* Then, while Martha had waited in the car with his son Domenico, Giuseppe led me to his family's fields. We traipsed through the rows of olive trees and ducked below grapevines, then paused to rest on a small, dusty hill within arm's reach of wild *fichi d'india*, prickly pears. There Giuseppe grew ruminative, speaking of his three sons and recalling that just a generation ago Italians had large families.

"But now no one has money to raise children," he said. "The children stay at home and live with their parents."

Walking again, we came across a stand of fig trees—his father's fig trees, Giuseppe said. *"Bello,"* Giuseppe whispered; the fruit was ripe. With the lightest touch you clench the plump fruit between your thumb and two fingers and pull. If it comes off easily, it's yours; if it doesn't, then it's simply not ready to be plucked. We gathered a couple of dozen and filled up a sack, which quickly became permeated with the red juice of the figs. We cleaned rows of trees of ripe fruit.

With the bread-making lesson, the view of Gimigliano, and even that fig-picking raid, Giuseppe was showing me life's basic necessities.

Whenever I visited Calabria, I brought the obvious gifts, things that I thought everyone could use: fancy soaps, fluffy towels, toys, hats, and T-shirts with "New York" or "Florida" written somewhere on them. They all were items that I'd picked up on my way out of the States. Giuseppe, for his part, would present me—even before the double-cheek kiss—with, say, a jar of roasted chestnuts soaking in sugar water. It was something I'd never eaten before. I still remember the distinct taste of the soft, wet, sugary nut. I brought my relatives what I thought they needed; they gave gifts that they couldn't live without. While I had shopped for the towels and Yankees hats, Giuseppe had picked and jarred the chestnuts himself. His gift was always the air, the views, or the food on which Calabresi exist.

When we filled up the sack with figs, Giuseppe hurried me back to the car. That evening, after we had stuffed ourselves with a king's banquet of Elena's cooking, he pulled me aside to the living room. He brought out the sack and carefully opened it. He reached his hand in and pulled out a fig that showed the telltale sign of ripeness, a swelled crack that was just ready to burst. I followed, and soon we made our way through the sack, reaching and eating, praising the quality of the full and juicy figs. Giuseppe half smiled, then grinned wide enough to show a silver eyetooth. Finally he erupted in laughter.

"What's so funny?"

"You like these figs?"

"They're delicious."

"They're not mine . . . or my father's."

"Whose are they?" I asked.

"Who knows, but when the owner wakes up tomorrow morning, he's going to scream."

This must be a pastime here, I thought. I recalled my father telling me how he had raided farmers' fig trees and peas—all out of boredom. I couldn't help noting the similarities between my father and Giuseppe. It was almost as if my father had taken me to Calabria, then handed me off to someone he knew could explain it to me better than he could himself.

I reached for another fig, which squished between my fingers.

Giuseppe sighed with pleasure. "There's nothing tastier than stolen figs."

Fig trees grow almost everywhere in Calabria. They grow along hills, on mountains, in valleys; they even squeeze their way through the stone walls of former palazzi. Their roots seek out any pockets of water. Figs are there for the picking. It doesn't take a Calabrese rhyme to explain what everyone already knows: " '*A fica è 'na cucca, che l'acchiappa si l'ammucca*" (or, in Italian, "*Il fico è un frutto molto buono ed ognuno vuole mangiarlo*"): the fig is a delicious fruit, and everyone wants to eat it.

The Greeks introduced the fruit to Italy, having brought it over from Asia Minor. Several varieties now cover the land. Calabria is the second-largest grower of figs in Italy, after Campania, accounting for 25 percent of Italy's production.

Almost all fig trees descend from the caprifig tree. For the most part, the caprifigs are inedible, but they have a greater purpose: they grow simply to help pollinate trees that produce edible figs. In order to grow fruit, many varieties of fig trees need the caprifig tree close by, for it houses a tiny female wasp that pollinates the other fig trees with the seeds of the caprifig. The problem for the wasp is getting to the pollen. The flower of the fig is buried deep within the fruit. As with Calabria herself, the beauty isn't always apparent on the surface.

Norman Douglas was amazed at the many varieties of figs; he counted at least eight types each of *neri* and *bianchi* figs. (Italians distinguish the color of figs as they do with grapes, as black and white: black figs are actually red, and white figs are green.) The Romans, who cultivated fig trees that didn't need the fig wasp, could select from a couple dozen types of fig. Of the figs grown nowadays, there are Pecoraro, Pizzolungo, Torchiaro, and Fraccazzano *nero*, as well as Melanzana *verde*, Melanzana *nera*, and Melanzana *corta*. But the most common fig is the Dottato.

An Italian proverb says, "*'A fica l'ha benaditta a' madonna.*" The fig is indeed blessed by the Madonna, for fig trees produce two harvests—one in early summer, the other in September. There is even a fig tree that bears fruit in December; its figs are known as *fichi Natalini*.

For the most part, the early summer figs are meant to be eaten fresh, right away; they rot quickly. The ones that grow in August and September are best for dry preserving; these can also be frozen, shipped elsewhere, then thawed upon arrival.

In Calabria, figs end the meal. They can be eaten fresh, dried, or preserved in rum syrup. They can be cut open, stuffed with almonds or almond paste, then baked. They can also be baked with walnuts, then dipped in chocolate. When they are served as an appetizer, they are sometimes wrapped in prosciutto for a perfect blend of sweet and salty.

In his classic book *The Food of Italy*, the great culinary writer Waverley Root remarks that not all of Italy cherishes figs. He points out the problem one may encounter when asking for a fig in Milan. Apparently, in 1162 the Holy Roman Emperor Frederick Barbarossa fought back a revolt during which his wife was led out of the city on the back of a mule. He made the men an offer: if they did not want to be hanged, they would have to present the executioner with a fig. Rumor has it that upon realizing how the figs would be procured, a few chose to be hanged. Those who chose to live followed the instructions: they were to extract a fig from the anus of the same mule they had led the empress out on—but with their teeth. They were to present it to the executioner, saying, *"Ecco il fico,"* then return it to the mule in the same manner from which it was taken. According to Root, this is the origin of a now-famous Italian gesture. By making a fist and sticking your thumb between your index and middle fingers, you are "making the fig."

In Italian, by changing just one letter, the word "fig" becomes sexual.

On our anniversary trip to Italy, my wife, Martha, and I visited friends in Perugia, where at a dinner party Martha described her fig-eating experience in Calabria, saying *fica* instead of *fico*: "Never had I eaten a fig so red, so plump, so juicy." The dinner guests began to squirm in pleasurable embarrassment. Our hostess, an Italian raised in South Africa, turned to Martha and said in English, "My dear, you've just been saying, over and over, the word 'cunt.' "

In Calabria everyone knows the seasons of the fig. *Alivu rùosso e fichi pittirilli*—When the olives ripen, the figs are still young. My grandparents knew it, and my father, even after decades of living without the yearly consumption of the fruit, knew it.

Calabria is the second-largest producer of figs, but as with much of her produce, she sees very little monetary return for its export. Unlike the truffles of the north, which are sniffed out by dogs and pigs, the figs in Calabria are ubiquitous, taken for granted, and little premium is placed on them.

Giuseppe may have taken some fruit from a neighbor's tree, but he knows that in a couple of months, when the trees produce their fruit in September, he may wake up to find that his own trees have been picked clean.

THE TIN MAN

A<small>N ARAGONESE CASTLE</small> tops the dense mountain village of Corigliano Calabro. Almost forty thousand people live along the coast and within this remote city, which seems to have been affected very little by the earthquakes that have continually ravaged the rest of Calabria. Douglas's "little town . . . whose coquettish white houses lie in the folds of the hills" is amazingly well preserved, though many of these houses lie empty.

Giuseppe and I walked up the sinewy cobblestone roads. He led, proceeding at a relaxed stroll, hands locked behind his back; he nodded at passersby and surveyed the building fronts, most of which were closed with heavy medieval-looking wood doors.

He looked at his watch. "He must have gone home."

"Who?"

"A friend. An old friend. We'll return tomorrow morning."

The air chilled in the early evening. As shopkeepers pulled their heavy wooden doors shut, the streets grew crowded with villagers on their way home for supper. This was the time of the *spassiaturu*, dialect for *passeggiata*.

Every city, town, and village in Italy has an unstated but universally understood time during which the entire population emerges from their houses in their evening best. No one discusses it; no one makes appointments to meet anyone; they all just converge to find one another out on the street.

The road led directly up to the front of the castle, but Giuseppe knew a shortcut that would take us straight in. We skirted the castle wall, which was a continuation of the sharp cliff. The drop would bring you nearly to sea level.

"Look." He slapped the side of the stone wall. "*Tufo*. Even here. *Tufo*."

We turned to face the sixteenth-century castle and, next to it, the Byzantine Chiesa di San Pietro. To the right was a single doorway—Giuseppe's "direct" way in. Leading off from that corner of the church was an enclosed portico with small openings at eye level; this tunnel of sorts ended at the castle wall, where stairs then led down below the courtyard. Through one of the openings, Giuseppe pointed to a doorway leading from the church. "The bride went through that doorway," Giuseppe said.

"To the castle?"

"First night," Giuseppe said, then added: "The duke had the right to spend the wedding night with any bride in the village."

Giuseppe must have seen the dubious look on my face. "It happened as recently as a hundred years ago. Really. The man came out alone. The bride never even made it out of the church."

The sun dropped as we walked up stairs cut into the mountainside. We came out with our backs to the castle, facing the piazza, which was packed with cars. Drivers maneuvered, inching back and forth, trying to get out of tight spots and home in time for dinner, which they would never miss or be late for. I realized that I hadn't had anything since that *panino* near Crotone, and I hoped that we would eat soon, too.

Giuseppe and I were staying in a hotel outside Rossano, a half hour away. Our rooms, down the hall from each other, were spare; the check-in counter also served as a bar, cigarette and newspaper shop, and cashier for a pizzeria down a narrow hallway.

Dinner was in a room the size of a small banquet hall. Only two of the fifteen or so tables were occupied. A man sat alone eating a bowl of spaghetti, and four men sat at one curve of a large round table, oddly close together. As Giuseppe and I took our seats, I saw why: a television was suspended over the kitchen doorway, playing the news, and tables were placed so a patron could watch while he ate.

I always thought of the Italian evening meal as a time for conversation. But in villages like this in Calabria, where virtually everyone returns home at lunch for the family meal, the evening meal is a time to relax and be entertained, whether at home or in a trattoria.

I ordered a bottle of red wine, *fatto in casa*, and a *pizza quattro stagione*, which when it arrived was the perfect blend of artichokes, porcini mushrooms, whole olives, and spicy *soppressata* on a lightly cheesed, thin-crusted dough. The drone of the newsperson bounced off the concrete walls and floor, a lonely sound in the big room. Our evening in Rossano ended with the meal.

In Corigliano Calabro the next morning, we parked in front of the same heavy wood doors and began our stroll back up the same steep road. It was nine o'clock, and within fifteen minutes the streets filled with mothers and children, shopkeepers and artisans. Giuseppe and I stood in the middle of the cobblestone road like a rock in the middle of a shallow stream of people. People nodded hello. Giuseppe looked at me and nodded toward something ahead.

Walking with perfect balance and placement of footsteps, a tiny man negotiated the curb. He wore a snap-brim cap and rose-tinted glasses. Giuseppe approached; the man glanced up and smiled shyly; Giuseppe put his hands on his waist indignantly. Now the man broke into a grin.

"*Pino! Come va?*" he called out to Giuseppe.

Giuseppe introduced me, and the man, who stood as high as my chest, took my hand with both of his. "*Piacere,*" he said—it's a pleasure—looking at me with crossed eyes behind the rose shades, his large smile revealing a single tooth clinging to the top front gum.

Antonio Bellitto was the *fabbro*, or village metalworker. Inside the shop's sixteenth-century wooden doors, tin colanders and copper funnels of all sizes hung on rusty nails. Sheets of copper were neatly piled on shelves. Three or four pictures of the Virgin Mary and the saints hung from the racks.

Antonio's tools included hefty metal-cutting scissors, a knife, a shoehorn, a hammer, pliers, and a blowtorch. He went to work, and Giuseppe and I looked on. With a knife he cut out a pattern in a piece of aluminum. His hands deftly rolled the piece into a cone. He soldered the ends and curved the rims with heat. He then added a heavy metal handle. He had formed a basic funnel, the way funnels had no doubt been made for centuries. He set it aside to let it cool.

Giuseppe presented Antonio with the map of Calabria that he had designed. Antonio looked over the map, his eyes following the roads, mountains, and coast. He pointed out cities that Giuseppe had marked with apt local symbols; with his finger, he followed the road from the coast to mountains and stopped at the image of the Castello Compagno, which crested his city.

"*Va bene,*" he said. "*Bellissima. Ah, ecco Rossano.*"

"We're going there soon," Giuseppe said, and winked at me. "*Una città molta antica.*" Then he told Antonio that the map was a gift to him.

"No, I can't," Antonio said. But he soon relented. He folded the map neatly and lightly placed it on a far shelf. He then pulled down two funnels and wrapped them in newspaper. He offered them to Giuseppe.

"Nino, I couldn't," Giuseppe said, and sighed.

Antonio forced them into his hands and shrugged his shoulders. "It's nothing," Antonio said. He picked up another funnel, wrapped it, and handed it to me. "It's simple, but it's a gift from Corigliano."

"*Grazie tanto,*" I said.

The cool metal heft of the funnel was satisfying to the touch. This was not molded plastic; it was simply made, but there was nothing cheap about it.

"Maybe he'll write about you," Giuseppe said.

"About me?" Antonio said with a hopeful lilt in his voice. "No, I'm just an artisan. He can write about the castle, but no, not me."

Now he took the funnel out of my hand. "Too small," he explained, and searched his shop, which wasn't much bigger than a hallway. "No, I don't have much today," he said, then took down a second funnel. "Take two, it's nothing."

I nodded, but it *was* something. The funnel—the raw copper and the silver solder—was more beautiful than even the most ornately painted ceramics of Tuscany. While Italy is full of specialized artisans, I have rarely seen as many as I did in Calabria. In northern Italy, mass-produced products are filling the shelves as in the rest of Western Europe and America, but in Calabria handmade goods—the stuff that Americans pay a premium for—are still less expensive than the stuff made in factories, and far more satisfying as well.

Rossano perfectly tops a mountain plateau, which seems to have been thrust up from the ground separated from rolling hills leading up to it, a mountain city that hangs in the clouds by itself. Fig and almond trees spread out from the base of the red mountain, but one's eye trains to the top of the plateau, where the red gradually lightens, and falls on the sand-colored Chiesa di San Marco from the sixth century, one of the Byzantine treasures of southern Italy.

Giuseppe stopped the car in front of the archbishop's palace, which houses the diocesan museum, the proud keeper of the Codex Purpureus, or the Purple Codex. This sixth-century manuscript is a copy of the Gospels of St. Matthew and St. Mark. Of the 400 original pages, only 188 pages remain.

I waited in the car while Giuseppe approached a stern-looking man standing by the door, which was closed. There were shrugs and pointed fingers. Then the man began what seemed to be a windy monologue.

Giuseppe walked back to me, rubbing his hands together. "Marco, it's really difficult to understand them. The dialect is so strange. Even for me. And I'm sorry, but the church and palace seem to be undergoing renovations—renovations that should have been done for the jubilee. So we can't see the Archiropita today."

Not wanting to admit defeat, he smiled and said, *"Ritorniamo."*

We'll return. For the Calabresi, it could be tomorrow, it could be five years from now, but we'll return.

The road leading out of the city was clogged with traffic. Boys and men of an indeterminate age came up to the cars stopped at lights, hawking batteries and cheap toys. Some offered to clean windshields. Their teeth were marred by dark stains.

"Marocchini," Giuseppe said. There was no judgment in his voice; he was just pointing out another aspect of Calabria. The Arabs were returning to Italy, and their first stops were Sicily and Calabria. Like the newly emigrated Albanians, the Moroccans were subjected to xenophobic prejudices.

Soon the traffic thinned out. The aroma of blossoming clementine flowers wafted through the open windows of the car. Far beyond the North African merchants and the fields of mandarins and clementines, the snow-spotted, sharp-peaked Pollino Mountains cut into the clouds. They signify the end of Calabria to the north and the beginning of Basilicata. Here Cerchiara di Calabria, our northernmost destination, is nestled within the mountains.

THE LOST CITY OF SIBARI

Gissing and douglas, and everyone before them, searched for the fabled city of Sibari, or Sybaris. They asked villagers, shepherds, and local historians, everyone they could, but they all left disappointed, convinced the city was just a myth.

Sybarites lived in such opulence that they were the envy of Magna Graecia. (Even today the word "sybarite" defines a person who is a sensualist, someone who lives a life of opulence and indulgence.) In 510 B.C., as legend has it, the people of Crotone invaded Sibari, plundered its great wealth, and burned it to the ground. The Sybarites fled to the mountain village that is now Corigliano Calabro, some historians say; those who didn't escape were taken into slavery. To vanquish Sibari forever, the Crotonese diverted the flow of the huge Crati River and submerged the city. Eventually Sibari became a name in legend only.

Today citrus fields occupy the land between the sea and the mountains, a narrow five miles, following the riverbed of the Crati, now a mere trickle. With so few flat, fertile areas in Calabria, farmers use every possible patch of soil within the groves of trees, so it's not uncommon to see smaller almond and fig trees planted in between the larger, leafier mandarin and clementine trees.

The mandarin trees are shorter and bushier than the clementines, and are more closely pruned. Clementines ripen as early as September, a full three months before the mandarins. Every fifteen years the trees are pulled up, and new ones are planted.

Giuseppe and I entered the tourist office of the Sibari archaeological site. Two men who had been smoking and talking stopped and looked up at us. We paid the admission and walked toward the grounds, whereupon one of the men rose and lugged himself toward us.

"You can only see the grounds with a guide," he said, neither lazily nor enthusiastically. He put on a jacket that marked him as an official park guide.

Within minutes Giuseppe had engaged him in conversation, and within minutes they learned that they had friends in common. Giuseppe seemed to know someone no matter how far off the well-traveled path he was. And if he was in a place that was truly foreign to him, he would strike up a conversation with a stranger anyway.

Now that Giuseppe was no longer just a curious tourist, the guide—his name was Angelo—gave us a special tour of the site, spicing his narrative with local history and lore. He brought us beyond the yellow ropes marking areas off-limits and steered us down the damp main road that at one time had led from the sea to what archaeologists believe had been a college. Water hoses snaked throughout the excavations, and he explained that the workers were still pumping out what had become marshland after the river receded.

The breeze from the sea carried with it the scent of orange blossoms. The excavations had actually uncovered the ruins of three cities built one on top of another. We walked along the main cobblestone road, which still showed the ruts from ancient carriage wheels. The road at one time extended out to the sea, and at the center of the gridded city, the cross street ran north to south. Now nearly three thousand years after it had been founded—and almost a hundred years after Douglas had given up his search—I stood at the site of a jewel in the crown that was Magna Graecia.

About forty years after the Crotonese destroyed Sibari, the villagers returned from their hideouts to try to rebuild their city, but the Crotonese fought them back to the hills and the sea. After another failed attempt, they returned in 444 B.C. and commenced to rebuild the city, calling it Thourioi. About a hundred years later the city fell once again, this time to the native tribes called the Bruttians (from Calabria) and the Lucanians (from Basilicata).

Not until about 190 B.C., with the help of the Romans, was the city, now called Copia, rebuilt successfully. Copia lasted until the sixth century A.D., when a malaria epidemic wiped out the population.

Now fig and olive trees surround the ruins of Copia's Roman amphitheater; you can walk along the floor of a Roman house and peer into a large bath lined with red tile. Grand column bases line the main street of Thourioi. And virtually all that has been uncovered of Sibari is the original layout and various pieces of gold.

The excavation of Sibari is one of Calabria's postwar success stories. Under the direction of archaeologist Umberto Zanotti-Bianco, who under Mussolini was imprisoned (much like Carlo Levi) in 1932, the serious research to find Sibari began. The first stone of Sibari wasn't uncovered until shortly after the war ended, and even then archaeologists weren't convinced that they had unearthed the mythical city.

The hum of pumps extracting water from the longtime riverbed throbbed and disappeared into the nearby marshland. My eyes followed the empty cobblestone road that led to the horizon when Giuseppe pointed to a mountain with two peaks, separated by a crescent slope. It looked menacing in the distance. Dark thunderclouds flanked the mountain. There was something primitive about it.

"The mountain is called Sellaro, named after its shape—a saddle. That's where we're headed."

We left the city and drove out of ancient Calabria onto a road barely two lanes wide. About a hundred feet along the road there was a flash of color and movement in the bushes. As we passed, I spotted two dark-haired women walking out of the brush onto a sandy tractor road that led into the mandarin groves. It was cold, and they wore heavy jackets and dresses.

"Prostitutes," Giuseppe said. "Albanian girls waiting for truck drivers and businessmen. They get dropped off here in the afternoon and get picked up late at night."

They weren't showing leg, as I would have expected, and they weren't calling out to us. They just stared. To judge from their wizened faces, they must have descended from the ancient Sybarite prostitutes themselves.

Twenty minutes later—twenty minutes that spanned twenty-five hundred years—we reached the resort village of Laghi di Sibari. There Sibari had been reincarnated as a West Palm Beach housing complex. Though its name translates as "Lake of Sibari," there is really only one large lake, shaped to give the impression that each row of condos opened up onto its own private lake—it had been man-made, with a channel cut to connect it with the Ionian Sea.

Laghi di Sibari was built in 1996 by an English developer. Like all new buildings on the Ionian Sea, it is populated only in the summer, although British and German tourists trickle in during the off season to take advantage of cheaper rates and less congested beaches.

Of all the tourist complexes on the Ionian Sea, Laghi di Sibari is perhaps the most attractive. Each villa has its own gated front garden and a dock. The sparrows' chirps carried across the lake. In the summer, streets are lined with oleander, which happens to be the name of the only hotel there, Il Oleandro. As in U.S. suburbs, streets and villas are named after the birds and trees that they've displaced. One villa has the name Il Cormorano, the cormorant.

Perhaps it is insensitive to criticize the hasty, ugly character of most other Calabrese tourist villages. They have brought income into a region that has always struggled economically, enabling the Calabresi to catch up to the rest of Italy. These new developments fill voids between places of historic interest, and in Calabria there are many voids to be filled.

"There is no crime here . . . now," Giuseppe remarked, and I knew this was a teaser to a story.

"About five years ago there were several robberies and thefts. The caretaker received a call from someone and caught the thief hiding in the bushes. So he shot him." He explained to me that all the *contadini*, the farmers, had guns to protect their crops and livestock. There is a Calabrese saying, *Paura guarda la vigne, non la siepe*— it is fear, not hedges or fences, that guards the vines—and while there's less handgun violence in Italy than in the United States, this saying still is the rule in Calabria.

In the center of the hotel complex, there was a bar, a restaurant—its doors closed—a sitting room, a patio for the large pool, and a shop that sold souvenirs and newspapers.

We stood at the bar, and a tall, large-boned woman appeared behind the counter. She greeted us with a nod and served us each a *caffè*. Afterward we walked into the shop and perused the racks of postcards. The woman followed us and took on the role of shopkeeper, with the same sour face.

"Gentilissima," Giuseppe began in his most formal tone, "may I show you a map?"

He pulled his map out of his briefcase and launched into his sales pitch, comparing her outdated postcards with his custom-made new ones.

I shuffled through the magazines and newspapers—most of them German—looking for news from the States. Italian papers covered little American news unless it had to do with fashion or music or sensational shootings.

The phone rang. The woman cut Giuseppe short to answer. While she talked, he whispered in my ear, "That's the wife of the caretaker."

When I didn't make the connection, he formed his hand into a pistol.

I thought that Giuseppe was working hard and getting nowhere, but when the caretaker's wife returned, they got down to business.

She commissioned a series of postcards. No, she didn't need to see his slide show; no, she didn't need to see anything else.

She spied me ardently turning pages of a week-old *Time* magazine. She smiled at me and said, "Don't worry, it's my gift to you. Come back when you next visit." While Giuseppe plied his trade as a photographer, the caretaker's wife worked hers, wanting to please the American traveler.

Here in this isolated resort that was all but shut down during the off season was where I found the only English-language periodical in all of Calabria.

THE KEEPER OF THE SANCTUARY

"FEEL," GIUSEPPE SAID as he plunged one hand into a pool of water. He had brought me to the Grotta delle Ninfe, or Cave of the Nymphs, one of a series of caves from which warm sulfuric water flows. It's believed that the Sybarites luxuriated in these warm baths.

I dipped my right hand into the light blue, seemingly bottomless water. It was perhaps eighty degrees, the warmest spot I'd felt in this chilly April. The smell of salt and sulfur expanded my nostrils, and the steamy heat opened my pores. My muscles felt as if they were sliding from my bones. My footsteps echoed above the constant sound of water falling.

The cave vault is over sixty feet high; stalactites taper to the ground as stalagmites reach up toward them. A narrow waterfall empties in the cave, behind which a sickle-shaped entrance offers an opening just large enough for a person to walk through. Now the proprietors have channeled the water to two large outdoor pools and two underground steam rooms. The baths have been converted to an inexpensive spa, where people can ease their muscles in the pool, cover themselves with mud, and lounge beneath rows of grapevines as they look out at the dark green olive and fig trees that color the sandy brown hills.

Giuseppe had insisted we stop off here on the way to the Santuario di Santa Maria delle Armi at the top of Sellaro, the saddle in the mountains. A newly built two-story house, white with a sloping terra-cotta roof, served as a lodge and restaurant; Giuseppe knocked on the door, and a small woman answered.

"Are you serving lunch today, or are you closed for the season?" Giuseppe asked.

"I'm cooking now," the woman said. "Why don't you come in and sit down?"

The aroma of fresh-baked bread, sweet and warm, wafted through the doorway. I must have taken in an obviously deep breath, because the woman pointed at me and snickered to Giuseppe. *"Ha sentito l'odore di pane"*—he smells the bread.

"Oh, he knows how to cook Calabrese bread. I showed him last week," Giuseppe replied proudly.

In no time the woman, who, in her flower-print apron and short wavy hair, could have been any Italian *nonna*, had set a table for the two of us next to a window that overlooked the valley. Two more people had appeared—a caretaker and a manager, evidently—but Giuseppe and I were the only ones eating.

The woman brought out penne glistening with olive oil and garlic. She set down a tin bowl of thinly chopped green chili peppers, which we crumbled over the *maccheroni* with our fingers. (I made the mistake of scratching my face sometime afterward, and the burn continued throughout the meal.) Next came an eggplant parmigiana, much lighter than what's served in the United States. The eggplant was thinly sliced and very lightly breaded. Tomato sauce gave the eggplant moisture, as did the cheese, just enough to add sharpness, that topped the creation. The flavors combined and melted even before the first bite.

A middle-aged man came to the table, bringing out a plate of *pitta*, a thicker version of middle Eastern pita that had been filled with a mixture of minced meat—pig fat and gristle—and baked with a coating of olive oil. Next came the *pizze alle contadine*: one pizza was served with chopped tomatoes on top, the other with *erbi di campo misti,* mixed field greens, a blend of fresh oregano and fennel tossed with olive oil.

Just as I finished my glass of spicy red wine, the man brought out *caffè* with Calabrese cookies, oval-shaped and the consistency of biscuits with a trace of sugar and a hint of anise. As we ate, we looked out the windows, enjoying the silence. White clouds passed above us, their lumpiness seeming to mirror the rocky land below.

All the while the middle-aged man sat a few tables away from us, impatiently turning the pages of a newspaper. When Giuseppe was finished eating, he addressed the man, who introduced himself as the proprietor, and they were off and running.

The Calabresi are wonderful at small talk. The weather, food, tourists, summer, postcards: only then was it time for business. While Giuseppe went to his car to get his briefcase, the man unloaded brochures on me describing his spa. He handed me one nicely colored book, bound with a thick cover. I flipped through the pages. The photos had a 1960s color-enhanced quality.

Giuseppe interrupted his own demonstration to explain to the proprietor that so much more could be done with the grounds. He recommended adding a bar by the pool, offering cool almond and fruit drinks. And landscaping, yes, landscaping.

The clouds hung low; their fluffy white color turned gray with black crevices. We passed through the village of Cerchiara di Calabria, which caps one of the foothills of Mount Sellaro. At the hill's pinnacle, we stopped in front of what had been the village's Norman castle. Earthquakes have leveled all but the very base of the castle. We continued up, to the next level of foothills. The buildings immediately dropped off; there were no stray structures, no fences, just the road, which the mountain had been reclaiming by tumbling rock down the side and sprouting weeds through cracks in the pavement.

As the car hugged the north side of the mountain, Giuseppe stopped. Below us, lush green grass spread across the valley. Nearby gaped the Bifurto Abyss, which, at two thousand feet down, is one of the deepest in all of Italy. Green grass grew around rocks like gums to teeth. A road wound through the valley and dead-ended yards before a rock formation.

"Beyond that mountain is Basilicata," Giuseppe said. "You can't get there from here."

We continued up toward the sanctuary. Giuseppe continually downshifted to gain speed; I looked off to the side and felt myself scooting closer to the inside of my seat. We had just topped the mountain, and when the road sloped downward, I realized that we were in the saddle. A dense pine forest with patches of sheep pastures surrounded us, but there was no sign of sheep, just stretches of twisted wood-slatted fences. It was only four in the afternoon, but it felt like dusk. The clouds emitted a sprinkle of rain.

Out of the bushes five or six dogs lined the road and snarled. A large sheepdog that looked part wolf led the pack. Her teats were swollen and hung almost to the ground. The other dogs were smaller and of an indescribable breed. One barely looked like a dog at all. We slowed down, and the dogs headed for the car.

One of the smaller dogs lunged at Giuseppe, smacking its nose against the door. As I turned to look out my side of the car, the she-dog leaped at me, grazing her teeth and nails against the window. I jumped back, brushing against Giuseppe, and saw a long string of slobber against the glass.

Giuseppe laughed, then inched down his window and barked back at the dogs.

The other dogs rushed the car, barking frantically. We got up to 25 kmh, but they kept up. One dog clung to the tail pipe, its back legs swinging out from under it. Giuseppe downshifted and punched the gas. I turned back. The dogs gathered in the center of the road behind us, barking.

Ten minutes later we rounded a corner and found ourselves at the Santuario di Santa Maria delle Armi. We faced the side of the tallest horn of the saddle, a crested rock formation out of which a long six-story stone building protruded. There wasn't a single car, not a voice, no one. The chestnut door had been set open, as if in expectation of us. We entered a long, narrow hallway with deep-inset windows overlooking the flat coastal land below.

At the end of the hall, two thick wood doors had been left ajar. Inside was the chapel with four rows of pews and a crucifix that, as in many Calabrese churches, took a back seat to a painting of the Virgin Mary. The altar wall, on which the painting hung, was rough with irregular cracks and protrusions; the altar itself had been carved into the mountain.

A second, even smaller chapel opened to the side. Here, I knew, was where the Archiropita, a work of art that was created by divine hands, was kept. Giuseppe and I squeezed in, having no choice but to lower ourselves to the kneeler. Someone had been praying here and placed a black-and-white photo of a woman at eye level; another photo of a young boy had been placed next to that of the woman.

Just above our heads, inside a silver tabernacle, two angels appeared to be holding a ten-inch silver plate. As I drew my head closer, I saw that it was actually a stone that bore an image.

"This is the Archiropita," Giuseppe said.

Only when you kneel does she appear. The image was of the Virgin Mary, formed by what looked to be a rainbow streak left by running water. Legend says a shepherd came across this stone with the visage of Mary in 1450. The sanctuary was constructed at the site a century later.

"Forty years ago two men stole this stone from its frame of angels," Giuseppe said. "But something must have happened that made them unload it; they must have felt like they were being chased. Because two days later, as the sun was setting, a woman saw a ray of light shoot up from the ocean. She called the police, who waded into the water and found the stone at the bottom. The image had reflected the descending sun's rays."

We followed a stairway that led up behind the sanctuary and came out onto a patch of green grass almost at roof level. A dog was chained to a fence. A hundred feet in front of us stood a small two-story stone house. The door opened, and a middle-aged man walked out. *"Buongiorno,"* he said, extending a hand.

The man wore a brown snap-brim cap and blue knit sweater. As he got nearer, the first thing I noticed were his eyes: the left was sharp and gray; on the right, a translucent film had begun to envelop the bottom half, covering the iris almost entirely. It was a sign of cataracts. I had often noticed cataracts or missing teeth or other ailments in people his age, who grew up in a time when good doctors weren't available in Calabria—and when Calabresi distrusted doctors anyway.

He offered the first words to Giuseppe, speaking in Italian rather than dialect. As Giuseppe spoke, the man offered a respectful glance in my direction and a nod. I nodded back and wiped away the raindrops that had been slowly wetting my face.

Finally, after explaining where he was from, Giuseppe introduced me and my book. "You see, he is a second-generation Italian, and he has family still here. He says everyone in the U.S. knows about Tuscany and Rome and even Sicily, but no one, no one, knows about Calabria."

The man turned to me and said in a measured British accent, "That is a wonderful idea." He shook my hand. As my hand was enveloped within his larger, rougher one, I felt that he had a finger or two missing. "Calabria, indeed, is an amazing region. We have cliffs that fall deep into two seas; we have Greek history, Saracen history, and our own Bruttian ancestry."

I complimented his English in Italian.

"Please, if you don't mind, I'd like to speak English. I love the language. You see, for thirty years I lived in London as a railroad worker. I worked on the tracks. But I missed my country so much that I decided to move back to my village, Cerchiara, and take care of the sanctuary grounds here with my wife."

"How long have you been here?"

"About twenty years now."

I imagined that only an Italian who has lived abroad, one who has already separated himself from his family, could live in near isolation, away from the village, away from the piazza and main corso.

He introduced himself as Ciccio Pistacchi.

"Can I invite you two for dinner?" he asked, returning to Italian.

Giuseppe looked at me, then turned to Ciccio. "I'm sorry but we can't. We have to make it back to Gimigliano tonight."

"A *caffè* before you leave, then?"

"Thank you, but perhaps another time," Giuseppe said, although I wanted to stay to talk to this Ciccio.

"Do return, it's magical here."

We said our goodbyes.

"Alas, I will have to wait another five years to speak English again."

"Five years?"

"Yes, it seems that only every five years does an English speaker make his way up here."

"Tourists?"

"Sometimes, though rarely. Often it's relatives from this area who have lived in England or America who come back, come back to the sanctuary."

The drizzle turned to thicker raindrops.

"Maybe the same dogs that attacked our car will be waiting," I said, jokingly.

"What dogs?" Ciccio asked, looking as if he'd never seen or heard them.

"Large sheepdogs, wild," Giuseppe said. "They literally attacked the car."

"Are you sure they were dogs? They looked like dogs?"

We both nodded.

"There are many wolves here, and boars . . . mean, wild boars. The wolves wouldn't attack the car, but the boars might."

We descended the mountain, and at the exact same place the dogs lay in wait. The large bitch led two others out onto the road. Giuseppe accelerated. The dogs charged and ran after the car. We flew by so quickly that I barely caught a glimpse of the other dogs darting out of the bushes. I turned around to see four more squat dark brown animals leaping out onto the road. They looked like dogs, but then again, I wasn't sure. Here in the middle of nowhere Calabria, a man speaks perfect English, and dogs that don't look like dogs attack passing cars.

Miles out, the sun shot through the clouds and sparkled on the waves of the Ionian Sea.

THE ALBANIAN PASSION PLAY

WOMEN CREPT OUT OF THE BUSHES and onto the crossroads. There were five in all, three blond and two dark. Their smileless faces and blue-eyed stares penetrated the car windows. I pressed farther back into my seat. A pair of legs in fishnet stockings peeked out below a long coat. The rest of their bodies were covered, so your eyes trained back to their high-cheekboned faces. There were young-looking women, girls almost, as well as a woman just past middle age.

About an hour outside Cerchiara di Calabria, Giuseppe made a detour through Albanian country to take me to a store his friend had in Spezzano Albanese.

"Albanians," Giuseppe said. "New Albanians. They are kidnapped and brought here as girls, sold on the streets until they're used up or die. Some their families have sold to pimps, knowing they'll never see their daughters again. It's a big business; they work with the mafia. But the Albanians are brutal; they care about no one. They have no code of honor. They kill, and they rape."

"I'm sure it's only a small percentage of the Albanians, just like it's a small percentage of Calabresi that are mafiosi," I said, recalling remarks I'd heard in the United States about the Russian and Chinese mafia.

Giuseppe paused, then went on: "And nothing is done here, because the Italian men buy them. Everyone buys them for a night or more, so no one complains."

At one time Spezzano Albanese, the second-largest of more than a dozen Albanian villages in Calabria, was a major trading center for people traveling from the Tyrrhenian Sea to the Ionian Sea and as far as Bari, in Apulia. Spezzano Albanese spreads across the hills above the only northern valley that offers easy passageway between the two coasts. On the next mountaintop over, in San Demetrio Corone, an Italo-Albanian college was founded in 1794. But Albanian immigration began centuries before.

After the Muslim Turks conquered Albania in the late fifteenth century, thousands of Greek Orthodox Albanians fled their homeland and set sail, just across the Adriatic Sea, for Italy, landing in Apulia. But they wanted to get farther away and kept traveling to the isolated mountains of Calabria, where they settled and still, to this day, speak their ancient language, a language that has incorporated so many local words that it's considered a dialect of Italian. They are known as the Abereschsh people, and while they have fully integrated into Italian society, they still maintain their customs, most visible in their food, churches, and holiday costumes.

Outside Spezzano Albanese, peach trees grow on V-shaped wood frames just high enough for a small truck to pass beneath, and while the frames lay the peach trees bare to the sun, the trees are sprayed or picked from below.

The mountains fell back and the hills rolled out as we approached Spezzano Albanese. Little of Calabria reminds me of anywhere else in Italy, but for a moment I felt as if I were in Tuscany or Umbria, on the train line between Rome and Perugia, for the valley here, as there, is an expanse of treeless pastures.

The town shopkeeper, Giuseppe Muià, a man slightly younger than I was, greeted Giuseppe warmly.

"I remember when your father ran this store," Giuseppe said, placing a hand on the young man's shoulder, a gesture he reserved only for those he was most familiar with, generally the kids who came into his own store.

Muià was short and thick-bodied, though he was not fat. Two other men stood by what seemed to be the village photocopier. Muià sold mostly stationery and books, but he also had racks of postcards and toys. As in most Italian stores, your eyes needed to adjust to the darkness; the high cost of electricity has made Italians energy-conscious.

"Pino," Giuseppe said, addressing Muià by his nickname, which was the same as his own.

"*Sì, Pino,*" Muià responded.

"Is everyone getting ready for Easter?"

"*Sì—*" He was interrupted by one of the men at the photocopier. There was a paper jam.

Muià gently opened the paper tray of the machine, a multitray behemoth with countless functions on its keypad. He treated the machine as a Calabrese housewife might treat her stove or refrigerator; it was kept immaculately clean. The two men stood back, reverently, speaking in a whisper.

"They're speaking Albanian," Giuseppe whispered in my ear. "I have no idea what they are saying. It's not Latinate. But there are a few words in Italian."

Muià came back.

"I overheard you talking," I said. "Was that Albanian?"

Muià shrugged his shoulders. "We were speaking in dialect. We just speak it among ourselves, but we also speak Italian. If you want to hear real, old-style Albanian, you have to go to Lungro. They are more isolated. There are more mountains, fewer travelers."

"I know that there are many Albanians moving to Calabria," I said. "It must be difficult for them to assimilate now. The language is different; the culture is different."

Muià straightened up, almost shocked. "No, there's no problem at all. We try to help them out, and the language is similar enough.

Here alone we have seven hundred new immigrants from Albania."

Giuseppe rolled his eyes and shook his head. "Yes, they are living here, but I don't think it's quite that easy. They don't have jobs, I don't see them working here in Spezzano, and how long will it be until the prostitutes move up here? Where do they live?"

"Prostitutes live everywhere; it's not just an Albanian concern," Muià responded.

"I don't agree. There is a difference, just like there's a difference between you and the immigrants . . ."

A woman walked in with her two daughters, carrying a piece of sheet music. Giuseppe and Muià suspended their argument.

Muià greeted her and turned to me. "Marco, look. It's the Passion play in Italian, Abereschsh, and Albanian."

He turned to the woman and explained to her who I was. "Would you mind reading to him the first few lines so he can hear the proper Abereschsh pronunciation?"

She stepped back and shook her hands. "No, no, no. I can't read. Maybe my girls can read it. They just came back from rehearsal."

"Or better yet," Muià said. "Maybe you can sing it for us."

The girls giggled, looked at each other, then broke into song. Abereschsh sounded more Slavic than Italian, with harsh *ch* and *sh* sounds.

The girls sang a verse from the Passion play, which in English is "Christ heard the noise, and couldn't get peace; it was Judas the traitor, with all those soldiers."

Criscti ghieghinej rumur
E nong senej riciet
Isc Iuda traditur
Me hith alto suglidet

They then sang it in Albanian:

Krishti gjegjënej rrëmur
E nëng zënej rrëcjet,

Ishi Iudha tradhëtur
E me gjithë ata suldet

And finally in Italian:

Cristo sentivo dei rumori
E non prendeva pace
Era Giuda traditore
Con tutti quei soldati.

"We have our own Albanian celebration the Tuesday after Easter," the mother explained to me shyly.

Each of these villages I visited felt foreign to me. Each had its own food, its own personality, its own language. I remember Giuseppe holding up his hand and, explaining how dialect works in Calabria, saying, "These are five villages." He pointed to his thumb and index finger. "These two villages share the same dialect." He pointed to his index finger and middle finger. "And these two villages have similarities in their dialect."

Then he pointed to his thumb and middle finger. "But these two villages can't understand each other."

Each town in Calabria was once its own city-state and developed its own Italianate language mixed with Greek, Albanian, Hebrew, or French, depending on which ethnic group lived there. Not until the Risorgimento under Garibaldi in the 1860s was there a movement to unify Italians under a single language. Heading the Fascist state from the 1920s on, Mussolini made it his goal not only to make the trains run on time but to make Italians speak the same language. Nowadays, however, the younger people have begun taking pride in their dialects.

Considering each village's distinctly different dialect, I could only imagine how foreign it must have felt for peasants traveling to even a neighboring village—especially at the turn of the last century. They could understand one another, but occasionally there would be a word, a single incomprehensible word, that made them realize they weren't among their own people. It's no wonder that when my grandfather moved to the United States, like so many other Italians, he sought out cities where his *paesani* had already settled. It's also no wonder that when my grandfather looked to marry, he returned to his hometown to find a wife.

LIMONCELLO AT GIUSEPPE'S

WE DIDN'T GET BACK TO GIMIGLIANO until after nine that evening, but Giuseppe's wife, Elena, had prepared a pesto al Genovese served with linguine, as well as sliced potatoes fried with porcini mushrooms, and kept it waiting for us.

Giuseppe and Elena's middle son, Domenico, had just arrived home from the University of Calabria in Cosenza for the Easter holidays. He brought his girlfriend, Francesca, with him. They both were quiet, introspective, and both had long dark hair that fell to their shoulders. She was studying linguistics, and Domenico was studying ecology.

We all sat at the table. Elena poured a glass of their wine for me and sparkling water for everyone else. Giuseppe and his wife are among the handful of people in all of Italy who don't usually drink wine with dinner. They prefer sparkling water, and they served their youngest son, Alessio, the orange soft drink generically called *aranciata*. In Calabria, and in Sicily as well, the *aranciata* is a darker red than elsewhere, since here soft drinks and orange juice are made from the heavier-tasting blood oranges.

After dinner, Giuseppe pushed back his chair, reached into the refrigerator, and produced a bottle of bright yellow *limoncello*, the sweet lemon liqueur served chilled after dinner. I felt my stomach warm with anticipation.

He filled my *aperitivo* glass. "We drink first; then we make the next batch. I know that in America you buy everything, but here we eat and drink what we make ourselves." Not entirely true, of course, but the thought of making my own *limoncello* rather than paying twenty-five dollars for a bottle back home did thrill me.

"Don't forget," I insisted, "my grandfather did make sausages and soppressata and wine—"

"Yes, yes. But did he ever make limoncello?"

I shook my head.

"So we will make two batches. One for you—the usual way. And then I'll give you instructions for Martha, with a little less alcohol," he said roguishly. Elena, Domenico, and Francesca sat back and laughed as Giuseppe bestowed upon me his exacting formula for *limoncello*.

He took out small lemons from the fruit bowl and counted them out on the table—sixteen in all. "But you can use ten larger ones," he said. From the cupboard he procured an empty three-liter bottle, a liter of 95 percent grain alcohol, and two bottles of water.

He grasped one of the lemons, and with a serrated steak knife he began peeling a thread of rind so thin that the white pulp was barely visible. "Lightly, lightly," he instructed. In less than a minute he had peeled off a single long thread of rind.

"Perfetto," he said, holding it aloft. He handed me a knife and a lemon—it was my turn—and I peeled what I thought was a perfectly thin piece of rind.

"Marco, be careful," Giuseppe said, pointing to the tiniest bit of white pith on the back side of the rind. The pith would make the liqueur too bitter.

I had finished five by the time he peeled his eleventh, which he brandished as another example of a perfect peel. He proceeded to cut the rind into small pieces, stuffed them into an empty liter bottle, then poured in the grain alcohol. He placed the liter of murky yellow liquid in the refrigerator.

"We'll let this sit for about twenty days and every two or three days open the bottle and scrape away the pulp that has floated to the top."

He explained the rest of the process, breaking down the ingredients for my stronger bottle and the less potent one, Martha's, which would be cut with milk.

So it was that on our first night back in Gimigliano, we ate pesto, a dish from Genoa, and drank *limoncello*, which comes from the Amalfi coast. When my grandparents lived here, these dishes would have been just as foreign as a burger and fries.

Giuseppe sealed the bottle and gave the top an extra slap. "It will be ready by the time you leave," he told me. "This will be your good-bye drink."

Part III

GIMIGLIANO

GOOD FRIDAY

"**M**Y NAME IS GIACOMINO. And this is Jesus Christ," a large man said, pointing to a thin, un-shaven man with blue eyes. These men confirmed my belief that, like my pale-complexioned, blue-eyed aunt Francesca in Danbury, not all southern Italians were short and dark.

Three men had just taken seats at the table next to me at Caffè Millennium in Gimigliano Superiore. The thin man actually did re-semble the common Jesus Christ of tacky paintings, with his longish light brown hair. The sharpness of his cheekbones and jaw balanced the gentleness of his eyes.

Giacomino, for his part, was a tall, meaty guy, also blue-eyed, with short, wavy blond hair. He wore a leather biker jacket, and his eyes blinked in a nervous tic. Both seemed to be in their late twen-ties or early thirties. The third man was older, probably in his early forties; he wore a few days' growth of beard.

Giacomino called over to me, "Excuse me, but who are you?"

"I'm from the United States, here visiting relatives."

"Come join us."

"That's okay, I've just finished eating anyway."

"No, no. Please come have a drink with us." Giacomino rose, cleared a space for me, then dragged over the extra chair from my table.

Jesus Christ extended a lazy hand. "Vincenzo."

"And this is Franco."

The older man turned to me and said, "Call me Gatto."

"Gatto?"

He let out the cry of a cat whose tail is being stepped on. "Yes, Gatto."

Earlier that Good Friday morning—before I met Jesus and his apostles—Gimigliano had begun to feel like a village in the clouds, its altitude isolating it from the surrounding region, carrying it off far into the puffs of cumulus. At the bar in Gimigliano Inferiore, I asked Maria for a cappuccino rather than my usual morning brioche and *caffè*, or espresso, as it's called in the States. I wanted something more than just a quick espresso. She smelled the container of milk under the counter and declared, "This has turned."

While no Italian will drink a cappuccino after ten in the morning, I found that even in the south very few people drank frothy milk with their espressos. Mostly, Calabresi prefer their coffee pure and strong with the added spoonful of sugar or, in the afternoon or evening, *corretto*, corrected, by a liqueur of some sort. Southerners prefer anisette or sambuca to the northerners' grappa. The liqueur is usually served in a shot glass and can be drunk alongside the coffee or poured in and mixed.

Outside, the market vendors had already set up their booths. Fridays they alternated between Gimigliano Inferiore and Superiore. This Friday was Inferiore's turn. Trucks with built-in slanted shelves hauled in shirts and underwear and socks and pants, from the kind of thin material sold in Chinatown in New York; the vendors were Moroccan and spoke only enough Italian—or, in this case, dialect— to haggle. The produce man, who usually drives through narrow village alleys in his pickup truck, hawking his fresh produce, had set up his own small, though plentiful, stand.

The real attractions were the food stands. Ordinary delivery trucks concealed self-contained gourmet markets. The truck's side panel extended out and was supported by poles, forming a shaded shopping area. A blue canopy attached to the metal panel extended another ten feet, lengthening the floor space for boxes of vegetables. Immaculate glass counters stocked with meats and cheeses were backed by shelves displaying choice selections of pasta and canned goods. There was even a cash register, adorned with pieces of stringy *cacciocavallo* cheese, a kind of provolone, shaped into horses and giraffes—an impulse buy.

Even in this driveway-size piazza, the villagers were given a choice. There were two of each of the food vendors. You might like Santoro's *cacciocavallo*, which resembled a large pear when hung, but the mozzarella at d'Amici's, ten steps away, was creamier.

Giuseppe would be busy for the next couple of days with family visiting for the holidays; today I had a few hours to explore my ancestral village before lunch at Zia Angela's. Leaving my grandmother's Inferiore, I set out for the Superiore of my grandfather.

The precipice of Superiore loomed above. The walk up was steep and long, and I usually had to stop halfway along the mule path and rest at the abandoned chapel. Not once during my stay in Gimigliano did I encounter a single other person along the mule path between the villages. There was simply no need for people to walk the twenty minutes between the two villages when you could drive there in five. Those who didn't have a car waited directly outside the piazza for the bus that ran every two or three hours from Inferiore to Superiore. I, too, contemplated the steep walk and decided to wait for the bus.

A mud-splattered Fiat pulled alongside of me.

"*Marco, che cosa fai?*" the driver asked. He was the thin man who supplied Maria's bar with his homemade wine.

"Waiting for the bus," I answered.

"Marco, it's a holiday. The buses don't run. Get in, I'm going up."

"*Dove vai?*" I asked.

"Back to work, at the farm. But I have to go through Superiore."

Giuseppe had once explained to me the differences between the villagers of Inferiore and those of the larger Superiore. The people of Inferiore tend to be closer and a bit warmer. If a stranger starts a fight with an Inferiorese, others will come to his defense. Not so in Superiore, where Giuseppe is from. During an argument, passersby may shrug their shoulders and simply watch. The people of Inferiore have the reputation, much like Calabresi all over the world, of being stubborn. The people of Superiore take the notion of *testa dura* one step further, accusing their downslope neighbors of holding a *testa di legno* on their shoulders—a head of wood, probably referring to the hard chestnut trees that grow in the surrounding forest.

The piazza of Gimigliano Superiore isn't in the center of the village like most piazzas in Italy; instead, it is at the entrance to the village. A waist-high wall encloses the piazza, with benches encircling the center. I strolled in.

When the Scottish writer Leslie Gardiner passed through Gimigliano in the 1960s, he thought the piazza was the obvious setting for *I Pagliacci*, Leoncavallo's famous opera about a troupe of performers who travel in the mountain villages of Calabria. Gardiner saw the piazza as a perfect amphitheater, remote, with the Chiesa S.S. Salvatore (which Gardiner found less than pleasing) forming the backdrop.

The story of *I Pagliacci*, named for a commedia dell'arte troupe headed by a husband-and-wife team, is tragic. During their stay outside one of the villages, the husband realizes that his wife is cuckolding him with one of the villagers. He knows his rightful duty. At the end of the night's performance—and the opera—as the couple are performing their curtain-dropping comedy skit, he rises and stabs his wife, then faces the audience and announces: *"La commedia è finita!"* I've seen the opera in New York City several times—it is a staple of the Metropolitan Opera repertory—and I'm always reminded of my grandfather shooting a man over my grandmother. *I Pagliacci*, which premiered in 1892, was realistic theater in a time when this kind of retribution was not only allowed but encouraged.

Now old men sat on a couple of benches, keeping warm beneath their wool coats. A wet breeze blew across the piazza. Ten boys played soccer with a semideflated ball only slightly bigger than a softball, using two opposing benches as goals. A tall, thin boy stood out as the aggressor. He was older than the other boys, maybe fourteen, and his kicks were precise but awkward. I soon realized that he had a limp, that his right leg didn't quite bend at the knee. It was as if he were swinging a two-by-four from his hip. But he got the ball where he wanted.

The few times the ball went astray and whizzed by the old men, they didn't even flinch, much less stop their conversation. A brown-and-black dog, sleeping at the far end of the piazza, rose and limped through the playing field, such as it was; the boys played around him.

By the time I got back to Inferiore, the temperature must have dropped to below fifty degrees. As I walked home down the alley, I heard the window to Zia Angela's open above me. "Marco, it's time for lunch," she called.

Sabrina and Masino, Luisa and Tommaso all were at the table; a space was cleared for me. Angela's mother sat at the same table with her back to the wall—the same spot she seemed to sit in all day, knitting, sewing, or shelling beans or chopping eggplant and zucchini.

Angela placed in front of me a bowl of penne with fava beans and a generous amount of pecorino cheese. I scooped a tiny spoonful of *piccante* from a clear dish. My body warmed. The meal, as Angela clearly knew, was the perfect comfort food for a cold day.

In Calabria during Easter, a bigger celebration than in the United States, the nuclear family becomes tighter. Here in Gimigliano the celebrations involved the entire village. Back in the States, because my family lived far away from me, I had been celebrating Easter with my wife and her Episcopalian family for the last decade. I felt as if I were truly celebrating Easter for the first time.

I posed the question to my relatives. "Are you walking the procession this evening?" I asked everyone.

"No, not this year," Luisa said. "We used to all the time, but . . ."

Angela grimaced. "I wish I could, but I can't walk for that long."

"But *you* should," they all said at once, encouraging me. "It's beautiful!"

"Do they have it in America?" Sabrina asked.

"I'm sure they do, somewhere. But I've never gone to one."

"Aah," they said. They looked at one another the way that Luisa and her friends had looked at me during the Palm Sunday service; the look said, "As we expected. They aren't religious in America, are they?"

Now Angela put at the center of the table a dish piled high with fried calamari, just out of the pan, along with fried anchovies and sardines baked in salt. Next came *salatulu*—a mixed pickled salad of peppers, eggplant, fennel, mushrooms (porcini, in this case, since they are abundant in Calabria), and tomatoes.

The wine was poured, and conversation continued. The dialect, a language that hinted of Greek and Arabic, was challenging no matter how much I heard it spoken throughout Calabria. When I took Italian in college, the dialect had been taught out of me. Now I kept hearing without understanding sounds and words that my father and grandparents spoke. Only slowly, and often with Giuseppe's help, could I decipher the linguistic tics of Gimiglianese.

For example, the *f* in *fava* is pronounced as *h*. So *fava* becomes *hava*. *Funghi*, spoken with a hard *g* in Italian, is said with a soft *g* in dialect. So *funghi* becomes *hunjee*. When a word ends in an *o*, the vowel turns into a *u*. Even the town's name, Gimigliano (pronounced "ji-mi-li-*an*-o") is pronounced "yi-mi-yi-*an*-o." So an Italian phrase as basic as *Io ho mangiato* (I ate) becomes *Ai umanyatu* in Gimiglianese.

Sometimes I understood; sometimes I didn't. Most times I just let the wine carry me off as I listened to the words glide by in a smooth legato.

After a long lunch, followed by a quiet siesta, and a *caffè* at Maria's, I made my way back to Superiore for the six-thirty Good Friday mass. I sat in the second to last pew, on the end, in order to get the best view of the beginning of the procession, which would follow the service. Carved in stone above the altar was "Ave Maria." Below, a human-size statue of Jesus was nailed to the cross. The veins and muscles bulged and seemed to pump from the light-colored flesh. Blood trickled from his feet, hands, and forehead, where the thorns dug in.

As usual, the pews of S.S. Salvatore in Gimigliano Superiore were filled only with women and children; the men stood at the back. The women and children rose as the priest started down the center aisle. I turned to the priest, half expecting him to be the same priest I'd met a decade earlier with my father, but this was a younger man, with large glasses. It wasn't until the reading of the first Gospel, about fifteen minutes into the mass, that the older boys and men slid into the pews.

Just as communion was given toward the end of the service, the church swelled with last-minute participants: Italians don't want to waste time with the prelude when they can take part in the main event. Four life-size statues appeared behind me: the Virgin Mary, Mary Magdalene, John the Baptist, and an angel.

Two men approached the altar, genuflected, then retrieved Christ. A line formed to bow and kiss His feet. Only women formed the line, it seemed. Southern Italian men, as Luigi Barzini noted in *The Italians*, refuse to drop to their knees at the feet of another man, and therefore they petition their prayers through the Virgin Mary. When the last woman bent at Christ's feet, the priest carried the statue of Him to the quartet of equally lifelike statues, then out the door. A chant rose from what must have been three or four hundred people.

I felt a hand on my shoulder. It was my uncle Mimmo's brother Gino, whom I had met earlier in the bar. He taught music to high school students in Catanzaro.

"Please, walk the procession with my wife and me."

I was happy not to have to walk the procession alone. Giuseppe's wife, Elena, wasn't feeling well that evening, and they had both decided to stay home.

Gino introduced me to his wife and his son, an eight-year-old with neatly combed hair, who, he proudly noted, was named Marco.

We followed the statues out the door, through the piazza, and down the only road connecting Superiore with Inferiore. The villagers turned into civilian police, wearing dark blue vests with silver reflective lining and carrying standard-issue flashlights. Although they had closed off the streets for the procession, a line of traffic had already begun to form on this main road, which was also the only road that led to Catanzaro, ten mountain miles away.

Gino, his family, and I fell in toward the end of the procession, along with about fifteen other people. The procession stopped; there was silence, then prayer led by the priest. It was the first station of the cross. By seven-thirty the sun had fallen behind the mountains, the last light beginning to dim.

There was a commotion behind us. One of the newly minted *polizia* was yelling at a man driving a small old commercial truck. The driver waved the guard away and pulled up behind us. His engine rumbled, overpowering the prayers. His lights lit up everyone's backs. The intimate magical spell was broken, but the procession crept on.

"Do you do this in New York?" Gino asked me.

"No. I'm sure it happens somewhere, but I've never done it." I remembered I had said the same thing to my relatives earlier this morning. I felt as if I were denying something and that after the next time someone asked me the same question, I would hear the crow of a rooster.

Gino thought for a moment. "But you are Catholic?"

"Yes," I said. "But it's not quite our custom in the United States to have such a big celebration for Easter."

Gino nodded his head, reaffirming some long-held belief he had about Americans. It may not have been the case with Gino, but many Italians, who've lived so long with a monolithic church that they confuse religion with nationality, have trouble understanding other religions in the world—or understanding that Catholics elsewhere in the world might not have the same ceremonies.

We stopped again. Far up front the prayers began. The truck continued to roar. The driver thumped his steering wheel and craned his neck to see how far ahead he had to go before he could turn off. Meanwhile, a Fiat Cinquecento lined up behind him. The older couple looked at us apologetically from behind the windshield. They realized that they had timed their ride badly.

"Are you eating at Angela and Mimmo's tonight?" Gino asked. "If not, you are more than welcome at our place."

I had stopped eating dinner at Angela and Mimmo's because they usually went to bed early, so this was a nice gesture on Gino's part. I realized he hated the idea of someone's eating by himself, but I decided to let him have the rest of this evening with his family.

"No, not tonight. I think I'll grab a quick pizza, then go home and read a little."

We had stopped again, and so had the truck. Several people turned toward the driver. He finally realized that he should cut the lights and turn off the engine. Silence, finally. Darkness. Dogs howled in the valley, and the driver, a large mustachioed bald man, looked out his window, picking his nose. As the praying emerged from the silence, people behind me and to my side began to move forward. Something brushed against my leg. It was the gimpy dog from the piazza. He nosed his way through my legs and cut his way through the crowd to the front, where all the action was.

After proceeding for almost an hour down the tight, winding road, we stopped at a curve. Directly above us, tucked in a cliffside cove, rose three crosses. Just as the priest walked up the hill, lights from the ground illuminated them. Now the truck driver, realizing that this was the widest, most convenient place to pass, started inching through the crowd.

The priest spoke to the crowd. An old retired man with his guard vest insisted that the truck driver turn off his engine. The driver yelled back. The priest stopped the service and frowned at the trucker, who relented. A moment after the silent standoff the priest, with a slight wave, instructed us to let the truck through. Eight cars followed; the priest stood impassively. The old couple passed us, and from inside closed windows, you could here a soft woman's voice saying, "I'm sorry," as the car, with its engine cut, rolled through the crowd and down the hill.

Italian men—and women, for that matter—hang out in groups. And in Calabria especially, this hanging out is an art form. You rarely see a person standing, let alone walking, by himself. Standing together, Italians unintentionally position themselves so that they can talk and watch the piazza at the same time. Everyone gets a view. When you're walking by yourself, all you see is a group quietly talking and staring at you. It's easy to feel intimidated. But once you engage the group in conversation, their unified wall breaks. One person will lean toward you or visibly bend his head. You feel yourself moving to one side, listening and talking, but also looking out, as the girls and women and old men walk by. You've become a part of the group, if only for those few minutes.

After the procession I strolled back up the hill, eager to get out of the cold and fill my stomach. I went into the Caffè Millennium, the only place to eat in Superiore. The first floor contained the coffee bar (two steps down was another room with a pinball machine and video game); a staircase led up to the dining room.

I greeted the bartender.

"You must be Marco," he said.

"Yes, how did you know?"

"Giuseppe said that you'd be stopping in tonight. I'm a Rotella, too," he said, "Domenico. Go on upstairs and have a seat." Even in his absence, Giuseppe was taking care of me.

The dining room was completely empty. I sat at a two-person table on the balcony overlooking the front door and above it, the TV. Domenico brought over his house wine, a light but intense red that was surprisingly smooth. A woman came out of the kitchen behind me. I ordered a *caprese*—sliced fresh mozzarella and tomato— then a *pizza quattro stagione* and a mixed green salad.

"Are sure you want the quattro stagione?" she asked.

"Sure, I think so," I said with a smile.

Two women and a man arrived and took a table behind me. One was a short dark-haired woman; the other had bleached blond hair. The man was tall, thin, and graying. Domenico stopped off at the table on his way into the kitchen and said something.

"Ciao, Marco," the blond woman said. "My name is Mirella. I'm Domenico's sister."

She urged me to stop by her house, then introduced me to the dark-haired woman next to her, Loretta, a weaver in town. Just then my pizza arrived.

"*Mangia, mangia, Marco,*" she said. "We'll talk later."

I thanked her and cut into the pizza. The crust was thin, and there was just enough cheese to cover the pizza without turning into goop. The artichokes were fresh; whole olives had been tossed about. With the first bite the flavor of the porcini mushrooms and the spicy Calabrese *soppressata* burst in my mouth. It was deliciously spicy and salty. I sipped the wine and felt satisfied. Then I realized why the waitress had made sure I wanted the *quattro stagione*: I was eating meat on Good Friday.

It was at this point that Giacomino, Gatto, and Jesus Christ walked into the restaurant and asked me to join them. Even sitting, Giacomino towered over the scruffy Gatto and the bearded Vincenzo.

Two beautiful women in their mid-twenties joined us at the table, and everyone exchanged a barrage of ciaos.

One of the women had full lips and dark brown hair with blond highlights. The other had dark hair that fell below her shoulders. Both wore big smiles. Giacomino and Vincenzo introduced them as Francesca and Rosanna. I remember Norman Douglas praising Gimiglianese women: "it would be difficult to find anywhere an equal number of handsome women on such a restricted space."

As they both sat down, Francesca kissed Vincenzo.

"Why do they call you Jesus Christ?" I asked Vincenzo, who was only slightly younger than I was.

Everyone laughed. Francesca giggled. She seemed to be picking her nose as she talked to Vincenzo. "He just becomes Jesus Christ this week," she said. When Francesca moved her hand from her face,

I realized that she was adjusting a nose ring. It must have been new, for the amount of attention she was paying it.

"For the Passion play," Vincenzo said. "You should come see it tomorrow night."

I'd heard about the Passion play, but I hadn't expected the leading actors to be this crew, for they were clearly the village punks. They dressed down when all the other villagers paid meticulous attention to clothing and grooming. They swaggered in and out of shops and cafés like this one, indifferent to formalities. They didn't look rough so much as bored. I couldn't help thinking that had I grown up here—had my grandparents never moved—I would have been one of them.

"Are you in the Passion play too?" I asked Giacomino.

Gatto leaned over to me. "Yes, he's one of the lambs."

Everyone at the table roared with laughter, and Giacomino ordered another liter of wine—and two more pizzas.

"So you're actually a practicing Catholic?" I asked Vincenzo. I was surprised that a relatively young man like him would be devout.

"No, I just look like Christ. I've been playing the part for years. Culturally, I guess, I'm Catholic, but I don't believe in the church. I'm more spiritual. I believe more in the beliefs of the American Indian. I want to go to the desert there. I believe in the earth. In nature," he continued. "You should see my art."

"You're an artist?"

"Yes, that's what I do. Come on," Vincenzo said, announcing that he and I were going to his studio and that we should all meet later in the piazza.

I took out my wallet to pay. Giacomino frowned. "No, no, no. Please. Marco." He put his hand on mine and directed my wallet back to my pocket.

As I left, another woman walked in. Large-boned with an ivory white face, she looked Irish. She waved hello and sat close to Giacomino.

Vincenzo led me down the main road, along a row of buildings, and directed me to an alleyway, then to a stairway in the back of a building, one in a row constructed of weathered stone, that looked to be at least a couple centuries old.

Vincenzo flicked on the light switch, and two naked bulbs illuminated the room. There was a cot and a small stove. Paintings hung on the wall. He seemed to work with maps. They had been cut and repasted, and the cities and countries and bodies of water were named in Italian. Some maps were replicas of nineteenth-century maps of Africa and China. There was a sculpture made of olive wood, and one of part of a shoe.

He had fashioned a chair of driftwood, adapting a German map of North and South America as a seat cover. A torn black umbrella hung from the back. Clearly Vincenzo was obsessed with places other than Gimigliano.

"Marco, what do you think?" He looked at me for a reaction; he was obviously pleased with his work. I was always wary of people too enthusiastic about their own art, as if their own praise made up for quality. But his work was much better than I thought it would be. I explained that I liked the desire to go to a place other than where you happened to be.

"But it's the desert in America where I most want to go," Vincenzo replied emphatically.

Back in the *Pagliacci* piazza, a group of boys was playing soccer. Gatto, Vincenzo, and Giacomino joined in, thrilling the boys. I stood with the women.

"To judge by his work, Vincenzo likes to travel," I said to Francesca.

"Yes, but he hasn't really been much out of Italy," Francesca said. "And wherever he goes, he always comes right back here to Gimigliano."

"It's pretty boring here, isn't it?" asked Rosanna, the dark-haired woman. "Not like in New York?"

"New York can wear you down," I said. "Here I can take in a village at a slow pace. I can appreciate it. And for me that's exciting."

"But for how long?"

The game continued. It began to rain. *"O, dio mio,"* Francesca said. "Do you want a ride home?"

I told her I'd stick around, and the two women took off without saying goodbye to the others. I stood beneath an arch that led to the main pedestrian road. Out in the piazza, the laid-back, self-conscious Vincenzo broke loose with the ball and scored a goal. He was much better than I had thought he would be, but then again he was playing against kids less than half his age. Gatto tended the other goal while smoking a cigarette.

The rain came down harder. A figure slumped its way across the stone; it was the gimpy brown-and-black dog from the procession, hobbling out of the rain.

Now it poured, and the players headed for cover under the arch. The kids dispersed.

Giacomino placed his hand on my shoulder: "We'll see you tomorrow night for the Passion play, yes?"

I said they would, and the four of us walked out of the piazza and down a street called Corso America.

THE SILK WEAVERS

"**F**UNGHI-CARCIOFI-FINOCCHI-PISELLI,**"** echoed a tinny voice amplified by a loudspeaker outside my window. It was seven in the morning. I was tired but pleasantly surprised that I wasn't hung over from the night before. The fact that the homemade wine was preservative-free saved me from a headache. As a matter of fact, no matter how much wine I drank in Calabria, no matter how drunk I got—and the fortified Calabrese wine is not for lightweights—I was never tight in the head the next morning.

"Funghi-carciofi-finocchi-piselli," droned the voice, which blended all the words together in a single breath, mushrooms-artichokes-fennel-peas.

"Francesco!" a woman's voice yelled out.

"Ciao, Maria," the loudspeaker replied.

"*Aspett', aspett'!*" the woman said. Wait!

"Don't rush," said the loudspeaker.

I pulled the curtains back to see a white Fiat pickup truck parked in the alley outside. The truck bed stood open at the back and on both sides, displaying four rows of cascading shelves full of fruits and vegetables. The vendor had everything from eggplants, potatoes, artichokes, and bananas to every green in season.

I shaved, got dressed, and started up the steps to the café.

"Marco," I heard Zia Angela call from above, *"prendi un caffè."*

Upstairs, Angela's mother and Marisa, Sabrina and Masino's daughter, were sitting at the table. Marisa was playing with her Barbie. In front of her was something large, folded in a towel, a typical Gimiglianese handwoven towel. Angela proudly pulled back the towel to reveal an entire skinned lamb.

"A-gnel-lo," Marisa said in a gleeful voice, pronouncing each syllable of "lamb."

"For Easter," Angela said. "It's from our farm."

Angela's mother pointed to her cheek and twisted her hand. *"Buona,"* she said. "Very tasty."

It was a beautiful, healthy lamb, perfectly skinned and dehoofed. There was not a trace of blood; its pink skin glistened, seeming almost translucent. I could tell that it had been killed only minutes ago; its dark eyes had not yet glazed over.

Most Americans would gasp if they were to see entire animals laid out on their dining room tables. In Calabria, though, there is no mystery as to where dinner comes from. Little Marisa kept playing with her Barbie; for her, this was just as normal as playing in front of newly shelled fava beans.

I drank a cup of coffee and bit into a brioche that came from a plastic bag. Even that tasted fresher than it would have in the States.

The old men in tweed coats and caps walked throughout Gimigliano Superiore in an early-morning stroll. It would be a lazy, quiet Holy Saturday. With their hands clasped behind their backs, the men don't avert their eyes when others pass. They acknowledge each person walking by, happy to offer a greeting. They knew that I was a visitor. They looked me in the eyes, smiled or didn't smile, and enunciated a *"Salve,"* a formal hello. They were curious as to who this stranger was and whether he was good or bad. Could he respond, was he mute, or did he have some kind of secret?

"*Salve,*" I said with a smile and a nod.

Their furrowed brows loosened; their clenched jaws once again fell into a comfortable position. They nodded and continued their conversation. I had passed the test.

I was walking to Lorella Biamonte's weaving studio. I had met Lorella the previous night at the Caffè Millennium, and she offered to show me her work before lunch. On the top floor of a house down the alley from the Chiesa S.S. Salvatore, she had set up shop with two other weavers, Maria Mangiacasale and Maria Critelli, the founder. I climbed up the stairs, and Lorella, who was short with unruly dark hair, showed me in. Three looms, one of which was antique, filled the front room. On one loom the three women wove throw rugs and place mats made of *ginestra*, or broom; another loom was for the weaving of wool blankets; the third was designated for finer items, such as silk or linen shawls as well as tablecloths and napkins.

"We all have degrees. I'm an accountant, for instance," Lorella explained. She was intense, somewhat humorless. "But instead of moving to the north to find work, we insist on living in our hometown, and we insist on making our own money."

Lorella pulled up a few cardboard boxes that had been stacked against the wall, produced some examples of their work, setting them out: two dish towels, one bright red with gold trim, the other cream with green olive branches and yellow birds. She displayed a rug made of *ginestra*; red-and-green designs jumped out of the white background. Finally, she placed in my hands a delicate, cream-colored tablecloth, tightly folded. I remembered seeing such table linens in my grandmother's house. Like all the others, it bore the distinctive design of all Calabrese weavers, a repeating pattern of diamonds within diamonds.

"Beautiful," I told her. "Can you make a living doing this?"

"We do well enough," she said sternly. "We belong to an artisans' guild, and we go to fairs and festivals all over Italy. In our way, by refusing to leave for the north and insisting on making a living here in the south, we are preserving Calabria."

Lorella was not a typical southern Italian woman. She was

straightforward, not shy, though not gregarious. I wanted to talk to her about so much, to ask her opinions on Calabria, on Gimigliano. But she was set on talking about her work and her collective, not herself.

"Where did you study?" I asked her, trying once more to get to know her.

"Not far, in Cosenza," she said, then returned at once to the subject at hand. "Now, the process of making *ginestra* is not complex. *Ginestra* is tough and strong and, when woven, becomes much softer."

She nodded to my notepad—a wordless instruction for me to take notes.

The rain began to fall late in the afternoon, and by seven o'clock it was still drizzling. I called my cousin Luisa about Vincenzo's Passion play.

"Marco, it's raining," she said. "They canceled it."

For some reason I thought that the Passion play would go on in spite of any weather. Instead, I offered to treat my cousins to pizza from the Golden Rabbit in Tiriolo. Masino and I drove the four miles, returning with the pizzas and *arancini*, stuffed rice balls. While we were eating, I told them about the people I'd met. They were impressed that I had run into the artists of the city. These outcasts, *vagabondi*, had a kind of celebrity aura about them.

I was able to meet and get along with even the most offbeat that Gimigliano had to offer. And that, oddly, had drawn me closer to my cousins. We sat back, drank homemade wine, and relaxed. Tommaso put on the end of a soccer game.

The rain came down in spikes. The wind whistled through the alleys and gaps in the windowsills. The curtains floated on cold puffs of air. I threw on an extra blanket and crawled into bed. Rain, then hail, sprayed against the window. The electricity went off, to return intermittently. At midnight the church bells rang for a solid two minutes; when the last chime of bell floated away, the lonely sound of rain pelting my windows returned. It was Easter Sunday.

PASQUA

AT THE BAR, Maria was wearing a neat gray skirt and a beautiful knitted black sweater. She had put on mascara and added color to her high cheekbones, but her eyes were sad. She placed the cappuccino in front of me, then opened the silver sugar dish for easy access to the spoon. These silver dishes are ubiquitous throughout Italy, and the welcome gesture of opening the dish usually accompanies the *caffè* when the bartender is not too busy.

I smiled at Maria and furrowed my eyebrows inquisitively. *"Buona Pasqua,"* I said.

"This is always a hard holiday," she said.

I was about to ask her why when the door swung open and a well-dressed gray-haired man walked in. He was tan and wore a beige camel-hair sport coat and nicely tailored pants. A wide Windsor knot separated his lapels, and a dark blue wool coat was draped over his shoulders. This was Maria's husband, Ciccio Paonessa.

He shook my hand, and with a sincere *buona Pasqua,* he motioned to Maria to pour me a drink. Three more men came in, dressed in jackets and ties. Maria set two glasses of brandy in front of us.

"No, I can't," I said. "Too early in the morning."

"Too early?" Ciccio said. "It's Easter!"

Everyone laughed. I sipped a glass of anisette, a licorice liqueur, that Maria had set down instead. It was a cold, damp morning, and all the men were huddled in the local bar drinking and telling stories. This is what it must feel like to be in Ireland—except there I'd be drinking whiskey rather than a sweet liqueur.

I offered to buy the next round, but Maria's husband, Ciccio, stepped back with his hands in the air. "What are you doing? You're a guest here. You can't pay."

The wine maker who had taken me up to Superiore the day before bought the bar a round of his wine.

After that was drunk, Maria's husband leaned over and said, "Have you ever had amaro?"

"No," I said. "What is it?"

"It's a special Calabrese liqueur, made from herbs over in Tropea."

Maria poured us each a shot. The drink warmed me as it went down. It was slightly medicinal but had a sweet aftertaste. There was no food in my stomach; my head felt light, and my body tingled. It was nine-twenty. Easter mass was to begin in ten minutes.

Mimmo Mercante, a tall man with a gentle face and a goatee, brought in his clarinet. He, like Gino Cantafio, with whom I had walked the procession two nights before, teaches music to high school students in Catanzaro. Another man, in his late thirties like Mimmo, brought out a guitar. In the back of the room, cutting through the sound of chatter and playing through the smoke, the two musicians broke into a Calabrese folk song. Mimmo's friend sang in a raspy voice that strained to keep the high notes from disappearing in his throat.

I ordered another *caffè*. Ciccio, smiling, held a hand up to Maria and insisted I have another drink instead.

"No, I really shouldn't. I'm going to Easter mass."

"Even better reason for another drink," Ciccio said. Clearly none of these men would be going to mass. While their wives worshiped, they would stick around and drink, decamping for the church toward the end of the service. Even so, they wore their Sunday best; church or no church, Easter in Calabria was still a holiday.

Myself, I was my grandmother and grandfather combined. I was dutifully going to mass but not before having a quick drink with my friends.

"I just ordered a coffee," I said, shrugging my shoulders as if to say, "Oh, well, maybe next time."

"Aaah, but this will make the coffee go down that much better." Maria's husband poured a shot of anisette into the *caffè* and patted my shoulder: I had no choice but to drink it down.

Maria smiled at me as if I were a lost child.

I smiled back. "Are you going to mass?"

She nodded. "But then my husband and I will go to the cemetery and leave flowers for my parents." She paused and ran a wet rag along the counter. "This is a hard time of year," she repeated.

I stepped out into the cool air and began a wobbly descent as the last church bells rang. The sun broke through the clouds for the first time in days.

I entered the church just as the doors were closing and found a spot behind a group of teenage boys in the back. I knew I must have reeked of cigarette smoke and sweet alcohol.

From the corner of my eye, I saw someone waving. It was Elena, Giuseppe's wife, who had brought her mother to mass. Obviously, Giuseppe and the his sons had decided to stay home.

I waved back, thankful that she wasn't any closer.

The church felt alive with energy. The yellow stucco walls seemed even brighter than the week before. Above the altar, in this church as well, Christ took a back seat to the Virgin. I focused my eyes on the statue of the Virgin Mary; the angels floating around her came to life.

"Marco!" came a voice that was something between a whisper and a yell. "Marco!" It was Luisa's son Francesco, in the very front pew. Now he strode down the center aisle where the priest stood, awaiting the music for his procession to the altar.

"*Marco, vieni,*" Francesco said, beckoning me with a cupped hand.

I pointed to the pew. "It's okay, I'll stay here."

He furrowed his eyebrows and frowned. I pointed to the priest and shook my head as a way of saying, "But it's too late."

Now the priest glanced back at me. I was sure he could smell the alcohol. I nodded deferentially, put on a dopey smile, and stumbled up the aisle. Francesco took my hand and walked me to the pew, where he put a program in my hand and gave me a hymnal opened to the correct page. As the procession began, I turned around and saw, a few pews behind me, Luisa and Sabrina and Zia Caterina and her friends; they waved, excited to see me there: a man at mass and in the very first pew.

After mass, Luisa and Francesco led me back to Zia Angela's house, where Sabrina and Masino had been waiting. The women busied themselves setting the table for the paschal feast. There were tagliatelle with tomato sauce and sliced hot green peppers; sausage frittata; sautéed fennel; and finally, the freshly slaughtered, perfectly roasted lamb with baby potatoes.

During the course of my stay my cousins had been curious about my role at home. Luisa and Sabrina marveled at my skills as a husband. I cooked, did laundry—and here in Italy I offered to help set the table for Easter dinner.

Whenever I mentioned the work I did around the house—cooking, cleaning, laundry—Masino and Tommaso looked on in disbelief, while Luisa and Sabrina nodded approvingly, praising me in front of their husbands. But no matter how much Luisa and Sabrina complimented me, I couldn't help thinking that they considered me just as much a candy-ass as did Tommaso and Masino.

"Here men don't do anything," Sabrina said. "They're lazy."

Tommaso wished me a *buona Pasqua,* then sniffed. "Marco, have you been drinking?"

I cringed and softly admitted that I had had a drink or two at the café.

"A drink or two." Tommaso turned to Masino and tilted a thumb sprouting from a cup-formed hand back to his mouth.

Just then we sat down for dinner.

"Make sure you pile up Marco's plate," Tommaso said.

"Why more than usual?" Luisa asked.

Masino stifled a laugh and added, "He needs the fortification."

"He needs what?" Sabrina asked.

"Yes, he needs food badly or else he's going to have a headache," said Tommaso.

"What's this?" Zia Angela said, serving me a double portion.

Tommaso feigned incredulity. "I can't believe it, that on Easter our American friend Marco has gotten drunk!"

"What? When?" all three women demanded.

Masino and Tommaso could barely contain themselves. I could tell they wanted to exploit my faults, especially after hearing how enlightened I was.

"They just kept offering," I tried to explain.

Sabrina cut me off. "Oh, yes, that's always the case with men. It's never their fault."

We finished the meal with apples, nuts, and lupini beans, and finally, *caffè* and a *torta di nocciola,* hazelnut cake, by which time I was drunk no more.

After dinner and a brief rest, I walked through the village by myself. The smell of wood fires filled the air. With everyone inside napping or spending time with their families I felt alone, and the usually comforting scent of woodsmoke made me want to be back in New York with my wife.

Gradually people emerged from their Easter afternoon slumber; the *passeggiata* swelled. I poked my head inside a large bar on the piazza in Gimigliano Superiore, where I immediately spotted Giacomino and another young man named Giuseppe. I joined them.

A discussion on Calabria's economy led to a conversation on finding work in the north, which then turned into one on the self-image of the Calabresi.

"They're hypocrites," said Giuseppe, who, in his twenties, was an accounting student at the university in Catanzaro.

"Hypocrites? Why?" I asked.

"The Calabresi are proud to be known as kind, warm, and open. It's a nice self-image to have," Giuseppe said, pushing his glasses farther up on his nose. He was one of the few men my age who wore glasses; in a country where looking good is an art form, most men and women wear contacts. "But while they help their own families and friends, they are arrogant toward others."

"Is that hypocrisy? Or is that just a stereotype that they enjoy?" I asked.

"It is a stereotype, but it's hypocrisy because they want everyone to believe it. The Calabresi are calculating, they are proud"— Giuseppe paused for a minute—"and they know exactly what they are doing. We are not just a bunch of stubborn, smiling fools."

Giacomino went to the bar and returned with glasses of wine for the three of us.

"It's almost insulting to say that we Calabresi are simply warm," Giuseppe continued. "We are just as warm as anyone else; we are just as calculating as anyone else. We are really not so different."

"Do you know what they call us up north?" Giacomino interrupted. "They call us *terrone*." His face crunched together and turned red as he enunciated each syllable, spitting out the word with all the hatred he felt.

Terrone translates as "of the earth." It carries the same impact, the same anger and disgust, as the word "nigger." Many northern Italians regard southerners—anyone south of Rome (or south of the Po River, according to extremists)—with much the same contempt as white Americans long bestowed upon blacks.

However, as immigrants—Albanians, Moroccans, Africans, Russians, Ukrainians—have arrived in Italy, the younger generation of southern Italians faces less prejudice than their forebears did. Prejudice now is directed at the immigrants—especially Albanians, Moroccans, and black Africans. Meanwhile, southerners call those north of Rome *polentoni*, or polenta heads, for their love of polenta, cakes of fried or baked cornmeal. But to me this term simply doesn't carry the same weight; it is akin to a black man's calling a white person a cracker.

Debora and Rosanna, two of the women I had met on Good Friday, came in smoking cigarettes, along with Stefano, Debora's younger brother. Stefano was in his final year of high school, where he studied the French horn and the trumpet. His dark curly hair framed a pleasantly inquisitive face.

"I visited America once," Stefano said in broken English.

"Where?" I asked in English, and when he looked puzzled: *"Dove?"*

"Ah, yes. Toronto," he answered.

"Oh, in Canada?"

"Yes, Canada. My relatives live there," he said, and we spoke of geography, as I explained to him that Niagara Falls, though in New York, is nowhere near New York City.

Thousands of Calabresi have settled in Niagara Falls and elsewhere in upstate New York, all along the Erie Canal, as well as throughout eastern Canada. When Calabresi think of America, their image is often of Canada. Just about everyone who emigrated from Gimigliano went to Niagara Falls, Toronto, or Danbury, and the Festa della Madonna di Porto is celebrated even in Toronto.

Giacomino put his arm around me. To me, he was like a gentle giant, though I suspected he was capable of exploding when provoked.

He handed me a book. "I know you are a writer, so I feel safe showing you this. I know you'll understand. I mean, not many people here do," he said. The title was *The Boss Is Alone*; the endpaper showed a flow chart of hierarchy within the mafia.

"You should read this so you can understand the mentality of people here," he said. However terrifying the mafia was, there was nevertheless a sense of pride in knowing that your countrymen were capable of influencing not just local politics but the entire government. I was surprised by how similar this complicated sentiment was to that in the States: while many Italian-Americans cry out against their stereotypical, derogatory portrayal in movies that glorify the mafia, just as many revel in the power the mafia dons wield.

"What effect does the mafia have here in Calabria?" I asked.

Giacomino shrugged. "The mafia isn't as strong now—Calabria isn't as isolated from the rest of Italy—but people are still cautious. It's just woven into society." I felt that he didn't actually know much about the mafia—in Calabria or in general—and definitely hadn't felt its influence firsthand. With another glance at the book, I realized it was about the Cosa Nostra in Sicily, not the 'ndrangheta in Calabria.

He opened the book to the middle, where a sheet of paper had been folded and tucked away. "But this is *really* what I wanted to show you."

He looked up at everyone to make sure that no one else was looking—everybody was busy talking—and carefully uncreased it with his large hands and presented it to me. Three short poems had been printed by hand on the lined page.

"Thank you," I said. I was genuinely touched—and happy to meet another writer. The Calabresi—Italians, for that matter—consider writing, along with reading, an antisocial activity.

"*Figurati, Marco,*" Giacomino said—it's nothing. Then he averted his eyes. "This is really embarrassing. I mean, it's personal, but then again, it's not."

At that moment Rosanna swooped down and plucked the paper out of his hands. "What's this? Is it poetry?"

"Rosanna, please," Giacomino said.

"Giacomino, is this yours?"

"Yes, but, Rosanna, I want Marco's professional eyes to read it."

"But poetry is meant to be read aloud."

"Rosanna," Giacomino said testily, then settled back in his chair, resigned.

"Ooh, this is juicy," Rosanna said.

She read the first poem, which was about ten lines long. She giggled at the outset, as did everyone else, but soon the laughter subsided. The poet was content to die upon merely breathing in the sweet scent of his beloved's skin.

"This is all *so* erotic, isn't it?" Rosanna teased. "Let's read the next one! It's titled 'Virginity.' "

"Let's read that one," Debora said.

Giacomino stood up and swiped the poems from her hand. "Rosanna, when you're able to understand poetry, you can read it."

We finished our drinks and headed out into the cold evening. Rosanna and Debora went home; Stefano, Giacomino, Giuseppe, and I went up to the Millennium for pizza and more wine.

"Marco, now for something even more personal," Giacomino said once we had settled in and removed our coats. "Can I ask a favor of you?"

"Of course. What is it?" I wondered what could be more personal than sharing one's poems.

"Do you like boxing?" he asked.

"Yes, I do," I said. I was a fight fan back home.

"Me, too. Who's your favorite fighter?"

"Roy Jones, Jr.," I said, naming a quick, powerful middleweight from Florida. "I didn't think Italians liked the fights."

"Not many. That's why it's embarrassing," he said. "And my favorite is Mike Tyson."

"Now that *is* embarrassing. He was great at one time, but now he's just a circus act."

"Yes, I know," he said. "But he's big and powerful. I was hoping that when you come back, you could bring a poster."

I said it might be hard to find such a poster in the States. "Boxing isn't as popular as it once was."

"I know, I know. It's too much to ask of you. Forgive me."

I told him I would do my best. Then I ordered another liter of wine.

"You know, I used to live abroad," Giacomino said, returning to our earlier conversation. When southerners talk about going abroad—*all'estero*—to work, they usually mean to northern Italy. "I tried to find work in Milan," Giacomino continued. "I wanted to do good, to make a living. But it's tough. I got involved with the wrong people." He waved his hand to dismiss the thought. "There's no work here, and only work for northerners in the north."

Stefano nodded in a way that suggested he sympathized with Giacomino's experience but thought there was more to the story. When

Giacomino got up to find the waiter, Stefano leaned over the table and said softly, "It's not like that everywhere. Some people feel it; some don't. I think Giacomino feels it more than others."

"And you, do you think you'll go north?"

"I don't know. If I can play French horn down here, I'll stay. Maybe I'll go to Toronto. Maybe I'll go with my sister to Rome to study." Debora was in her third year at the University of Rome.

"I'll leave," Giuseppe said, with a tone of disgust.

It was getting late. We drank the wine, paid the tab, then walked out once again into the cold, wet night.

"I could use some coffee," Giacomino said.

On the other side of the piazza we ran into Gatto and Vincenzo, who decided to come with us to a small dark café along Corso America. The only other people in the place were some rough-looking guys about our age, who had clearly passed the evening drinking.

When we walked in, one of them was talking about a woman he knew, whom he described as a slut. Giacomino turned to the speaker, a wiry man in a leather jacket and with a couple of days' beard, and said, "I don't think you should say that."

"What the fuck do you care?" he said with a shrug. "She's not your girlfriend; you hardly even know her."

Giacomino drew closer to the man. "I just don't think you should say that, especially a pig like you."

Before I could even take a sip of my coffee, the two began swinging at each other, and everyone else squared off, with each fighter's friends halfheartedly trying to break up the fight. I had the impression this was a ritual that each group was tiring of. Finally the combatants were separated, and Vincenzo and Gatto led a struggling Giacomino outside.

I had witnessed many tense situations, many arguments in Italy, but I had never seen Italians come to blows. I had always thought that for Italians, the verbal assault was enough, a pressure valve that allowed them to let off steam instead of completely blowing up. But Giacomino's pressure valve seemed to have popped off long ago.

I paid for our undrunk demitasses of *caffè* and walked out along the alley. I found Giacomino and the others huddled in the shadows of a building, their hands in their pockets, their breath visible in the cold air.

Stefano offered to take me home.

Giacomino came up to me and put a hand on my shoulder. "I'm so sorry. Forgive me. I was an asshole. I didn't want you to see that."

"*Figurati,*" I said. After all, the Calabresi, like Italians in general, are known for their passion.

PASQUETTA IN SILA

WHILE *PASQUA* IS CELEBRATED WITH FAMILY, *Pasquetta*, the day after Easter, is celebrated with friends, and in Gimigliano it's celebrated in the Sila.

Sila Piccola, one of the three ranges of the Sila massif—an expanse of more than twelve hundred square miles and at an altitude of nearly sixty-five hundred feet—begins just north of Gimigliano, in the heart of Calabria. Deep forests of pine, beech, and chestnut trees blanket most of the region. The Greeks once had all but cleared the forests for their shipbuilding industry, leaving barren, windblown mountains. The Romans had deforested the region for the same reason (as they did the rest of Italy), but since then the Sila forest has been relatively untouched by agriculture and industry.

The Sila massif now contains the largest national park in Italy. This is the only region in Italy where wolves, bear, wildcats, and boar roam the dense forests, along with a species of slender tiny deer. It is also home to deadly vipers.

I rode with Luisa, Tommaso, and Francesco, while Sabrina, Masino, and Marisa followed in their car. Everyone had dressed up for the dinner. I had been happily surprised when they invited me to join them; I finally felt as if I had gone from being a distant relative to a friend.

We passed through dense swaths of pine forest with deep brown soil and many lakes—some natural, most man-made. We crossed a dam over the Alli River, the same place where Angela and Mimmo had taken Martha and my parents to their summer cottage. One afternoon we saw wild horses lapping up the cool water on the distant banks.

"At certain times of the year here," Tommaso said, "you can snow ski in the morning, then go to the beach in the afternoon."

From the winding mountain roads, the peaks to the north, cleared of trees, looked as if they were capped with snow. Giuseppe had once explained to me that many of the mountains had been stripped down to rock for the clay from which terra-cotta roofs and fine pottery are made, most of it going to the north. Unfortunately, the Calabresi as a whole were never able to profit from this industry. Individual landowners sold tracts to northern excavators, and even the contractors who bought state land failed to keep their promise to hire more than a few Calabrese workers, with the better-paying positions going to the owners' northern relatives. But now the Gimiglianesi regard the Sila with a great sense of pride, as a respite from everyday life.

Out of this seemingly remote wilderness we emerged into a cluster of condominiums and four-star hotels, with cozy white houses and restaurants with peaked roofs and dark-brown wood trim, smoke streaming from their chimneys, that seemed to have been transported directly from Switzerland. We had reached Villaggio Mancuso, a tourist destination for skiers all over Calabria that is known as Little Switzerland. Just as the Calabrese coast has been referred to as the poor man's Riviera, so the Sila is a downscale Alpine resort.

When I looked closer, there were signs that we were still in southern Italy. In the small zoo, you could catch a glimpse of the tiny Calabrese deer. The stores sold packaged porcini mushrooms, jarred *'nduja* and *piccante*, as well as vacuum-sealed packages of *soppressata* and sheep cheese; tchotchke stands sold figurines and toy guns carved from the region's pine and chestnut trees, miniature wine jugs hand-sculpted from the region's clay, and ornate walking sticks and pipes carved from Calabrese olive wood (though they are manufactured in Milan, as their tiny stickers announced).

And of course there were packs of the usual harmless stray dogs. Many of them obviously had wolf blood, but constant contact with humans had rendered them as docile and needy as stray puppies. You would find yourself being followed by three or four, all of them looking longingly up at you.

For the noon meal, the cousins and their friends had reserved half a restaurant, Il Semaforo, named for the streetlight outside, the only one for miles. Since the intersection was no larger than those elsewhere in the area, it seemed as if the streetlight had been put up just to supply the name for the restaurant. There were eight couples, and as is typical throughout Italy, each had only one child. We sat at a large L-shaped table, the men in the center and at the bend of the L, the wives and children at the ends. Immediately liters of wine were set on the table, and my glass was miraculously filled.

"Let's make sure *l'american'* finds out what good eating is," I heard someone say.

The table had been set with *cacciocavallo* and pecorino cheeses, hard and soft, and with breads and Calabrese meats—salami, *soppressata*, prosciutto. An army of waiters placed in front of us *scilatelli*, or *maccheroni al forno*—baked penne with tomato sauce and mozzarella. A man my age walked in and sat next to Tommaso. His face brought to mind pictures of my dad and my uncle Frank in their twenties; he had my uncle's profile and my father's jet-black hair. And like the two of them, and me, he had the stereotypical dark olive southern Italian complexion.

"Marco," Tommaso called from the other side of the table, "here's a distant cousin of yours, Tommaso Rotella."

I walked over to introduce myself. Tommaso, my newfound relative, poured me a glass of wine, and we toasted. We noted resemblances in features, but after a list of potential relatives yielded no matches, we drank some more and concluded that surely we must be related somehow, if only distantly.

Next, the waiters served *conchiglie*, small shells with porcini mushrooms and peas in light cream sauce. The wine kept coming. Masino and I began talking about Italian soccer, and he was pleased to find that I could keep up with him. I had been following Reggina, from Reggio di Calabria, which for the first time shot up from Serie B to Serie A (the top league of Italian soccer). We talked about Catanzaro's team, the very mention of which elicited boos and hisses from around the table. The Italians are harsh fans when their teams are performing poorly. Way down in Serie C-2, the lowest rung of professional Italian soccer, Catanzaro struggled to reclaim its glory days of the 1970s, when it had blossomed at the top of the Serie A teams.

"Next week is one of Catanzaro's last games," Masino said. "We'll go."

I was thrilled at the prospect of attending my first professional soccer game—even if it was a lowly Serie C team.

The waiters cleared our *primi piatti* and served the *secondi*: sliced breast of goose stuffed with pepperoni, prosciutto, and bread crumbs, accompanied by fresh carafes of wine.

The Calabresi eat with gusto, and I was pleased to see that it wasn't only my father and I who ate quickly. Within fifteen minutes our plates were cleared and a second *secondo* arrived: a *vitello scallopine* sautéed in olive oil.

Someone stood up from the only other large party in the restaurant and waved me over to his table. It was Tonino Ventura, my uncle Tom's doppelgänger from my flight into Calabria. He introduced me to his wife and two daughters, his mother and father, and the rest of his cousins. He told the story of meeting me on the plane. It was obvious that his family had heard the story before, but his own interest seemed as keen as ever.

When I returned to my seat, I found that several platters of roast lamb and potatoes had been set in the center of the tables.

Luisa's husband, Tommaso, broke out into the popular old folk song—for my benefit, I knew—"Calabresella Mia." Luisa covered her eyes in embarrassment. The other men joined in. Some stretched their arms around the friends next to them.

At last dessert was served. It was surprising in its sparseness after all the rich food; it was a mix of fruits and nuts, with platters of hard cookies.

Tommaso ordered bottles of *prosecco*, Italian sparkling wine. Corks popped and champagne overflowed onto the tabletop. Luisa's face turned hard. She looked at her sister, who frowned.

"Imbriago," I heard her say. Drunk.

An older couple walked in, waving to everyone.

"Unbelievable, Marco," Tommaso said. "Yet another relative. You're related to the entire village."

He introduced me to my uncle and aunt Ciccio and Maria Critelli as he offered them champagne.

"I remember your father," Ciccio said as we touched glasses. "Forty years ago."

He seemed genuinely disappointed that I hadn't been brought around to see them sooner. I had been a bit surprised at this, too; I'd have thought it would have made it easier for Angela and Domenico to distribute the responsibility of entertaining me. But wonderful hosts though they were, I was learning that they weren't the most social of my relatives.

Masino, Sabrina, and Luisa began packing up to go. Many of the wives left with each other, leaving the cars with their husbands. I wanted to stay and looked to Luisa for her thoughts. I could tell she was angry with Tommaso. She waved for me not to get up. "No, stay," she said, sounding as if she meant it. "Have fun."

The party moved outside, wine bottles and all. It was already eight o'clock.

I kicked around a rubber ball with some kids behind the kitchen. Then I picked it up and began dribbling.

"Come on, Michael Jordan," one said.

I tripped over my rubbery legs. Then eight of us, I and seven preteen kids, improvised our own hybrid of soccer and basketball, using clotheslines as hoops. I overshot, and the ball rolled into the back door of the kitchen, where the chef and his two female assistants were cleaning up.

"So you're the American?" he said. "I'm also a Rotella, but I'm from Tiriolo, the next village over from Gimigliano." We shook hands, and he offered me a glass of wine.

"Have you ever been to Toronto?" he asked.

"No, but it seems that all of Calabria lives there, or has at one time."

"I used to work at a restaurant there," he said. "I never learned English. Where did you learn Italian?"

I told him what little dialect I knew I had learned from my father and grandparents, but that I had studied Italian in college.

"Marco, Marco!" the kids called behind me.

I thanked him for the meal and told him it was one of the best I had ever eaten. He shrugged it off. "Next time you come back to Calabria, stop by for dinner."

When I got outside, almost everyone had cleared out. Only my cousin Tommaso, Tommaso Rotella, and a couple of their friends remained.

Tommaso wobbled over to his car. No one including me seemed to care, or notice, that he was very drunk. "Marco, it's time to go."

I sat in the front seat and Tommaso Rotella crawled into the back. "You're all right," Tommaso said, slapping me on my shoulder. I didn't know what had made him think I wasn't in the first place, but it was another sign that I had gone beyond simply being the American relative. His mood became sentimental.

"You like Bob Marley?"

"I do."

He smiled a drunken smile and pushed in the tape. We set out for Gimigliano, the three of us singing along to "No Woman, No Cry." When the tape ended, Tommaso steadied the wheel with one hand while he popped in another tape. "Vasco Rossi," he said. The song "Stai con me in città" came on, and the two Tommasos commenced singing along with the Bruce Springsteen of Italy.

When we parked at the piazza at Inferiore, Tommaso shook my

hand, placed his other on my shoulder, and looked at me squarely, without a smile. *"Buona sera, mio amico,"* he said, then turned and stumbled down the alley to his home.

I looked at Tommaso Rotella and shrugged.

"The wine, the food, music, the sun setting. He gets a little sad," he said.

LA MADONNA DI PORTO

FOR SIXTY YEARS my grandmother sent money every month to the Madonna di Porto. For sixty years she prayed to the Virgin, whose image she had posted in every room except the bathroom. And the one time she returned to Gimigliano, she took off her shoes and walked barefoot the three miles from the village to the Chiesa della Madonna di Porto.

In June, fifty days after Easter, at Pentecost, the population of Gimigliano and the surrounding municipality swells from about thirty-five hundred to more than twenty thousand. Pilgrims come from all over Calabria; they return from their adopted homes in northern Italy, elsewhere in Europe, Canada, and the United States. They come from South America; they come from Australia. They come on their naked feet, they come with prayers, and they come to cry.

The Madonna di Porto arose from a cult of Mary worshipers, specifically of the Madonna di Costantinopoli, a phenomenon of southern Italy that began sometime around A.D. 430. In 1528 the Gimiglianese made their own appeal to the Virgin to spare them from the plague.

Almost a hundred years later earthquakes devastated the area, killing thousands of Calabresi. The Gimiglianesi pleaded once again to the Virgin but realized that their petition needed its own painting, its own icon. In 1626 the region's archpriest commissioned a painter from the neighboring village of Gagliano, called Marcangione, to paint the Virgin.

Marcangione must have suffered some kind of creative block because for days he couldn't begin. One morning he awoke to the sun filling his studio. When his eyes had adjusted to the light, he looked over at what he expected to be a blank canvas, the beginning of another fruitless day. But there, illuminated by the sun's rays, was a portrait of the Madonna in vivid blues and reds, with the baby Jesus at her breast.

The miracle didn't stop there. Just over another hundred years later, in 1753, a petty thief, Pietro Gatto, fled Gimigliano late one afternoon after having committed a crime. The sun had begun to set. In the failing light he lost the trails. He must have wandered from mountain to mountain into deep forests. The air became colder. He skirted the rocky edge of a mountain, then, seeking a vantage point, decided to climb it. On the way up, his foot slipped into a hole that he soon realized was large enough to enter. It was slightly warmer there, so for shelter he climbed inside. He could stay there until the morning. That night the Virgin appeared to him in a dream.

Pietro awoke knowing just which way to go. When he got out of the wilderness, he visited the local priest to confess his sins and to tell him his dream. He explained that the Virgin had instructed him to build a tiny chapel in her honor at a bend in the Corace River known as the Porto, or port, for its stretch of flat riverbanks. Here the miraculous portrait of the Madonna would be held when it wasn't at the church in Gimigliano Superiore.

The chapel was built, and every year at Pentecost the painting is carried on the shoulders of a dozen men from the church in Gimigliano Superiore along the winding three miles to the Chiesa della Madonna di Porto along the Corace River, the entire stretch packed with pilgrims. Never mind that the painting was never sanctioned by the Vatican as a true miracle. For the villagers in Calabria, the Vatican is too far away to pay it any attention. And after all, in 1984 Pope John Paul II did bless the painting.

The Porto holds a small festival the first Tuesday after Easter Sunday. Ciccio Paonessa, Maria the café proprietor's husband, drove me to there in his red Fiat Panda, which he told me he drove only when he went hunting in the mountains. As always, he was well dressed in a light tan cashmere sport coat and pressed gray pants. A handkerchief poked out of his pocket, and his brown shoes shone. He was a manager at the Banco di Napoli in Catanzaro, and it seemed that he held a local political position as well.

"I'd like to show you something," he said, "a wonderful place to go to clear your head."

The barely paved road hugged the mountain, and chestnut and pine trees grew right along its edge. A dirty sheep darted out from the trees, followed by another and another. Then a shepherd with his crook walked in front of the car without even glancing at us. On the other side of the road, on a raised mound, two rams faced each other. The shepherd paused to look at them. Then they lowered their heads and struck with an impact that seemed to shudder through their bodies from cranium to bottom. They dug in and attacked again, and again.

An identical Fiat pulled up behind us.

"*Aah, il sindaco,*" Ciccio said. The mayor.

He motioned for me to get out of the car, and we walked back to the other red Panda. Ciccio introduced me as a Rotella from the United States. The mayor nodded without smiling and extended his hand with a perfunctory *benvenuto*. He was handsome and stylish, reminding me of an Italian Bryan Ferry. His wife nodded to me from the passenger seat as his young son played with Pokémon figures in the back seat. By then the sheep had crossed the street, and Ciccio said goodbye as we headed back to the car.

When we got above the tree line, Ciccio pulled off the road onto a dirt-packed plateau. We got out and walked to a promontory. The sun had just begun to burn off the clouds.

"Hmm," he said somewhat disappointedly, and continued looking around. He guided me by the shoulders to my left toward a series of valleys and lower mountains. He pointed to where the mountains stopped.

"That's the Ionian Sea," he said. The haze slightly obscured the ocean. Then he turned me 180 degrees and had me look out. Here I could see an expanse of blue. "That's the Tyrrhenian Sea."

From this point, with a turn of my head, I could see both oceans: one in front of me, one behind. Here at the narrowest point of the entire boot, the center of Calabria, the land is only about twenty-five miles across. To get from Gimigliano to Naples by train, you have to backtrack to Catanzaro on the Ionian Sea, cut through the mountains and valleys to Lamezia on the Tyrrhenian Sea, then head north to Naples. I imagined the trek my grandparents must have made to get to their ship at Naples. They left their village in a carriage or by mule to Catanzaro, where they took a series of trains to Naples, then a ship to New York. The trip to Naples alone was such a long journey that by the time they boarded the ship, they must have known they were leaving their village forever.

Vendors at the Porto had set up rows of booths in front of the church, offering underwear, shirts, salami, cheeses, and music cassettes. African vendors set out elephants and lions sculpted from wood on colorful blankets. Ciccio stopped a dozen times to shake hands with people he knew from Gimigliano. One of the salami vendors offered us hot espresso.

Behind the church, Ciccio introduced me to the monsignor, a tall, thin gray-haired man who wore dark-framed glasses. When Ciccio explained who I was, the monsignor took me into the chapel, which was filling with pilgrims, and from a table handed me a pamphlet about the miracle. A stream of water flowed up from some underground source into the chapel, surrounding a small altar. Pilgrims bent down, filled vials with the holy water, and kissed them as they popped the lids on.

"If you write anything," the monsignor said, "the Madonna di Porto will be the most important part of your book."

On the way out Ciccio stopped to talk to a friend, and I stopped at a stand selling cassettes. Along with pop music from the sixties and seventies, there was Italian folk music recorded in the forties and fifties.

I reached for a tape of tarantellas. If any one music defines Calabria, it's the tarantella, literally a dance to rid oneself of a spider's venom. The high-pitched drone of the *zampogne*, or bagpipes, wails in the foreground as drums thump out a rhythm, the music gradually picking up momentum as the dancer goes into a euphoric state.

Calabrese folk songs dominated the rest of the shelves, half of the tapes featuring versions of "Calabresella Mia," the popular folk song Tommaso had drunkenly sung the night before. A section was devoted to the songs of Otello Profazio, Calabria's famous high-voiced bard who sings Calabria's story as he strums mournful chords on his guitar. There was also a section labeled "Musica della mafia," generic pink, blue, and yellow cassette cases with labels that must have come out of a typewriter or someone's home computer.

I asked the vendor, a middle-aged man with smoke-stained fingers and large glasses, what kind of music this was. "Oh, just another style of folk music," he said, shrugging. "Sung about mafiosi."

This music was performed by musicians hired to play for mafiosi bosses throughout Calabria. Songs of revenge and pledges of faith to the *'ndrangheta*, they are sung in the style of *stornelli*, or narrative tales—a style very similar to that of Otello Profazio. Many of these songs were also sung by Calabrese *contadini* working their fields. The line between folk music and mafia songs was often blurred. The only difference now is that the *musica della mafia*—or at least public performances of the music—is officially banned in Italy.

We ended the trip with a coffee back at Maria's bar, where Maria's sister was serving. Outside, a man passed by with his mule laden with firewood.

"Aah, the last mule in Gimigliano," Ciccio said.

One of the regulars, a short old man with no teeth and a nose that looked as if it had been partially sheared off in some sort of accident, came up to me and muttered something in dialect that I understood: "Are you married?"

"Yes," I said.

He said something in return—this time I caught only "donkey" and "wife"—then let loose a hearty laugh. I looked to Maria for help. She was flushed red, as was her sister.

"I can't understand him," she said, averting her eyes. "He's crazy and a bit drunk."

The old man ignored Maria and repeated what he'd said, this time with gestures. I turned to Maria, who nervously served my coffee. When he repeated himself a third time, she scolded him. By then I finally understood what he was saying: "I'll give you a day with my mule if you give me a night with your wife."

I called Giuseppe just as he was closing the shop. I was worried about Elena and concerned because I hadn't heard from him. I had missed seeing him and his family over the Easter holidays.

"Marco, *come va?*" Giuseppe asked.

"Not bad," I said. "How is Elena?"

"She's doing much better now. We actually had to bring her to the hospital. But she was fine by Easter." He paused, then added, "We didn't hear from you."

"I thought I'd let you have some time with your family."

"Aah," Giuseppe said, and with that mere sound let me know that I could have, should have, called. "So, Marco, are you ready for a short trip?"

"Yes," I said, barely able to conceal my excitement.

"I'll meet you in the piazza in twenty minutes," Giuseppe said. "Let's go to Maida, the village of your writer, Talese."

LA STRADA DEI DUE MARI: MAIDA AND TIRIOLO

I T WAS *Unto the Sons*, written by Gay Talese, that offered me my first glimpse of Calabria and of Italian-Americans of Calabrese descent. It gave me the tools to begin to understand my grandparents and the choices they made, as well as the Italian-American culture in which my father had grown up. It is not an exaggeration to say that the book spurred my exploration of my Italian self.

Forty-five minutes from Gimigliano—fifteen as the crow flies—is the town of Maida, Talese's ancestral village. Maida was the last holdout of the French during their brief rule of the Two Sicilies. In 1806 the Spanish Bourbons had asked the British to assist them in reclaiming their land from the French. The British, heavily outnumbered by the French, landed and defeated the French at the Battle of Maida. That battle proved that Napoleon's army could be defeated, and it is after this battle that the London district Maida Vale was named.

I was envious that Talese could trace his ancestors' participation in any battle. He had spent months researching his book in Maida, and as a first-generation immigrant he had access to first cousins still living in Italy who could tell him stories of their family's past. By the time I arrived in Gimigliano, as a second-generation Italian-American, most of the people who remembered my grandparents, and especially their parents, had long since died. I could continue to dream that these immigrants, who were looked down upon by many Americans, had performed important deeds, lived celebrated lives back in Italy, but I could never prove it.

The valley of Lamezia opened up as Giuseppe and I headed into the descending sun. There, along the gentle slopes of olive trees, the sand-colored city of Maida quietly rested, its once-mighty Norman castle now a worn cap on top of sagging shoulders. Newer buildings filled the valley, through which a bumpy old mule path road led us uphill, through a narrow opening in the castle wall. Dwellings had been carved into the thick sandstone walls.

We drove to a brightly lit *tabaccheria*, a kind of cigarette and candy store, that opened onto an empty large piazza. I asked the owner, whom Giuseppe had known for years, about the city's Italian-American biographer. "Ah, Signore Talese. Yes, that was about twenty years ago, I was just a kid then. But I remember Signore Talese writing here. He lived . . . you know, I can't quite remember where he lived. But he was respected here."

The talk returned to business, and he and Giuseppe caught each other up on the events of their lives. Then the owner's wife came down from their upstairs apartment to say that dinner was almost ready.

"Aah, Giuseppe. I had no idea you were here," she said politely. The owner sighed and said that he should close.

"Well, Marco, we should probably head out ourselves," Giuseppe said. "Time for dinner."

The sun had long since set, and lights from villages across the valley sparkled like those of ships at sea.

"Marco," Giuseppe began, "you went to college, right?"

"Yes," I said.

"What did you study?"

"I studied Russian literature."

Giuseppe turned to me, startled.

"But why?"

I explained to him that it was the first literature that I loved, when I was in high school. After that I had studied acting and dance, and ballet dancing had made me want to study Russian.

"Just like my son Luigi," Giuseppe said. "I mean, he's involved in theater and dance. I'm paying all this money for him to study something that he will never make a living at."

I told Giuseppe I was sure my father had felt as he did and reassured him that it is possible to make a living in dance, albeit a small one. I was sure everything would work out.

Giuseppe glanced at me. It didn't seem that I had convinced him.

The road back to Gimigliano took us through Tiriolo, Gimigliano's wealthier sister city. It lies on the other side of the Strada dei Due Mari, the Road of the Two Seas, which connects the Ionian Sea with the Tyrrhenian. With about three thousand people, Tiriolo is slightly smaller than Gimigliano but has many times the amenities. The village's *passeggiata* runs along a breathtaking promontory overlooking the distant city of Catanzaro and the Ionian Sea. Unlike Gimigliano, the streets are lined with cafés, jewelry stores, restaurants, and cell phone outlets. The sidewalks are cleaner, and the stores have lighted windows and marquees.

In both Gimigliano and Tiriolo, silk weavers make a living, but Tiriolo has successfully marketed itself as the place to go for silk shawls and table linens. Both villages are known for their octogenarian women in traditional dress, but the difference in costume is indicative of everything else: while the Gimiglianese costume is beautiful in its austerity (a black dress with black embroidery on the bodice, worn over a white blouse), the Tiriolese costume has bright red and green colors woven in.

But what truly casts Gimigliano in shadow is Tiriolo's stature as a city of antiquity. Many classicist scholars placed Odysseus's marriage to Nausicaa there. After his ship is destroyed at sea, Odysseus is washed ashore at what is now the Gulf of Sant'Eufemia, where the Lamezia airport now stands. He awakes to find three "fair-braided" girls washing clothes. One light-complexioned maiden, Nausicaa, catches his attention. "I am at your knees, mistress," Odysseus says. "Are you some god or a mortal?"

Sometime in the early 1990s the people of Tiriolo cleverly decided to erect in the village square a statue depicting the meeting of the two lovers. From this point, the highest in Tiriolo, you can see the beaches of Lamezia, where the mythical sailor washed ashore. From the square, the street curves away from the buildings to a promenade lined with benches overlooking the valley. Giuseppe slowed the car and pointed to Catanzaro in the distance, and the Ionian Sea just beyond, where Nausicaa's father set Odysseus back on his course home. Looking out that way, I was struck by the parallel between Nausicaa's father's allowing her husband to leave for a better place and Calabria's allowing her sons to leave for work, for food she couldn't provide.

That night Elena showed me how to make the simple dish of sautéed chicory, the green we had pulled from the ground during my first days in Gimigliano. She had gathered it in the woods above Gimigliano.

"I like picking chicory," she said. "I like the walk, and it's so peaceful."

After she had cleaned and scrubbed the chicory, she boiled it in salted water until it was tender, then sautéed it with garlic and oil and mixed in some grated pecorino and bread crumbs to make a delicious *contorno* that brought together crunch, tenderness, and bitter richness.

It brought to mind the fairy tale of the three sisters and the dragon. I wondered if those three sisters ever missed gathering the chicory, which seemed to me to be an integral part of enjoying the dish. I wondered if they missed the comforting, smoky taste.

THE POTTERS OF SQUILLACE

Y OU CAN TELL which city is controlled by the mafia," Giuseppe said. We were driving past Bianco, a small, decrepit city on the way up the coast to Locri. "Everything is falling apart; everything is abandoned."

We were returning from far south on the Ionian coast, almost to the point where the coast rounds back up to Reggio, facing Sicily to the west, then joins the Tyrrhenian Sea. The cities here are known for sequestering, or kidnappings, and while we were only two or three hours from Gimigliano, it felt like a different world.

"The mafia moves in, they open a restaurant or a store that competes with others in the city," Giuseppe explained. "They lower their prices so far down that the other companies lose money, then go out of business. All that is left is the one restaurant that doesn't provide good service. Any money they make is siphoned off by the mafia, and only people in the mafia work there."

We passed through the town of Bovalino, which looked abandoned and run-down. But even on our brief traverse I counted eight Land Rovers and Ford Explorers.

Giuseppe pointed to the west. "It's a different world in those mountains. A different people." He paused. "At one time the name alone made Italy wince. Aspromonte."

Dark and rocky, the distant mountains even looked eerie. Sharply rising granite cliffs dissuaded any thought of travel through them. The absence of greenery made them look like lunar terrain. This was where, beginning in the 1970s, the mafia began taking people it had kidnapped and holding them for ransom. First it preyed on wealthy local citizens, but soon it realized that more money could be made from wealthy northerners. Before long, the kidnappings took on the regularity and smoothness of any other business transaction.

Then the police got involved. Once it was known that someone's son or wife was kidnapped, the government would freeze the family's bank accounts to prevent money from going into the hands of the mafia. But leads on the culprits were weak, and no one spoke out. The code of silence, *omertà*, would not be cracked in Calabria.

When weeks and months passed without a break in the case, family members, desperate to free their loved ones, would borrow from friends, colleagues, distant cousins. Villages would quietly take up donations until the family could pay to have its son or daughter returned. And the police would still be looking under the rocks of the Aspromonte.

When police intervention prolonged the process, the mafia resorted to more drastic tactics. In July 1973, American billionaire J. Paul Getty, who was living in Rome at the time, received a letter with a ransom demand of seventeen million dollars for the return of his seventeen-year-old son, Eugene Paul II. At first the older Getty refused to pay as a matter of principle. Five months later the Rome newspaper *Il Messaggero* received a box with a lock of hair and a severed human ear as well as a note saying that unless the ransom was paid, Getty's son would be returned piece by piece. Getty paid what was thought to be about two million dollars, and his son was returned. The last reported kidnapping had occurred a few years before my trip. That time the police had found the victim after he had been held for a year and fed only every other day.

"You're wondering how they got away with this?" Giuseppe asked, seeing my mouth hanging open. The mafia preys on the poor, he explained. "If you don't have money, you'll do anything. Only shepherds and farmers live in that region. The mafia hides the person with the help of locals. They offer a solid amount of money that no one can turn down."

He paused. "There are so many caves up there. There are no roads—only trails made by humans and mules. Nothing else. Anyway, they pay each shepherd or farmer to take a captive to a certain point, and then they pay someone else to pick up that person and lead him to another point. Then they pay another person. The last person is in charge of feeding the captive, and how much the captive eats depends on how generous, or humane, that person is."

We drove on in silence. "Also, it's a different culture there," Giuseppe said. "The people live in remote villages, only one road in. A few of them speak Greek . . .

"But that hasn't happened for a while," Giuseppe said.

We pulled into the village of Roccella Ionica. I slipped away while Giuseppe was meeting with one of his clients and went to sit in a small grassy park overlooking the Ionian Sea. A train track separated the park from the rest of the town, and in the center of the park two Roman columns rose against the backdrop of ugly 1980s apartment buildings.

I sat facing the ocean, with the sun burning my face and my notebook on my lap. I had noticed a teenage boy circling me, then leaning against the railings facing the beach. He walked over to me.

"What are you doing?" he said, sitting down next to me. Pimples spotted his face, and his teeth had bands for braces but no wires. His dirty hands were as dark and oily as his spiked hair.

"Just writing. Noting what I see."

"Where are you from?"

"Where do you think?"

"Torino?"

I shook my head.

"Milan?"

"No," I said. "New York."

He paused and looked me over. "My uncle lives in Brooklyn."

"Oh, what does he do?"

"He owns a restaurant," he said. Then he turned to look somewhere behind me.

"I used to live in Brooklyn," I said.

"His name is Mimmo Metici," he said, looking behind me again. Bells rang behind us as the gates lowered across the tracks, closing us off from the rest of the city. "Tell him his cousin Aldo . . . of Italy . . . said hello."

I wrote his name on a blank page of my notebook.

He looked behind himself as if he were searching for something.

I decided that it was time to start heading back, and when I stood up, he stood up with me.

"Can I have that?" he said, pointing to my notebook.

"Why do you want my notebook?"

"No, the page that you wrote on."

I eyed him. He looked nervous.

"Sure, here you go," I said, and tore out the paper from my notebook.

"Thanks," he said, crumpling the paper and putting it into his jacket. "Just tell him Aldo said hello." He ran off past the park and behind a building on a side road. I got to the gate in time to see him hop on the back of a moped behind another boy who had the same hairstyle. They sped by me and over the tracks. In a land where suspicion bubbles, this greasy kid was just as curious about me as I was about him. But here, it seemed, curiosity could get you in trouble.

Giuseppe and I were traveling along the Ionian Sea of Calabria by the same route Aeneas took on his journey from Greece. From the sea he saw the columns of Caulonia and the city of Scylaceum, or Squillace. But he steered clear of this city, knowing that harsh winds and rain wrecked ships when they sailed too close.

Soon then we saw Tarentum's gulf, or Hercules'
If the old tale be true. There, dead ahead,

Rose the Lacinian goddess on her height.
Then Caulon's towers and Scylaceum,
The coast of shipwreck.

The Greeks who settled the city called it Skylletion. Aeneas desperately wanted to leave the Calabrian coast, which he cursed:

The shoreline to the west, a part of Italy
Lapped by the tide of our own sea: the towns
Are all inhabited by evil Greeks.
Here the Locrians found a colony
And Lyctian Idomeneus with soldiers
Took the Sallentine Plain . . .

From the vantage point of a Norman castle above the city of Squillace, I looked out toward the sea. The sky was clear, and the ocean remarkably blue with gentle waves. Just up from the shore stood the Guglielmo coffee company, which supplied its full dark ground coffee throughout Calabria. When it roasted the beans, imported from Africa or South America, the winds carried the scent all the way up here. Farther above us were the remains of a Norman castle, which had been leveled in the earthquake of 1783. The outside walls were all that was left standing.

Squillace is perhaps best known as the birthplace of Cassiodorus (480–575), a poet and secretary to the Byzantine emperor Theodoric the Ostrogoth. An aristocrat, Cassiodorus rose through the ranks to become an important statesman before retiring to Squillace, where he built a monastery whose monks devoted themselves to copying and preserving important books and papers of philosophy, theology, and science.

Giuseppe and I ate at a local trattoria. It served penne with tomato sauce, along with fava beans cooked in a pot and garnished with pecorino and bread crumbs. The beans gave a slight crunch when you bit in, then a fusion of the warm soft middle and the cheese. We ate *fraguni*, too, a kind of calzone filled with ricotta cheese, egg, and parsley.

After lunch Giuseppe and I walked down the narrow streets, which were clean and empty of cars and people. We passed a small bar in what had once been called the Quartiere de Giudei, or Jewish Quarter, which centuries before had housed a small but thriving population of Byzantine Jews who lived on the Ionian Sea. We walked past a shop that made and sold pottery. Giuseppe checked the door, but it was locked. We passed another pottery shop, also closed, and then reached another. The door was cracked open. We walked in to find a large room stocked with various pots, bowls, and platters. Along the wall hung tiles and ceramic fish.

"Hello. Can I help you?" a voice asked from behind a door. A young man came out. He had longish hair and was tall and thin.

Giuseppe introduced himself and then me. The man offered to take us up to his workroom and show us how he threw clay.

The potter used machines that had to be pedaled with the feet, and clay only from that region. Like the artisans in Umbria, these potters painted their pottery with only those colors that were traditionally used. In the same way that the pottery of Deruta (the town in Umbria famous for its pottery) is yellow and green, with bold red, which reflects its terrain (yellow sunflowers, reddish earth), the pottery in Squillace reflects the color of its surroundings. The potters incorporate the bright blue of the sea, the green and yellow of the fish. The base color was a light red, almost pink. The colors are not as bold as those in Umbria, and the lines not as sharp, tending to fade into one another. A pink might blend gradually with a faint green outline.

As had the women weavers in Gimigliano, these potters had formed a pottery guild. Where there wasn't industry, the Calabresi put to use the work they knew. While the artisans might have been able to earn a better living in the north, they chose to stay here in Calabria to make a living doing what they loved.

Giuseppe was thrilled to come across this potter. He knew that he could sell the potter's handiwork at his store in Gimigliano. The man was excited at the prospect as well and gave Giuseppe samples of his work. Giuseppe said he would call to work out a price. When

I next visited Giuseppe in Gimigliano two months later, he already had two shelves stocked with the potter's work.

Calabria held for me the prospect of handmade goods, of a simple lifestyle, but along with this rustic living came an antiquated criminal organization that prospered in the rugged mountains—mountains that are inhabited by people who hold the same beliefs and fears as they had in the nineteenth century. Here I was in Italy, one of the most popular tourist destinations in the world, yet I was wandering in a region so remote, so forbidding, that at times I could hardly believe it was the same country.

CATANZARO

I T MUST HAVE BEEN DIFFICULT for immigrants to leave Gimigliano. To go northwest to Naples, my grandparents first would have had to backtrack by train southeast to Catanzaro. With a population of more than one hundred thousand, Catanzaro is the second-largest city in Calabria, and it serves as the political seat of the region, with the bureaucratic feel of a state capital like Albany, New York.

It is still a regional hub today—not only can you still catch the train west to Lamezia, where you can continue north to Naples or Rome, but you can take trains or buses north to Apulia and south to Reggio—and for that reason Catanzaro was often my point of entry into Calabria. And so it happened that I gradually warmed to a city not generally considered the most attractive in Calabria. Invariably, whether arriving from Naples or Lamezia, I would miss the last train to Gimigliano and would have to stay in Catanzaro for the night. At other times, during my stay in Gimigliano, I would take the train to Catanzaro to exchange money, to travel elsewhere in Calabria, or just to spend time in a bigger city.

Catanzaro was built between the ninth and tenth centuries on a ridge of rock that lies at the southernmost part of the Sila massif. While its location has brought occasional devastation by earthquakes and landslides, it has also protected the city from intruders throughout the centuries.

Catanzaro was once a beautiful, thriving Byzantine city, but centuries of earthquakes have erased its glorious architectural past. The city has collapsed on itself; where buildings were destroyed, new ones had been built in the same place on the same streets. The buildings have changed, but the city's labyrinthine, winding streets remain, and access is almost as difficult now as it was in earlier times.

The main road, Corso Mazzini, is a serpentine two lanes that slither along the thin mountain ridge. It is often congested, and most guidebooks, if they mention Catanzaro at all, advise leaving one's car on the outskirts. Since the main way to get to Catanzaro is along a series of suspended bridges, this means that during the daytime these bridges become suspended open-air parking garages.

The Ponte Morante joins the ridge of Catanzaro to a lower ridge to the south. Built in 1967, the bridge is the pride of Calabria, and especially of Catanzaro, whose citizens will tell you that it was the first single-arch bridge to be built in Italy, the second in Europe. To the north, a web of suspended bridges allows direct access from Catanzaro Lido, the touristy beaches two miles to the east. A concrete runway winds up the cliff like a Matchbox car track. At the top, at the center of a figure eight, is a lone stoplight.

George Gissing visited Catanzaro in 1897 and found it a refuge. He was treated nicely, ate well, and was able to rest his sick body. A certain Signore Paparazzo sometimes joined Gissing for dinner at his hotel. Signore Paparazzo soon revealed himself to be the owner of the hotel and proprietor of the restaurant. He told Gissing that he could procure anything his guest wished, provided, of course, Gissing not dine in any other establishment. "It would give me a bad reputation," Paparazzo explained to him. To Gissing, Paparazzo was the ultimate annoying opportunist.

It is Federico Fellini, however, who is credited for popularizing the hotelier's name. In *La Dolce Vita*, Fellini bestowed it upon one of his main characters, a wily, pushy photographer. Soon the name Paparazzo was attributed to tabloid photojournalists, first in Italy, then throughout the world.

The hotel where Gissing stayed no longer exists, and no one I asked remembered where it was. Instead, I always stayed at the Albergo Grand Hotel, which proved to be more convenient than grand (it was just off the elevated highway system and within walking distance of the train station). It never changed in the decade that I visited there. The same drab brown carpet extended to the drab tan walls, and the same heavy cream-colored curtains—always drawn—blocked the sun. It was a hotel for businessmen and lawyers—the courthouse is just across the street—making up in efficiency what it lacked in charm.

Because Giuseppe had met me at the airport this trip, I had not yet visited Catanzaro, so I decided to take the train in from Gimigliano, behavior Giuseppe and my family thought extravagant. Before checking in at the hotel, I decided to cash some traveler's checks. I selected a bank from half a dozen that dotted Corso Mazzini. I took a number (a civilized system, I thought), looked up at the number just called, and realized that I would have at least an hour to wait. I decided to check in at the hotel in the meantime.

The same dark-haired clerk who had always checked me in approached the counter. He never smiled and always looked at me as if he had never laid eyes on me before.

I greeted him with a friendly hello nevertheless and asked him how he was.

He looked up and answered, "Fine, thank you," then looked back at my passport. After a pause he asked, "And will your wife be staying? Or have you brought your father this time?" He flashed me an uncharacteristic grin, letting me know that beneath the formality he knew exactly who I was; I was a Calabrese son.

When I returned to the bank, I was still ten numbers away from the window. When my number was finally called, the clerk handed me a ream of paperwork to fill out. She looked at me as if I were going to rob her, or my traveler's checks were counterfeit, or my exchange would break the bank. She told me to take my paperwork to the supervisor. After another ten minutes the supervisor called me to his cubicle, checked my passport, asked what I needed the money for, then told me to go back to the same teller.

The woman looked at me as if she had never seen me before, so I had to explain the transaction all over again. She took my paperwork and traveler's checks with a sneer and brought them to two more supervisors to sign. Finally, the lire were presented to me as if they were gold bullion. It had taken me nearly two hours to exchange my money, thanks to a banking system that had jumped directly from postwar hard currency to ATMs, bypassing the traveler's check phase of tourism altogether.

It was now lunchtime. On the way to Da Salvatore, my favorite trattoria, I stopped off at a bookstore for some mealtime reading. The shelves were stocked with translations of books by American writers such as Stephen King, Tom Clancy, and David Baldacci Ford (David Baldacci had been asked by his Italian publisher to adopt an American surname because Italians don't believe that Italians write good thrillers). I asked a young clerk working there what Italians liked to read, and he shrugged with a smile and said, "Not much." But the shop had the Touring Club Italiano guidebook to Calabria that I had been looking for since I had first arrived, so I paid for it and headed on.

Da Salvatore was packed, but as it was my home away from home—even if it had been a couple of years since my last visit—the maître d', Massimo, managed to find me a table.

"*Ciao, signore . . . come si chiama? . . . Rotella? Sì . . . Rotella.*" Massimo still remembered my name. "How are you?"

"Fine, thanks," I said, and shook his hand. He was my height, with a full head of dark hair and a smooth, tanned complexion.

"Dining alone?" he asked. I nodded, and he directed me to a table in the middle room, against the window and a direct shot across to the kitchen. When he brought me a carafe of red wine and a bottle of sparkling water, I ordered an antipasto of spicy Calabrese meats, soft cheeses, and pickled eggplant. I followed that with a tagliatelle bolognese, then, reading all the while, moved on to a parmigiana di zucchini, which was a layered casserole of zucchini and eggplant with eggs, mozzarella, salami, and tomatoes.

I finished with a cup of coffee, paid eleven dollars for the excellent meal, then returned to the hotel for my siesta.

When I awoke, I joined the city in its awakening *passeggiata*. The streets filled with the sound of whining *motorini*, mopeds, and mufflerless cars. The sidewalks were packed with people. I stopped into a store that specialized in Calabrese candy. I noticed a picture of a person in a red-and-gold eagle costume.

"That's the mascot for the Catanzaro team," the store clerk said.

"Great, I'm going to the game this weekend," I answered.

"Really?"

"Yes, with my cousin."

"They were great in the 1980s, you know—Serie A. Now . . ." His voice tailed off. "Well, now they're not so good, of course."

We both looked down in mutual disappointment, as if a moment of silence had been requested.

"Which seats do you have?" he asked, hopefully.

"I don't know, I think they're the cheaper seats outside."

"Good, you'll be sitting with the fans."

I stopped off at an establishment called the Mallard Pub. It was dark and cozy, with exposed wooden beams and an impressive selection of beers on tap. It looked as if it had been transported directly from Ireland. I later found out that it had. An Irish company set up Irish pubs throughout Europe, and although Italians aren't pub drinkers, Italy does get its share of British and German tourists whose stomachs never quite get used to the copious amounts of wine the Italians drink and who prefer a pint of homestyle brew. Here in Catanzaro, though, I couldn't imagine too many Britons dropping in for a drink.

Close to eight in the evening, I decided it was time to eat. A pizzeria called the Giallorossa, named after the colors of the Catanzaro soccer team, occupied two stories of a building with exposed rafters inside, which gave it the feel of a country farmhouse. The ovens were on the first floor. On the second, families ate in one room, while the other two were packed with men, young and old. The blare of television echoed off marble wood and stucco. I realized that I had happened upon the Italian equivalent of a sports bar, which in Italy had taken the form of a pizzeria, for food must be served at any social event.

A strong breeze to my back rushed me along Corso Mazzini to my hotel. The palm trees that lined the street swayed in the wind, the fronds sawing together above me. Drops of rain began to fall. At ten-thirty, Catanzaro was tucked in early for the night, just like a country village.

I T WAS AN EARLY FRIDAY MORNING, and I struggled to keep pace with Masino as we trotted through Gimigliano getting signatures from villagers for the upcoming presidential elections. Everyone knew Masino, and Masino talked to everyone he knew. He talked as quickly as he walked, sputtering out the beginnings of sentences and then breaking off to turn to me smiling and say, "Marco, Marco, Marco."

Masino, my cousin Sabrina's husband, worked for the commune of Gimigliano in the official records department, which consisted solely of his boss and him.

Voting turnout is high in Italy, although just as in the States, no one believes his or her vote really matters. Still, Masino needed signatures verifying that each house's occupants were alive and therefore eligible to vote. He would knock on a door trying to locate a given person, but that person never seemed to answer. Instead, a next-door neighbor—always a woman—would poke her head out of the window and say something like "She's shopping" or "She's at her mother-in-law's" or "I think she and her husband are still in Torino." It seemed as if no one we wanted was answering the door, but the neighbors always did. On the rare occasion that we did get the intended registered voter, the person would whine, "Masino, do I really have to sign? This is silly."

"Yes. It's the law," Masino would respond with official neutrality. "And the sooner you sign, the more quickly you can go back to cooking and I can go home."

We stopped off for an espresso *corretto*. No sooner had the old man served the coffee than we were back out the door making our way down Masino's list.

"I think it's great that you want to be an Italian citizen," Masino said. Earlier we had spoken with his boss about my ongoing attempts to get Italian citizenship. "Yes, fantastic. This way"—he patted my back—"you will then be Italian."

I knew that for me to be considered an Italian citizen, my father would have to be considered an Italian citizen. Even though my father had been born in the States, I only had to prove that he had been born before one of his parents had given up his or her Italian citizenship to become American. Easy. I knew that my grandfather had served in World War I on the side of the Americans—and paid for the privilege of citizenship with bullets in his stomach and leg on French soil—but my grandmother, who had lived in Danbury, Connecticut, for more than sixty years, had never learned English and had never given up her Italian citizenship.

On my first visit to Calabria, my cousin Luisa had dug up my grandparents' birth and marriage certificates. I assembled them, along with the birth certificates of my father and me, into a beautifully organized portfolio with Italian and English translations and took it to the Italian Embassy in New York. My counselor there, a young woman, seemed to be impressed with my presentation. As she turned the pages, she hummed a positive "Mmhhm, mmhhm, good, good . . . oh, wait."

"Wait, what, wait?" I stuttered.

"You are tracing your lineage through your grandmother," she said.

"Yes, my grandmother, that's it. She never gave up her Italian citizenship; she was loyal to her mother country."

"I'm sorry, but you can't trace your lineage through a woman who was born before 1936," she said, closing my folder.

"But why not?"

"Women were not Italian citizens before then."

My grandmother, who had held Calabria closer to her heart than almost anything in the world, was not even considered a citizen by a country whose men petitioned their prayers through the mother of all mothers? The consulate officer must have seen the disappointment in my face. "What about your grandfather?"

"No, he became a U.S. citizen."

"Hmm, but when?"

"Right after World War One."

"Let me tell you something. You know, records were not so good then, and if your grandfather was a typical southern Italian, he was probably skeptical about any government and was loath to leave a paper trail. He probably got his citizenship in a name different from his birth name."

I didn't quite follow.

She explained further. "All you need from the Justice Department is a letter saying that they have no record of this man—under this name—as being a citizen of the U.S. And there you have it."

It was kind of like stealing figs: if you didn't have any on hand, you found another way to get them. You could also look at it this way: the Italian government had stolen my grandmother's citizenship from her; I would look for what I needed on the branches of another tree.

On the way to Sabrina's and his house, Masino and I stopped off at the village's bocce court. Bocce, developed in ancient Rome, is a cross between horseshoes and shuffleboard and is played throughout Italy. The bocce court in Gimigliano stands above the main road that connects Inferiore with Superiore, a single court surrounded by a chain-link fence. You enter through a wood hut that serves as a clubhouse, where an older man and young boy were just preparing to play. Each had his own bocce set in a hard case, the balls shiny silver and carved with circles and spirals in various patterns.

"Marco, this is another Rotella, Filippo," Masino said.

"That's my grandfather's name," I said as I introduced myself to the older man.

He examined me and said nothing. He offered his huge hand.

"Maybe you two are relatives," Masino said.

"Do you play bocce?" Filippo asked.

"I've never played," I answered.

He looked at me skeptically, then placed a ball in my hand. It was heavier than it appeared.

"We'll form teams," Masino said. "You and Filippo, me and the kid."

"But I've never played," I protested.

Masino walked over to the club hut and dug into a cooler. He pulled out three bottles of Czech beer and gave one to each of the adults.

Masino tossed the small rubber ball, the *pallino*, that serves as a marker. The goal of the game is to get your bocce ball closest to the *pallino*. I was the first to bowl. I had watched the game a couple of times and thought the trick was to toss it with my palm down, giving it a spin backward so it wouldn't roll too far. The ball hit where I had intended, but with too much force, and it rolled out of bounds.

"Ahhh," Filippo cried. "What was that?"

I tried again. This time the ball fell shorter and rolled to a point that I would have considered quite close to the *pallino*.

"No, no, no," Filippo said.

Masino took a turn, each bowl getting close to the *pallino*. Then Filippo went. He bowled and struck out Masino's ball, allowing his to land a few inches closer. The boy bowled, and his ball landed just a scratch closer yet.

"Aim here," Filippo said, pointing with his foot. I tried again.

The boy looked on quietly, but Masino hooted me on. "Come on, Rotella, come on."

I had noticed that the other three bowled underhanded, so I decided to try it that way. This time my ball came closer than Filippo's but not as close as the boy's. I thought it was my best bowl yet.

"No, no, no," Filippo raged. "You're changing your style! Overhanded, underhanded, overhanded—which one is it? Decide."

I knew that Italians were passionate about bocce—arguing and yelling were a major part of the game—but I couldn't believe that Filippo, knowing this was my first time playing, wouldn't take it easy on me. I went back to my original style of pitching, but my nerves were shattered. My bowl went wild, and this time even Masino responded with a pitiful "Boh."

"Drink another beer," Filippo said. "It might help your game." And that was the last thing he said to me for the rest of the game.

As we put the balls away, Masino came up to me and patted me on the back. "Okay, bocce's not your game," he said. "But tomorrow we'll go to see Catanzaro play football. You'll be able to watch."

I extended my hand to Filippo and thanked him for allowing me to play.

He put out a limp hand, shrugged, and said, "I don't think we're related."

That night at dinner I discovered that my cousin Sabrina was the gourmet cook of the family. She served a feast that consisted of shells filled with ground pork and tomatoes, a lasagne with pesto and béchamel (to which Masino added his mother's homemade *piccante*), a tart filled with ground pork and covered with bread crumbs, a *pizza rustica* stuffed with prosciutto and mozzarella, and *soppressata* in a heavy tomato sauce.

Several of their friends from the *Pasquetta* in the Sila had joined us, and everyone was conversing in dialect. At one point Tommaso—we both were well on our way to getting drunk—turned to me and said, "When you and Martha get pregnant, you should come to Italy so the baby will be born Calabrese."

It was then that I realized that citizenship was only a formality. I would never be Calabrese in their eyes. The Calabresi are born on Calabrese soil.

Early the next day Masino and I drove to Catanzaro for one of the soccer team's final games of the season. I couldn't believe that the graffiti-covered, unfinished concrete walls, not much taller than a house, were actually the stadium. Somehow I had expected a miniature version of the Meadowlands. The poor standing of the team obviously dictated that little money went to them. In Italy soccer is a business, and only the best teams attract the wealthy sponsors who can pay for good players and fancy stadiums.

We passed through low arches with the hundreds of other fans, bundled in heavy jackets against the wind and rain. The field, surprisingly well manicured, was a couple of stories below. The stadium had been dug into the side of a mountain; the other side, beyond the away team stands, was the edge of the cliff. Looking down into the arena, I felt as if I were attending a gladiatorial contest in a minor village's coliseum. One section of the stands was sheltered and had wooden seats. The rest of the seats were formed of concrete, and in the middle of the curved section of concrete mass two or three large pine trees had grown. The fans surrounded this display of Calabrese earthiness with a swirl of bright red and yellow flags and jerseys. This section is called the *curva*, where the dedicated and truly rowdy fans gather.

The visiting team, from Gela, a port village in Sicily, was greeted with boos. Catanzaro came on the field, and immediately the fans, or *tifosi*, began a rally of cheers, songs, and chants that continued throughout the game.

Catanzaro scored within the first few minutes. The war cries revved up a notch. A leader banged a large drum out in front of the fans, and they pulsed and hopped to every beat. The stadium shook.

At halftime, Catanzaro was leading, 2 to 1, and I decided to walk around. There were no T-shirt vendors, no long lines for beer and hot dogs—just a few carts that served hot espresso in shot-size plastic cups with lids. The stadium was filled almost entirely with men and boys. I counted seven teenage girls around us in the lowest-priced seats and five older women sitting with their husbands in the sheltered section.

Catanzaro scored a final goal in injury time. This win meant that Catanzaro would have a chance to advance from Serie C-2 to Serie C-1 for the first time in more than two decades. One of the players pulled off his shorts and threw them into the stands. The fans rushed the field.

"Marco, Marco, Marco!" Masino cried. "It looks like football is your game!"

Part IV

A JOURNEY SOUTH

COSENZA

A T ONE TIME the Busento and Crati rivers rushed through mountain valleys and converged as one. On this spot, Calabria's indigenous people, the Bruttians, founded Cosenza as their capital. As the Greeks began settling Magna Graecia, they took control of the city from the Bruttians. While building the Appian Way to the north, the Romans wandered down through Calabria, settling around and building up Cosenza. Surrounded by mountains and the two rivers, Cosenza was, and still is, a serenely bucolic peninsula.

After he sacked Rome, Alaric the Visigoth left the city in A.D. 410 for Sicily, where he thought he might retire for good. With a convoy of soldiers to carry his gold and booty, he skirted the Italian coast and cut through the Greek Sila. When he looked down upon magical Cosenza, he immediately fell in love with the place and decided to rest there. His pit stop lasted for months. Alaric probably settled into a place right on the river, where he could be lulled by its powerful currents. But the river was also a bed of malaria-carrying insects, and Alaric probably contracted the disease. Just before he died he ordered that all his possessions be buried at the confluence of the two rivers.

Calabria has a history of diverting the flow of rivers. The city of Sibari was lost for centuries when the people of Crotone diverted the flow of the Crati River. Alaric's treasures were forgotten for almost a thousand years, until the Middle Ages, when efforts were made to alter the flow of the rivers long enough to recover them. But no one has ever found—or ever admitted to having found— Alaric's gold and silver.

I took the local train from Gimigliano to Cosenza, a three-and-a-half-hour ride to cover the distance a car could make in an hour and a half. The two-car diesel train cut northwest through the Sila Piccola, passing dense stands of chestnut trees and stopping at villages with such names as Cicala and Castagna—cicada and chestnut. We chugged through farms and fields of sheep until we entered a pass.

On the other side, raindrops speckled the train window, and the landscape was shrouded in mist. We followed a river to the right, and gradually buildings began to appear against the hills beyond. Cosenza is known as the city of five hills.

The train stopped and the conductor announced, "Cosenza Centro." I got out and walked across the tracks, past the station and through a dirt parking lot. Across a small but busy street I saw a block-wide Victorian building with a sign that read ALBERGO CEN- TRALE. As I approached the entrance, I pictured a grand hallway with plush, albeit worn, couches on either side. Instead, after my eyes had adjusted to the relative darkness, I saw that there were no lightbulbs in the fixtures and that the hallway leading to the front desk was flanked by couches that looked as if they belonged in a college dorm.

"A room for three nights, please," I told the attendant. He was probably in his late twenties but had large eyes and a sad face with a downward-turned mouth that made him look ten years older.

He flipped back and forth between three or four pages of the register. "You can have a room tonight, but unfortunately all our rooms are booked for the next few days," he said apologetically.

"Booked?"

He frowned and apologized, *"Mi dispiace."* He looked through the book again and said, "Check with me tomorrow around noon; perhaps someone will have canceled."

He showed me up to my floor by way of a gated elevator. My room contained a single bed against an opened window that looked out on the courtyard. A small TV with a broken knob sat on a movable table in front of the bed. The bathroom was clean with the usual showerhead, curtain, and drain in the tile floor by the toilet. For thirty dollars a night, I could have done a lot worse.

I called Luigi, Giuseppe's oldest son, who was preparing for exams at the University of Cosenza, which was the newest university in Calabria and had a good reputation. Luigi was studying theater and was a member of a theater company that reminded me of the avant-garde Theater for the New City in New York. He said that he might be able to meet me the next afternoon before he went to work at the theater.

I had visited the university the week before, while returning from Spezzano Albanese with Giuseppe. Built in the 1970s on a mountain crest, the university had one of the oddest layouts I'd ever seen. It was long and thin, with buildings attached to buildings like the cars of a train. There wasn't a single square or other communal unifying place that I could see. It was as if the university were mimicking the shape of Calabria itself.

It was now early afternoon, and the sun had broken through the clouds and morning mist. I decided to explore the old town. The Busento River separated old Cosenza from new, although these days, thanks to Calabria's long drought, the mighty rivers that had buried Alaric the Goth and his treasures were reduced to a mere trickle, and about a hundred feet of dry land now lay on either bank. My hotel was on the new side of town, and when I walked across the bridge to the *centro storico*, the historic center, I was immediately transported back in time. Like many southern Italian cities, Cosenza owes its layout to the Greeks. The Romans rebuilt the city on its original lines, and the Normans and Angevins, alternating rule with the Arabs, built upon the Roman city. And, like many Calabrese cities, Cosenza grew and prospered throughout the Middle Ages.

In 1509, Cosenza gave birth to Bernardino Telesio, perhaps Calabria's most famous philosopher, who wrested scientific thought from the grips of the church and brought enlightenment from Calabria to the rest of Italy.

But the growth of Cosenza—and Calabria—was stalled when the Spanish Bourbons gained control of southern Italy, cutting it off from the Renaissance of the rest of Italy.

Because Cosenza stopped developing during the Spanish rule, the old city is like a time capsule, with its tight medieval alleys and terra-cotta roofs. In the 1970s the government gave money to anyone who would relocate there and renovate the old buildings. After only a couple of years' work, light finally broke through the boarded doors and bricked windows. Families reclaimed ancestral houses that couldn't be given away; newer families, tired of living in the newer cities, hungered for a Renaissance their forebears had never experienced. Artists moved in. A bookstore opened in a snug corridor, and new restaurants took hold. By the 1990s there were coffee shops that offered the students of Cosenza places to hang out.

I followed the steeply cobblestoned Corso Telesio, one of the only streets wide enough to fit a car. Most of the roads sprouting from it were alleys that began or ended with a series of cobblestone steps. The road led past the cathedral, a Gothic structure that had been destroyed in 1184 by an earthquake and rebuilt by Frederick II at the same time as he was adding onto the Norman castle that towered over the city. Inside, it was dark and spare, and my ears tingled in the hollow silence.

It had been hours since I ate the brioche Angela gave me before I caught the train, and I was hungry. I remembered that someone had recommended for lunch a restaurant called L'Arco Vecchio. It lay at the very top of Corso Telesio, just under the shadow of the castle. Under the arch of the old aqueduct was the restaurant.

The headwaiter was setting tables. A nice-looking heavyset

young man came out of the kitchen, wiping his mouth with a nap-kin.

"Are you open for lunch or just dinner?" I asked, seeing that no one else was in the restaurant at noon.

"We open at one," the man said with a large smile.

"I see," I said.

"Perhaps you'd like to look around our city," he said, looking at my guidebook.

"I just did."

"Have you seen the castle?" he asked.

"No, I haven't," I answered, somewhat curtly. Most Italian res-taurants start serving at noon, and I was somewhat annoyed that this man, having filled himself with what I was sure was a delicious meal, was telling me that I had to wait an hour. "I was hoping to do that after I ate."

"It's about a fifteen-minute walk. *È bella.*"

I nodded and said I'd see him in an hour.

The fifteen-minute walk was more like half an hour. Not a soul was around, although just across the street, almost on the castle grounds, was a new apartment complex. I walked to a ledge that of-fered a view below of the city, which wrapped around three sides of the mountain. The medieval city clung close beneath the mountain but was dwarfed by the new city, which filled the valley and rolled up the sides of the five hills.

A van was parked along the ledge, and when I turned to explore the castle, I noticed that there were two people in it. A man leaned over a woman in a red sweater, her dark hair with blond highlights falling over her shoulders and onto the back of the seat as he mas-saged her breast. They hadn't noticed me, or if they had, they didn't much care. Her fingers dug into his hair.

The castle was still. Nothing hung on the chipped stone walls, and I could see into the grassy courtyard. I heard the tinny sound of a radio or television deep within. I followed the sound through two rooms until I came to a long, dark room where a twenty-something man in what seemed like a museum uniform sat on a wooden chair, staring at a small TV. The light from the TV illuminated his face, and a heater glowed red at his feet.

Very slowly, as if mustering all his energy, the man raised his head and turned to me.

I walked closer. "Do I pay you?"

The man opened his mouth and furrowed his brows. "What?"

"Do I pay you?"

He waved me away as if swatting a fly. "No, just go." He locked back into the same position in front of the TV. I saw that he was watching one of Italy's many game shows featuring topless or scantily clad women. On this particular show, a large-breasted blonde wearing a tiny bathing suit was leaning over a glass table and blowing on a toothpick, trying to get it to roll through a simple maze. One of the cameras was set under the glass tabletop.

I walked through a series of empty rooms, my footsteps echoing, and emerged into the courtyard, where the sun beat down on the weeds and rubble. I was surprised to see that someone else was there. A woman sat in the sun, sketching part of the wall. We exchanged smiles; then she turned back to her sketch, still smiling. Her long, dark hair fell onto her shoulders and covered her face. She brushed it back behind her ears.

I found an arch that looked out below the castle. The van was still there, and the man had cleared his seat and had moved on top of the woman.

I circled back to find that the woman with the sketchpad was gone.

The moment I stepped into the restaurant, I inhaled the rich smell of grilled meat and tomatoes. The heavyset young man came out to greet me.

"Are you open now?"

He gave me a look that said, "Of course, why wouldn't we be?" even though I appeared to be the lone diner.

I asked the waiter to bring me the house specialties.

First he brought out a liter of the house red wine, and soon after that an antipasto selection of pork balls stuffed with bread and deep-fried, followed by an assortment of stuffed vegetables: zucchini stuffed with eggs and prosciutto, served warm and drizzled with olive oil, and eggplant stuffed with artichokes, breaded and fried. Placed generously with them were roasted yellow and red peppers, also drizzled with olive oil, and flavored with a hint of oregano and lemon.

"Everything is brought from the owner's farm," the waiter told me. "Even the pigs and fowl."

An older waiter joined us. He had relatives in Toronto. He wanted to make sure that the food was to my liking, and he assured me that on days other than Monday, the restaurant was very busy—especially at night. This led us into a conversation about how well the restaurant did and how hard he had to work to support his family. As the rest of Italy got richer, Calabria, while still a relatively inexpensive place to live, was getting more expensive, too.

I asked him why Calabria was still poor. Was it the farmland, which was rich only in small patches? Was it the lack of industry?

"The mafia," he said casually, neither embarrassed nor secretive.

"How, exactly, does that affect business?"

"The mafia is everywhere," he said. "We all have to pay. You pay." He smiled and stood by as the other waiter brought out my first course, an amazing fusilli, corkscrews tighter than even my grandmother made, with Calabrese sausage and tomato sauce.

I drank another glass of wine just in time for the main course, pork fillets stuffed with zucchini and smoked *scamorza* cheese, which tastes like a combination of provolone and mozzarella. An orange sauce had been drizzled over the stuffed pork, and edible orange rinds garnished the plate.

"Mostly the blood oranges are from Sicily, but we grow our own here," the young waiter said. "And of course, the pig is 'free-range.' " I tried to picture a pig roaming the hills.

To finish the meal, he brought out a *tartufo di Pizzo,* a chocolate and hazelnut gelato molded around a soft, syrupy chocolate fudge, then covered with a crunchy chocolate coating—"a specialty of the region"—and surrounded by small, tart *fragole di bosco,* wild strawberries.

When the older waiter brought the bill, he apologized for the expense and said that coffee and dessert were on the house. The New Yorker in me did a quick calculation and estimated that one of the best meals I'd eaten in all of Calabria had cost me under twenty-five dollars.

On the way back to the hotel, I stopped off and sat on the steps of the cathedral. Children yelled across the piazza, and a baby laughed on the balcony of a fourth-story apartment, playing in the sheets hanging on a clothesline. The screech of swallows cut the air, and the cooing of pigeons echoed from the alleys. The local artist had set up a chair outside his workshop, which also doubled as his gallery, and began cutting wood with a circular saw. Hammering came from inside a twelfth-century building. The sound of construction echoed throughout the old city.

With all my walking that day, exploring each alley and tiny piazza, I was able to work up another appetite—albeit a small one. About nine that night, I stopped off at a pizzeria close to the hotel. It was hidden in an alley behind two cinder-block apartment buildings. I ordered a pizza with porcini mushrooms and drank wine and sparkling water. A group of men was at one table; an older couple at another; a teenage boy and girl, obviously on a date, sat in the corner; and a family took up the large rectangular table close to the kitchen.

Everyone faced the large TV over the serving station. I'd come in at the midpoint of a made-for-TV movie, titled *Com'è l'America*, about a Calabrese family in the 1950s trying to assimilate into American culture. It seems that the mother and two teenagers have been sent for by their husband and father in America after years of separation. She finds him working on the railroad—and a complete drunk. In order to support the family, she finds work as a seamstress. The son is a high school track star who battles discrimination. The story covered everything that Italian immigrants might have experienced, from alcoholism and abortion to falling in love, but nothing about the location was recognizable to me. It definitely wasn't an East

Coast city, and it was too cold to be California. I thought perhaps the story was set in the Midwest or Colorado, but I couldn't think of anywhere except Denver where Calabresi would have emigrated—and there were no mountains in the movie. I figured that the set must have been fabricated by the Italian movie industry. Then the obvious occurred to me. It was Canada, somewhere between Niagara Falls and Toronto.

During World War II both Canada and the United States, fearing their common enemies Japan, Germany, and Italy, created internment camps. Most recently, the Japanese camps have become subjects of movies and novels. But few people realize that Germans and Italians were also held captive.

Italians refuse to talk about it, or they downplay the situation, saying that they went along with it to prove that they held allegiance to their adopted countries. After the war the Italian economy tumbled, and Calabria felt it the worst. One of their largest waves of emigration from Calabria came directly after the war. Because of the strict quotas the United States had set on Italian immigration, many Calabrese immigrants opted to move to Australia, Buenos Aires, and, of course, Canada. To the Calabresi, America included Canada.

The next morning I left the hotel (I later learned that it had been filled with traveling businessmen) and moved to the heart of the new city. The streets were busy with pedestrian and automobile traffic. Shiny new stores cast their light on the wide sidewalks. A store selling Diesel jeans, the Italian Levi's, dominated one large intersection, and just across the street were two bookstores.

Cosenza, with its university and beautiful setting, appeared to be the cultural and economic capital of Calabria. Not coincidentally, it is Calabria's northernmost large city.

I met Luigi at the larger of the two bookstores. We surveyed the shelves looking for good books on Calabria. He had just finished an exam and had a couple of hours free before he had to go hang lights for a dance performance at the university.

We came across a book, *Sull'identità meridionale* ("On Southern

Identity"), that Luigi said he had used in one of his sociology classes. I asked him about racism in Italy, namely, prejudice toward southerners in the north.

"It exists, but I think it's worse for my father's generation, those who desperately needed to leave to make money," Luigi said, "the ones who took just any job up north."

He pulled out another book and put it on my stack. "But in almost any Western country the youth now are more accepting, don't you think? They're bought up with more education and understanding of other cultures. Now when I go north, it's for art, but I don't feel I have to go there to make a living. I really think I can do it here. And I'd rather. But of course, I'm only in college now. Everything is possible. We'll see."

I remembered Giuseppe's worry that Luigi would be just a poor artist, someone out of touch with the real world. Their relationship reminded me a lot of mine and my father's when I was Luigi's age. Also, like me, Luigi was growing up in a time of prosperity that freed him from the anxiety about the future that his father had experienced.

"My father works the same grueling hours that his parents did," Luigi said. "But not on the farm. He spends all his time at the shop or traveling. It's almost the same peasant determination that drives my father, the same that his parents felt, that got him off the fields." Luigi paused. "But of course, I realize that my father is making enough money to put us through college."

Luigi put one more book on my stack, a book on the food of Calabria. "This might be interesting, yes?" he said. "I know that your grandmother cooked Calabrese food for you, though she might not have cooked *everything* that we eat here."

A young blond woman, with a sharp nose, blue eyes, and thin pink lips, had been perusing the shelves next to us, and I'd had the sense that she'd been listening to our conversation. She turned to us now. "You know, there is a great bookstore down around Via Piave that has so many different books on Calabria's history." Her voice was soft but strong, and her blue eyes sparkled, but she spoke seriously, without the slightest trace of a smile.

"Thank you," Luigi and I said, almost in unison.

"My pleasure," she said, and turned back to the shelves.

"I've been meaning to ask you," I said between bites of my pizza. "What are your thoughts on the mafia here?"

Luigi looked up and wiped his face. We had just finished a couple of *arancini*, rice balls filled with ground meat, tomatoes, peas, and cheese that had been deep-fried to the bright color of orange.

This was one of the questions that I had not intended to ask everyone. It embarrassed me, for my sake and for the sake of my father, who wanted me to come back from my travels with a picture of Calabria as beautiful as the stereotypical view of Tuscany. And so did I. I didn't want to play into the stereotypes about southern Italians as ne'er-do-wells and mafiosi. I saw potential for growth everywhere in the region, but I couldn't help asking myself, "Why has Calabria not gotten further along?"

One obvious answer was unfortunately the mafia, but of course no one would speak about it. When asked, people simply shrugged their shoulders or pointed to the next town.

"Again, the young people don't fear it because they didn't grow up with the violence of the seventies," said Luigi. "While the mafia is on the streets, there's no violence on the streets; when there's no violence, the mafia goes out of your everyday consciousness. But I think the violence is cyclical. When times get hard, the violence will return."

The restaurant started filling up. We talked more softly, almost conspiratorially. Luigi continued. "But then now, in this entire world, who is not involved with the mafia? People say that Berlusconi has to be, or else he wouldn't be president. Look, even great artists—they say Gianni Versace was."

We talked about the mysterious circumstances surrounding the fashion designer's death, then got up from the table and walked outside.

"Even your President Kennedy was involved," Luigi continued.

A few streets away we came across the address the woman had

given us for the bookstore. There was no storefront or sign, just an ornately carved door to what looked to be a residential building with the name of the bookstore below the buzzer. We rang. The door opened partway, and a well-groomed old man in a tweed coat appeared.

"Is this the bookstore?" I asked.

"Ah, yes. Please come in."

He directed us into a smallish room filled with books in plastic wrappers. He placed a catalog in our hands, and we studied the titles, most of which were books praising the glory of Calabria. It didn't take us long to realize that this was a Freemason shop, a fact we acknowledged with a glance at each other. Italians love conspiracy theories, and the Freemasons are often the subject of these theories. Many Italians believe they run the country—as ultrasecret and powerful a society as Yale University's Skull and Bones is rumored to be. Another man walked in, and they both eagerly presented us with books, waiting for a reaction. Not immediately finding what we wanted, we thanked them and said goodbye.

The heavy door closed behind us.

"Amazing," Luigi said. "But you know there are people who believe that both the mafia *and* the Freemasons control Italy."

Four men were gathered inside the Duomo Art Shop, across from the duomo in the historic center. Two of them were painting; the other two sat on small wooden benches.

The eldest of the men, the one whom I had seen the previous day working outside his studio, introduced himself as Giuseppe. He painted murals of the city, much the way that Ferdie Pacheco paints Ybor City, Florida, or Howard Finster depicted his rural Georgia. Giuseppe pulled up a heavy wood footstool and asked me to sit and join them. He had white curly hair that came down to his ears and wore a blue painting smock.

I told them where I was from and what I was doing in Calabria.

The other men beamed with excitement that a son of Calabria

had returned. Each told me a story about a relative who had emigrated to the States or Canada, never to return.

"So what have you seen of Cosenza?" they asked.

"Almost everything of the old city and a good part of the new," I said. "But I'm most intrigued by the legend of the treasures of Alaric at the bottom of the Busento."

"Oh, yes," Giuseppe said. "Well, all anyone has ever found were a few gold coins. Roman coins. But those are all over the place."

After a while I excused myself, promising to stop by again the next day. Giuseppe walked me across the piazza to the restaurant, Bella Calabria, which he described as one of the best in Cosenza.

The maître d' greeted us.

"This is Signore Rotella, a friend of mine from New York. Treat him well."

Like L'Arco Vecchio, where I had eaten lunch the day before, the restaurant had exposed chestnut beams on white stucco ceilings. I ordered a plate of *mozzarella di bufala* and tomatoes, which were served sprinkled with oregano, not basil, and a liter of light red wine that was slightly chilled and a little effervescent. The waiter served dessert to a couple in the far corner who were speaking English with an American accent. Aside from the former railroad worker back in Cerchiara di Calabria, this was the first time that I had heard English in weeks, let alone from the mouths of Americans.

I approached them. "I'm sorry for interrupting, but I couldn't help overhearing that you were speaking in English."

"Oh, my, yes. I had no idea you weren't Italian," the man said.

"My family is Italian, but I'm visiting from New York," I said. "Where in the States are you two from?"

"The States? We're from Canada," the woman said. She was in her fifties and looked as if she had spent most of her life on the beaches of Hawaii.

"Sorry for the assumption," I said, knowing how much Canadians hated to be mistaken for Americans. "What brought you to Cosenza?" I felt like my father: I wanted to hear them say that they were awed by the beauty of Calabria, that they had read about it or been intrigued by this mysterious part of the country, that this was their destination, not merely a resting point on the way to somewhere else. I wanted to hear that they had chosen Calabria.

"Well, we just spent a couple of weeks in Sicily—I'm a travel agent," the woman interjected, "and we are just checking out all the hotels. We were on our way to Naples, but because it was getting late, we decided to stop here in Cosenza for the night."

Oh, well, so it was just a stopping point.

"Yes, but we did spend some time in Reggio to see the Riace figures," the man added, referring to Calabria's most prestigious artifacts, two pre-Greek warriors that had been raised from the Ionian Sea.

"And we stopped for a short time in Tropea."

"How's the trip been so far?" I asked, still hopeful.

"Well, we were underwhelmed with the food in Sicily," the man said. "I'd heard that it was so good there. Perhaps we just selected the restaurants poorly."

"But we've been pleasantly surprised by the food here in Calabria," the woman said. "It's simple, but that's what I think is so good about it."

When I told them what I was doing in Calabria, the man commented, "Well, I'm sure you must have read Norman Douglas's *Old Calabria.*"

"Yes," I said, surprised and happy that he had even heard of the book.

"It seems like things haven't changed much since his time," the man said. "Except the food is better."

At that moment, the waiter placed in front of me a plate of tagliatelle with zucchini.

"We'd invite you to join us, but we are just finishing," the man said. But when I had finished my bowl of spicy *zuppa di pesce*, they were still at the table.

"You know, it's getting a little dark," the woman said. "And we don't know this city. Do you mind walking with us?"

"I'd be happy to," I said. And I was.

I said goodbye to the waiter, and we walked out together. A table of men who had been seated just after me looked up at us as if they were hearing English spoken in their city for the first time.

"You know, we have about two hundred thousand Calabresi living in Toronto," the man said.

"I'm beginning to realize that," I answered.

Swallows flew above us. We headed down Corso Telesio; the dull lights from the windows of medieval buildings flickered as if they were candles. As we approached the bridge, I looked down at the Busento River, and beyond at the Crati. Moonlight shimmered at their joining point.

THE PERFECT SHOT

"HERE IS TOO MUCH WORK in too short a time," Giuseppe said. "And not enough money. The Calabresi won't commit. They don't think ahead. When you try to sell postcards early in the year, they say it's too early. Then in June or July, when you come by again, they say it's too late. They want everything at that moment."

We were strolling the promontory of the Tyrrhenian seaside village of Pizzo. Giuseppe wanted to take me around the Tyrrhenian Sea, from Pizzo down to Tropea. He was frustrated with business and the Calabrese way of conducting it.

"Ah, Calabria." Giuseppe sighed.

"What about Calabria?"

"It will grow, but slowly. It will never attract the tourists like the rest of Italy," Giuseppe said.

How lucky, I thought selfishly.

"What about living someplace else?" I asked Giuseppe.

"If I could make a living that I liked, I'd leave tomorrow," he said.

"And you wouldn't miss Calabria?"

"Of course I'd miss it. But there's sentiment, and there's work."

The piazza of Pizzo, which juts out into the sea, with the castle to the south, was packed with cars. The market had opened early that morning. What few fishermen there were these days had brought their catch. Teenagers, half hanging on their motorbikes and against the tufa wall of the promontory, cuddled and made out, oblivious to us. Cafés and restaurants lined the piazza, with outdoor tables covered by red-and-blue umbrellas. Pizzo is now known for its gelato more than for its fishing industry. Even the local Nostromo tuna-canning factory had been bought and moved to Spain, where labor was cheaper. Cement factories had been moved to the outskirts of town. The road to the factories, Giuseppe explained, is lined with fields of *cipolle*, sweet onions. Again, not even industry is far from nature in Calabria.

When I was in high school, my grandparents came to visit us in Florida for the first time in years; we usually visited them in Connecticut. We lived close to a golf course, at which my grandfather shook his head as if disappointed with the wasted use of land. But he nodded approvingly at my father's garden, planted with Florida's tropical climate in mind.

"Pa, look at these, Pa," my father said, pointing to the largest tree in the backyard. "Bananas, Pa. And over there, I'm growing oranges and lemons." They walked onto the pool patio. "And down here, Pa," my father said, "are pineapples."

My grandfather stopped. *"Giusepp', dove i pomodori?"* Where are the tomatoes?

My father tried to explain that the roadside stands sold beautiful red tomatoes. My grandfather stood in silence, then out of his pocket he brought a plastic bag full of his own tomato seeds.

Two days later, when my father got home from work, he looked out the kitchen window to see that part of the backyard had been transformed. Sticks—strangely straight sticks—poked out of the tilled earth at regular intervals. At about that moment the phone rang. The next-door neighbor was calling to say that he had seen my grandfather walking along the golf course, pulling up all the flags, and snapping them across his knee.

From that point on, my father grew tomatoes.

Pizzo's piazza overlooks a Norman castle built in 1486 by Ferdinand I of Aragon.

During the brief time that Napoleon ruled southern Italy, he placed his brother-in-law Joachim Murat in charge of the region. Murat, an otherwise ineffective ruler, established strict laws against treason, which became punishable by death.

Gay Talese beautifully captures the end of Murat's reign in *Unto the Sons*. While Napoleon focused on Waterloo, the Bourbons, with the aid of the English, had taken back the Kingdom of the Two Sicilies. Murat, who believed the people of Calabria were enamored of him, sailed from Corsica to Calabria to begin a campaign to reclaim his throne, which had been taken by the Spanish. Murat left his ship on rowboats and rowed to the sandy shore. With a small coterie of soldiers, Murat marched up to the city, ostentatiously waving his hat as his gold spurs sparkled and jangled with every step.

A crowd began to form around him. He felt as if all of Calabria were backing him. Soon more people joined in. A padrone who had once served under him appeared before Murat and asked, "Who are you?"

"You know who I am." Murat laughed.

"I do not," said the man.

"I am Murat, your king."

"You are not our king. Ferdinand is our king," said the man.

The villagers jeered Murat and, with sticks and tuna spears, closed in on him. He and his soldiers broke away from the mob and ran for the shore with the villagers at their heels. The soldiers filled the boats and set off. As Murat tried to jump in his boat, legend has it, one of his flashy gold spurs got caught in a net. He tried to rip free, but the villagers grabbed him. Those who witnessed the attack talked of how violently the mob treated him. They ripped his hair from his scalp as easily as they tore the clothes from his body. They spat all over him.

Two days later, inside the castle, the people of Pizzo tried Murat for treason under his own law and placed him in front of a firing squad. His last request was that the squad aim at his heart and spare his face. He refused to be blindfolded. His body, with an unmarred face, was sent to his wife, Napoleon's sister Caroline.

In Pizzo there is a saying: *"Gioacchinu a fattu a legge, Gioacchinu a patiu."* Joachim made the law, and Joachim died by the law.

From Pizzo, Giuseppe took me to a place just north on the Tyrrhenian coast. Many areas on this coast resemble the Amalfi coast, with villages perched on cliffs—but over clear blue water that washes small spits of white sand, rather than sheer cliffs with stony beaches. Fifty to a hundred feet from shore, rocks thrust out of the blue like the backs of ancient dragons. Some have caves into which one can row a boat. Inside, the bright blue water shimmers from below, like the famous Grotta Azzura of Capri.

Legend has it that in the 1700s a ship crashed against some outlying rocks and sank, leaving the sailors to swim to shore. The sun was beginning to set when they finally washed upon the sandy beach. They looked up at the rocky cliffs, wondering where they were. About a quarter of the way up the sun illuminated the inside of a cave and a barely noticeable path leading up to it.

When they reached the cave, the sailors carved sculptures there as an offering of thanks for their safety. The statues in what is now called the Chiesa di Piedigrotta were formed from tufa and chalk. The statues of varying sizes, from lifesize to miniature, depict biblical stories. They blend with the stalagmites. The back wall drips with water. A few feet in front of the wall, an altar is centered between two stalactites. Candles burn on crisp white cloths. A painting of the lactating Madonna, the same as in Gimigliano, hangs on the moist wall above the altar.

Sculptures have been added throughout the centuries by local artists. In one corner, the cave floor curves upward to meet the cave ceiling. On this slope, figurines of eighteenth-century peasants, each about six inches tall, roam the terrain. Tucked into a crevice, a life-size sculpted Madonna is surrounded by fresh carnations and roses. A little stone girl wearing a peasant robe kneels at the Virgin's feet.

Giuseppe took a deep breath and whispered to me from the entrance. "Marco, do you remember the postcard I gave you of this?" he asked.

I did. I recalled how crisp the image on the postcard was, how much grander the sculptures looked in the photo than in person.

"I waited all day here. I paced around the entire cave, looking for the right angle. When the sun set over the water, I thought I'd get the best shot. But it still wasn't good. Then as I was walking out of the cave, just after the sun had set, I turned to see the place light up." Giuseppe brushed his forearm across his brow as if he were wiping away sweat. "I had my picture."

WHEN CENTURIES COLLIDE

I T ALL HAPPENED HERE! Here, in Calabria!" the voice said, through a tinny amplifier. "Great explorations and medical advancements were accomplished by Calabrese ingenuity."

Giuseppe and I stood in front of a white storefront, to the side of a larger-than-life-size ceramic statue of a nineteenth-century peasant churning milk over a fire smoldering with olive branches. He wore a white cap and had a black mustache very similar to Giuseppe's.

There were two entrances leading into the same building, but one sign for both: IL FARO—MOSTRA DEGLI ANTICHI MESTIERI DI CALABRIA (The Lighthouse—An Exhibit of Calabria's Traditional Professions).

"Look how eyeglasses evolved from just a single curved piece of glass," the voice intoned. "And with the help of scientific Calabrese research, doctors were able to graft skin from one part of the body to another."

The voice emerged from the exhibition room. A man in his fifties wearing a tweed jacket and bow tie walked out, talking into a microphone that was connected to a speaker strapped to his waist. A herd of grade-school children, mesmerized, pressed close behind him. His name was Benito Badolato.

"He's from the Gimigliano area," Giuseppe said proudly. "Remember the day you flew in? Remember the photos of the museum book? That's him."

Giuseppe described Badolato as being very smart, very creative, but a bit absentminded, "like a professor." He had conceived of and put together this museum in 1999.

We walked into the museum hall, which was long and narrow with glass cases flanking a corridor that two people could barely fit through together. In each case a detailed diorama depicted lifestyles of nineteenth-century Calabrese workers. Each figure stood about five inches tall and was set against a background appropriate to his work. The scenes reminded me of the best model railroad sets. In one diorama, a gray-haired mustachioed man (who also happened to resemble Giuseppe) roasted chestnuts over an olive branch fire. Beside him, a dead chicken hung outside a chicken wire hutch. Miniature pots and pans decorated shelves. The terrain was rocky and dusty.

Another diorama depicted the three major phases of the wine-making process. The first scene showed a man mashing the grapes in a large chestnut barrel with his feet; the next showed another man pressing grapes with a manual winepress in a smaller wine barrel made of olive wood (similar to the one my grandfather used in Connecticut), and in the last diorama, my favorite, the vintner was sitting down, accordion at his side, drinking wine from a wicker-covered bottle. Every essential Calabrese occupation had been covered—the making of pottery, umbrellas, olive oil, and bread. There was even a scene of women washing clothes and getting water from the river.

Signore Badolato had cornered the kids in the small main room, where they could purchase postcards—Giuseppe's, of course. He worked the cash register while continuing to speak over the loud-speaker at an auctioneer's speed.

Signore Badolato noticed us and signaled to Giuseppe that he'd be with us momentarily. We poked our heads into the other room, the museum of science and industry. A three-foot-long model of a locomotive filled the center display box. Each part of the engine—the headlights, the wheels, the insulator—had been identified by handwritten white labels. From each label sprouted a copper wire with a red arrow that pointed to the part in question.

Not all these displays claimed Calabrese invention, but one that did caught my eye. A man was sitting in a doctor's office, probably in the early part of the last century. The doctor was standing over him, directing the patient's arm to the patient's nose. When you looked closer, you could see that the patient's arm was actually strapped to his head, and his biceps was indeed resting on his nose. Was this some sort of medieval torture? The display was labeled "The First Human Graft: The Invention of Plastic Surgery." I immediately thought back to the noseless man in Gimigliano who wanted to trade his mule for my wife.

When a bus arrived to pick up the kids, Signore Badolato turned to us, obviously thrilled to see Giuseppe. He told me to make myself at home. He invited us to join the next group, which was starting anytime now . . . but on second thought, no, that would not do. We should come back some other time. Yes, perhaps this afternoon; no, maybe tomorrow or the next day. But we could visit his factory, just on the other side of town. The newer section. Oh, and I should make sure Giuseppe brought me to the gift shop, where his daughter, wife, and son worked.

We never did make it back for the tour.

About twenty minutes from Tropea is Capo Vaticano. There are at least twenty tourist villages, hotel complexes—all with tennis courts and pools—and a few water parks for kids around the Tropea region. Just ten years ago this small region of Vibo Valentia, the toe's spur, formed its own province. And because of tourism and the region's promotion of its agricultural industry, Vibo Valentia is now one of the wealthiest provinces. And within Vibo Valentia, Capo Vaticano is one of the most beautiful, and expensive, areas in Calabria.

If Vibo Valentia, the peninsula that juts out into the Tyrrhenian

Sea, is Calabria's Amalfi coast, Tropea is Capo Vaticano's Positano. Like a hat on an old man's head, the village tops a rocky crag jutting into the ocean. Tropea is Calabria's major tourist destination. It was founded sometime during the Roman Empire, but its streetscape is entirely Norman and Aragonese. With narrow streets winding between buildings of stone tufa, the entire city seems to have been constructed on a miniature scale. While walking through a maze of walls, you may suddenly stumble upon a hidden alcove where four or five tables have been set with red or blue checkerboard tablecloths, as I did.

A menu was posted on the wall in Italian, though a German translation had been handwritten next to it. Palm trees grew on one side of a tufa wall; grapevines covered the intimate sitting area behind which was the kitchen.

The sun warmed me. At last it was spring in Calabria. One alley connected to another, which then opened onto a tiny square that in turn led to a garden. Giuseppe and I finally came out at a moderate-size piazza dotted with white plastic tables and multicolored umbrellas. It was midday, and only a few tables were taken. Not yet hungry, we continued our stroll.

We followed the main road from the piazza down a slope until it ended at a waist-high wall. A long and fairly wide beach of light-brown sand, the color of all the buildings of Tropea, stretched to the water, which was so clear and blue that you could see a boat's shadow on the white ocean floor. There was a hotel at one end of the beach; inside, I could see a tropical piazza, with palm trees and wood chairs and fences. Beyond, wooden piers reached out into the sea, mooring private yachts and ferries that went regularly to Sicily and Stromboli, as well as to the rest of the Aeolian Islands.

A rock island stood to the left of Tropea; on its top rested the medieval sanctuary called the Chiesa di Santa Maria dell'Isola. At one time it was a convent that could be reached by a footbridge from where we were standing. The bridge had eroded and crumbled over the centuries until it was finally torn down, and the convent was relocated. I took one last look down at the water. A man in a boat rowed around the rocky crag and entered a cave just big enough for the boat. A couple on horses cantered down the beach.

South of Tropea the miles of secluded tourist villages are broken only by an isolated acre or two of summer camping parks, a haven for German tourists. Roads snake around the province, offering quiet access to private residences, all of which are hidden by wild foliage, stone walls, and gates. The weeds at the sides of the road are not trimmed; nothing's manicured. But tucked inside those overgrown trees and bushes are some of the most expensive houses in Calabria. Here doctors and lawyers from the north keep houses to which they sometimes retire in the summertime or on long holiday weekends. At those times military guards will patrol the neighborhoods, and helicopters hover, protecting Italy's politicians from assassins and kidnappers.

The area is known for its fields of *cipolle*. We drove through the onion fields with the windows down, breathing in the sweet aroma, which smelled like freshly cut parsley and scallions. The bright green fields expanded for miles, ending suddenly at the edge of a cliff.

We followed a dirt road through brush and bushes until it widened into a parking lot. We left the car, opened a wooden gate, and walked up a trail of stone steps to a wood frame building. Below, a cement pathway wound through a garden of meticulously arranged flowers, sloping down to offer a view of the distant sea. As I looked out to the horizon, where the garden ledge ended and the sea began, I was struck by the glorious melding of deep green grass and bright blue sea.

A young blond woman walked out of the garden.

"That's the garden restaurant," Giuseppe said. "I've been here; they serve a wonderful gelato."

A teenage girl walked out of the restaurant. She, too, had long, straight, shiny blond hair.

I motioned to Giuseppe and gestured an inquisitive "Who is she?"

"German," he said. "Germans come out here and fall in love with the sun. Some stay the summer; some decide to stay forever. They marry local Italians and have children."

Giuseppe called to the older woman. "*Mi scusa, signorina.* What month do you open?"

The woman answered in perfect Italian, "Beginning of June." She smiled, then walked away.

Giuseppe turned to me and said, "I think she's Italian. But she looks German."

I could see how Germans, or anyone from northern Europe, would fall in love with this place and decide to live here. And as the European community gradually meshed, I could imagine Germans beginning to move down and open up businesses, such as garden restaurants.

"In any case, we'll have to wait for our gelato," Giuseppe said.

The port village of Nicotera Marina lies on the south side of the Vibo Valentia spur, fronting the beach road and extending back in a grid of one- and two-story buildings about eight or ten blocks square. The wide main road was dusted with so much beach sand that I could barely tell it was paved. The grid formation is unusual in Italian villages, as are the detached buildings, with porticoes or balconies that shaded parts of the sidewalk. I turned around and faced the range of hills that climbed just behind the city. I felt as if I were on the set of a western movie, someplace in Colorado. Barely a soul strolled the street; it was almost a ghost town. Nicotera Marina came alive only in the summer.

Giuseppe had a distinct sweet tooth—for gelato. It led us, like a bloodhound's nose, down the street, to a gelateria by the sea. With the lights out—as in most Italian establishments during the day—I couldn't tell that there was life behind the glass, which reflected only the undulating waves of the ocean. Inside, though, we were greeted by the proprietor, an older man with a healthy paunch, and sparkling glass and metal counters. Giuseppe ordered a tropical orange, banana, and coconut cone. I ordered a pistachio-hazelnut combination, which the owner stuffed between two pieces of sweet, doughy bread: an Italian ice-cream sandwich.

The sun had finally warmed away the chill that had filled the first part of my stay in Calabria. We drove the car two blocks toward the sea and two blocks across and parked in front of a *tabaccheria*. A dark young man was standing outside, reading a paper in the sun. His black hair fell in waves across his forehead, illuminating cold blue eyes. He had a small nose, and his hands were wide and thick and looked as if they were made for manual labor. But this was Francesco Lococo, a *tabaccheria* proprietor.

Inside, Giuseppe had laid out his portfolio of postcards. Francesco quickly picked out the ones that interested him and walked around the counter to address me.

"It must be boring here," he said. "Nothing like America."

"Yes, but it's the weather, the scenery, the slow pace that I'm interested in," I said. I meant it, but it had become my pat response, which relieved me of the chore of describing my life in New York and set people at ease.

"We have nothing but sand and ocean," he said.

"We have nothing but people and buildings and cars and terrible smells."

"It must be beautiful."

We exchanged impressions of our own countries—characteristics that seemed boring to us but exotic to each other. Francesco paused to look out at the ocean. "We do have Greek ruins here. Greek ruins everywhere. But there's no money to excavate. We just build on top of them."

I doubted that there were ruins here, but he assured me that the entire area had been mined for granite in ancient times.

He brought out a magazine on boat racing and flipped to an article written by Giuseppe Chiaravalloti, president of Calabria. The article praised Calabria's wine-making industry; its arid mountain ranges, its coastline; its sun-dried tomatoes, capers, figs, and oranges. By the end of the article I realized that he had written a treatise comparing the virtues of Calabria with those of California. It made sense. After all, Calabria, while no Rome, had even provided the setting for a few of Piero Pasolini's films as well as for several spaghetti westerns. I wondered why the Calabresi who came to the United States hadn't settled farther west.

"So do you think that Calabria is on its way up?" I asked Francesco.

He thought for a moment, then grinned a grin that was neither proud nor apologetic, but somewhere in between. "Calabria is tranquil," he said. "It grows, but it grows slowly, quietly. It doesn't have the bang that Sicily, for instance, has."

Of course Sicily itself had only recently shaken off its mafia taint and begun to enjoy the fruits of tourism. I wonder if this was his way of not jinxing Calabria's progress—like Giuseppe's habit of answering only "Not bad" when asked how he is.

Just then Francesco's wife drove up with their two kids and spoke to him in an urgent tone. "I'm so sorry," Francesco said to us, moving for the door. "Come back, we'll continue business."

When he was gone, I said to Giuseppe, "He likes to talk about his village."

"Yes, of course," Giuseppe said. "He prefers talking to paying."

We went home by way of Vibo Valentia, the provincial capital of the newly formed region of the same name. We were discussing corruption, and Giuseppe was explaining that allotments the government had handed out to contractors to build factories or shopping centers "don't always go where they need to." Often the contractors would lay the foundation, build a frame, then take off with the rest of the money.

"In Italy, the state helps the thieves." Giuseppe sighed. "Those who are clever get away with it."

Giuseppe's cell phone rang. He talked in a low, almost defeated voice, then hung up. "Problems, always problems," he said. "I have to go to Apulia tomorrow to see a client who claims his shipment of postcards was not what he had ordered."

We stopped at an intersection just outside Vibo Valentia. On the other side of the road stood half-constructed buildings that illustrated what Giuseppe had been telling me. Roofless concrete shells stood among pits of excavated land and piles of debris that no one had had the money to clear.

Two Moroccan boys came to our windows selling individual packets of tissues for a thousand lire, about fifty cents. Giuseppe ignored them and looked at me. "Has anyone given you money today?"

"No," I said, not understanding his point.

"Me neither," he said, then looked out at the boys. "But *they* want money."

"But, Giuseppe, they're poor," I said. "They don't have anything else."

"The government lets them get away with it because they are poor." Giuseppe vented. "They show the same leniency toward the Gypsies, who steal and rob. The Africans and Gypsies get shorter sentences for the same crimes that Italians commit, because the government believes that poor people don't know any better." He finished with a grumbling *aaaah* of exasperation at his own situation and the situation around him.

The road narrowed as we entered the old city, traffic slowing as the buildings crowded up on the sidewalks. Pedestrians overflowed onto the streets. The sun was setting, and the lights were coming on in the cell phone stores, shoe shops, record stores, pizzerias, and flashy boutiques.

From here the road cut a straight path through the city center, where it dipped slightly, then shot directly up to a partially restored fourteenth-century Angevin castle that was lit from below. If I looked straight ahead, I could be on any Manhattan avenue. The moment I looked to either side, the city fell to fields of wheat. On the outskirts of town, I knew, lay the ruins of a Greek Acropolis, as well as the remains of a Doric temple.

"So day after tomorrow, Marco, what do you say about going to Apulia?" Giuseppe asked, a sly smile spreading across his face.

"I wish I could," I said to Giuseppe. "But I really should get to Reggio before I leave for home." I told him I'd call him when I got back.

Giuseppe nodded, but his smile slipped away.

REGGIO DI CALABRIA

I HAD ARRIVED in Reggio di Calabria in the early afternoon. The train tracks cut a swath through this long, narrow city of almost two hundred thousand, Calabria's largest, which sits on Italy's toe and overlooks Sicily. Reggio has the greatest expanse of poor urban housing, and it has been a poor city for a long time. Much of the region was leveled during the 1908 earthquake (a similarity with California that Calabria's president didn't mention). Messina, Reggio's twin city in Sicily, a couple of miles across the Strait of Messina, was also destroyed, but with better allocation of money it was rebuilt quickly and attractively, while the economics and politics of Reggio never permitted such reconstruction. Instead, the city built slipshod apartments between the sharply rising green-and-brown Aspromonte Mountains and the gray ocean, where a thin tract of white beach runs the length of the city.

On the train in, we passed through stations covered in graffiti until we stopped at the ocean port of Villa San Giovanni, where entire trains are carried aboard ferries across the Strait of Messina. Engineers have decided that the spot just north of here would be the optimal point to build a bridge linking Calabria with Sicily, just over two miles away. Such a bridge has been debated since Mussolini's time, but the talk now seems to be turning to action, and the proposed designs look a great deal like San Francisco's Golden Gate Bridge.

I checked into the Albergo Miramare, which has a grand lobby with polished wood trim and rich-looking leather chairs. At this time of year it was not much more expensive than other hotels, of which there were surprisingly few for a port city. The bar, with burnished oak tables, had wide windows from which you could look down at the boardwalk that lined about a mile of Reggio's beaches. An outdoor breezeway, on both the bar level and the balcony above, could be set up with tables, but on this weekend because there were official guests, probably judges, all tables had been taken in for security, and an Uzi-toting military guard was posted on each floor. Lamps and palm trees lined the streets of the center city, and the buildings were painted a dull yellow that reminded me of old photos of Havana, Cuba.

Every brochure of Calabria features four items: clear blue water lapping a rocky coast; sunsets over forested mountains; a string of hot red peppers; and the bronze warriors of Riace. The statues were discovered in 1972 by scuba divers who came across the raised arm of one of the warriors only twenty-four feet below the water's surface, about six hundred feet off the coast of Riace, close to Locri on the Ionian coast. The Italian government thought they should be displayed in Rome, the Sicilians proposed Palermo, but Calabria wasn't about to relinquish this relic of her glory days. And so, in the guarded basement of the Museo Archeologico Nazionale, set up on pedestals, stands the pride of Calabria, warriors from an era when the Greeks first started settling Reggio, or, as it was called then, Rhegion. With no glass around them and with their shields and weapons long vanished, their proximity and upraised arms make them seem almost human. At a distance, they look like two uncir-cumcised gay men dancing at a disco.

While Reggio is far from being Italy's most beautiful city, its *passeg-giata* is renowned for its incredible views of the lights of Messina. In the evening I joined the couples holding hands, groups of teens talk-ing to each other, and children running around their parents on the wide boardwalk called the Lungomare Matteotti. This was the first city I visited where I knew no one, and it was here that I felt my first pang.

Like most people who visit Italy, I love the food, the wine, the communal evening strolls; I am drawn to the exuberant, expressive atmosphere. I never expected to feel alone in one of the most socia-ble countries in the world. Perhaps it's precisely because Italians are so social, however, that the solo traveler, however outgoing, can feel an acute sense of loneliness.

I turned away from Sicily and watched everyone stroll by me. The only other person I saw alone was a man in his thirties, leaning against the railing, talking on his cell phone, and looking around anxiously. A moment later a woman wearing stylishly snug pants and high-heeled sandals walked up to him, dropping her cell phone into her purse. They embraced, clearly relieved to have found each other. I thought of my wife back in New York. I wanted to look out over the Strait of Messina with her, feel with her how the breeze cooled the air. Italy's beauty is meant to be shared.

I struggled with the idea of introducing myself, perhaps slid-ing down on a bench next to an older couple who were watching everyone else walk by. Or maybe I'd ask directions of a group of Italians my age, then segue into a conversation. I might even get up the courage to approach a group of Italian girls, whose embarrassed giggles I always found endearing. But it's intimidating to approach a group of any size, and in Italy there's no such thing as solitude. In fact, in Italian the word for "alone," *solo*, also means "lonely." Italians are simply never by themselves, or when they do find themselves alone, usually when they are in transit, they talk on their cell phones. After a while anyone

I approached would wonder why I was alone, why no one else was with me. Eventually that person would start to feel uncomfortable.

I gave up on the idea of initiating a conversation and continued along the *passeggiata*. I walked past a surprising number of Africans, Asians, and Arabs; some of them were selling their wares, but others obviously simply seemed to be joining the evening stroll with the Italians. It was the only place in Calabria, and one of the few places in Italy, where I encountered such a blending of cultures.

I turned once again and gazed out over the strait. It was once believed that a city lay submerged beneath the water and that at certain times you could see it emerge. This illusion was noticed by King Arthur, who is said to have been mesmerized by Reggio. It was known as the Fata Morgana, Morgan's Mirage, a name attributed to the king's sister, Morgan le Fay, who dabbled in sorcery.

Even today it is said that if you look across the strait—with the correct positioning of the sun and just the right amount of ash from Mount Etna floating in the sky—a glistening city emerges. The apparition is actually the reflection of Messina.

With not even the hope of a mirage, I decided the best way to soothe a lonely soul was to do what any Italian would do: eat. I walked farther into the city along Corso Garibaldi, Reggio's major shopping street and its second *passeggiata*. But at night the ornately wrought iron streetlights gave the postwar buildings an unwelcome romantic glow, and I turned off and made for La Bracieria, a restaurant that specializes in Calabrese-style grilling.

I was drinking a glass of red wine when the appetizer came. The waiter set down an embarrassingly large portion of thinly sliced grilled eggplant, zucchini fritters, and an assortment of cheeses and meats, a single order obviously meant to be shared. When I looked up to acknowledge the waiter, I realized that everyone in the restaurant was stealing glances at me, some with sympathy, some with curiosity. I felt like the molting goat in a petting zoo that none of the kids wanted to touch. It seemed that everyone in Italy had at least one family member to take care of him, to eat with him. I remembered a discussion I'd overheard in Rome. Two Italian women were talking about an old man who had just gotten up from a nearby table.

"He's crazy," one woman said.

"He's just quiet," said the other.

"No, he's a little off."

"What makes you say that?" the second woman asked.

"Well, look at him. He eats by himself."

It occurred to me that while I was eating antipasto and drinking homemade wine, I was fantasizing about having a beer in, of all places, a rural Irish pub. There solitude is a common experience and an accepted concept. You can guess that the man sitting next to the empty barstool that you are about to take will be just as eager—especially plied with enough beer—to hear your story as you would be to hear his. In such places even the lonely have company.

The restaurant began filling up. The waiter brought out my first course, which was *bucatini*, a thick, hollow spaghetti, tossed with porcini mushrooms and zucchini and baked in a terra-cotta pot.

"Are you here on business?" he asked.

"Kind of. I'm visiting relatives in Catanzaro," I said.

"Aah. So you live, what, up in Torino?"

"No, New York."

"So you're American?"

"Yes."

"Do you know Rick Steves?"

"Just by his books," I said, commenting on the author of America's ubiquitous travel guides to Europe.

"I'm in one of his books *and* in one of his videos—*Rick Steves' Tuscany*," he said, becoming excited. "What are you doing here?"

I launched into my biography.

"You should write one about Tuscany. It's beautiful, and that's where all the tourists go." The waiter paused. "During the summer I work at a restaurant in Siena, and I'm one of the waiters in his video. You can see me. I'm serving the pasta and instructing on how it's cooked."

"Maybe tourists don't come here because they don't know about it."

"We get tourists from the north, some Germans, but hardly any Americans," he said. "Reggio is just a stopping point between Naples and Sicily. They don't really come to visit. They're here long enough to get on ferries."

The table in front of me, a group of young couples, had been glancing in my direction. The waiter went up to them. He must have explained what I was doing because they turned to me and nodded, and a few of them raised their glasses.

I wasn't quite hungry enough for a second course, so I asked for the check.

The waiter brought out a pear tart and a tiny glass of chilled liqueur. "These are our house specialties. We welcome you as our guest," he said.

The tart was small but rich, and the liqueur proved to be *bergamotto*, made from the citrus fruit that resembles tiny oranges and is the distinctive ingredient in Earl Grey tea and perfumes all over the world. The tree has very specific climate requirements, and Reggio is one of the only regions where it can thrive.

Back at the hotel, I decided to have a quick drink before going to bed. A wedding reception was taking place in the dining room, and the lobby was filled with tuxedos, evening gowns, and gorgeous people. I sat down in a corner of the bar, and one of the bartenders poured me a Maker's Mark. He introduced himself as Nino, and I told him my name and what I was about.

"How's Reggio?" he asked.

"Better than I thought. Nicer, cleaner."

He nodded his head, but seemed neither to agree nor to disagree.

"But I want to go to the Aspromonte," I said. "I want to go to . . . Roccaforte."

He stepped back. "Roccaforte, boh," he grunted. "That's far. I mean it's just up the coast, but it's deep in the mountains." He paused for a moment. "Why do you want to go there?"

"I need to hear Greek."

"I'll take you to the Greek department at the university," he said, and smiled. "Anyway, it's a dangerous area. A few years ago anyway."

I shrugged my shoulders and thought, How dangerous can it be?

"I'll make some calls. I'm sure I can find someone to take you," he said. Then another bartender tapped him on the shoulder. The wedding party needed another round.

GARIBALDI, MUSOLINO, AND TONY BENNETT

I HAD JUST DOWNED TWO BRIOCHES and a cappuccino at the breakfast buffet in the hotel bar when Nino approached me. "Signore Rotella," he said, formally, "tomorrow morning Roccaforte is good for you?"

"Sure," I said.

"Pino will take you."

"Who's Pino?"

"Pino's Pino. Don't worry. He knows all the roads. Meet him out front at about eleven. Actually, he'll be parked down the street at the corner."

"How will I know who he is?"

"You'll know."

On Corso Garibaldi I tried hard to find the bus to Gambarie. I wanted to stop off at Santo Stefano, hometown of Giuseppe Musolino, the Calabrese Robin Hood.

Their history had taught the Calabresi to trust no one. Since the time of the Bruttians, the Greeks, Romans, Arabs, English, French, and Spaniards all took bites out of Calabria until, eventually, they left her to fend for herself. As a result, the Calabrese peasantry became secretive, especially toward anyone new, and they learned to turn to those who would fight for their needs. Criminals to others, brigands were their sustenance.

During times of war, between France and Spain, for instance, brigands formed guerrilla armies that assisted any group they thought would benefit their countrymen best. In any history book about Calabria, the story of brigandage is told; its spirit evolved into what is now the mafia.

The mafia took root in Calabria as the expression of peasant law, even though its members were officially considered criminals. It continues to exist partly because the Calabresi fear the criminal element into which it has evolved, which has long since stopped representing the people, but also because some of them don't want to disrespect the body that has governed them for centuries.

One name that every Calabrese mentions with pride is that of Giuseppe Musolino, a brigand of the early twentieth century who was as beloved by the Calabrese people as he was feared and abhorred by the government and military.

I walked the length of Corso Garibaldi, trying to find out where and when the bus to Gambarie stopped. Everyone had an answer, none of which was the same. I asked the owner of an outdoor *edicola*, a newsstand, in front of which was supposed to be a bus stop.

"I think it's every hour," he said. "It should be coming soon."

"I've been waiting for about forty-five minutes," I responded.

"Hmm," he said, "that's odd." He called out to an old man standing on the other side of the store. "Nino, the bus to Gambarie. When does it stop here?"

The old man shook his head. "Does it stop here? I thought they changed that two years ago."

The shop owner turned back to me. "Maybe that's why I haven't seen it," he said apologetically. "I don't think it stops here anymore."

A man walked into the shop. "Ciao, Luigi." The store owner addressed him. "Tell me, do you know where this gentleman can get the bus to Gambarie?"

"Ah, Gambarie's beautiful. Nice views, good day hikes in the mountains."

"I'm not really going as far as Gambarie," I said. "I want to go to Santo Stefano."

"What's in Santo Stefano?"

"The birthplace of Musolino," I said, fearing that this new information would create further confusion.

"Oh, yes, of course. He died here in Reggio. Did you know that? In a hospital. It's pathetic that they let him die like that."

"Yes, well, that's where I'm trying to go," I said, looking at my watch. I had already lost an hour, and I knew that the last bus returned at three. "The hotel said that I could catch the bus here." How was it that no one here knew how to get to a point only an hour away that was not only the birthplace of a Calabrese hero but a ski resort to boot?

"Aah, that's the problem," the old man said. "The people at the hotel don't take the bus. You have to go to the train station to get the bus."

By the time I got to the train station, I had lost almost another hour. Again I asked around, and again no one knew which bus went to Gambarie. The little clock sign in the bus information booth indicated that the staff was on its break and wouldn't be back until eleven; it was already a quarter after.

A bus pulled into the station. I walked over to the driver. "Can you tell me the bus to Gambarie?"

"It's this one," the driver said.

On Italian noncity buses, there are always two men working. One drives, while the other accepts payment and gives out receipts.

I asked the ticket man if he could let me off at Santo Stefano and when the next bus could pick me up.

He looked up at me. "But this is the last bus for the day. The last one going up and the last one returning."

"Can I get a taxi from there back?" I asked.

"It would be hard, and anyway, it would cost too much," he said. "But we'll figure something out."

He walked up to the front of the bus to begin his ticket collecting. *"Scusa, signore,"* he called out to me. "Sit here." He pointed to the front two seats, usually reserved for the ticket collector. When he finished collecting tickets, from a nearly full bus, he sat down and pulled out a map. I explained that I had two more days in Reggio before I had to go back to Catanzaro.

"Then you could come back tomorrow?"

"I can't. I'm going to Roccaforte."

The ticket man leaned back in his seat, but said only, "That's a distance. Deep in the Aspromonte."

The driver, who had a larger build and wore dark sunglasses, turned to me and said, "Do you like jazz?"

"Yes," I said.

"Big band?"

"It's one of my favorite kinds of music," I said.

"Good. I love the American pop standard," he said, enunciating the words in heavily accented English.

We drove through the suburbs of Reggio, gradually gaining altitude, until the paved streets and cramped apartments gave way to steep slopes with valleys dropping far below. Orange and lemon trees grew on the mountainsides. I had seen olive trees grown on such steep mountains, but never orange trees. Well outside Reggio, the bus driver flicked on his portable tape player. I could just barely hear a trumpet calling out over a slow, measured rhythm.

"When we get to Santo Stefano," the ticket collector said, "you and I will get out and Napoleone"—pointing to the bus driver—"will head off for Gambarie—you don't want to see Gambarie, do you?"

"No, not this trip."

"Good. Next trip, when you come back to Reggio, you'll go to Gambarie."

"Okay," I said. It seemed that almost everyone I talked to, once they knew that I was of Calabrese descent, assumed that I would return. Or perhaps this was the Calabrese idea of time in play: if I didn't return next year or the year after, surely I'd come back within ten or twenty.

"Va bene. We will find out what we can about Musolino."

We drove in front of a town that looked as if it was accessible only by mule. A steep drop to a trickling ravine separated the road from the village on the other side of the gorge.

"This is Podargoni," Napoleone, the music man, said. "Do you know . . . aah, *come si dice* . . . Tonio Bennett'," he said, with an accent on the last syllable as if to say "Benetto."

"Yes, of course, Tony Bennett!"

"Yes, I think he comes from there," he said. "Or maybe somewhere around here. Yes, yes, it is Podargoni."

I could hear my father proudly crowing, ". . . and Tony Bennett, now he's Calabrese!"

Within these deep crevices and deceiving plateaus, Giuseppe Garibaldi and his army of Red Shirts encountered their toughest battle in the struggle to liberate Italy from Bourbon rule. In every Italian city, major streets and piazzas have been named for him and for other men responsible for uniting Italy: Giuseppe Garibaldi, Count Camillo Benso di Cavour, Giuseppe Mazzini, and King Vittorio Emmanuelle. (However, some Italians in the north may be heard cursing below their breath, "Garibaldi didn't unite Italy. He divided Africa!")

It was here at the Battle of Aspromonte in September 1862 that Garibaldi suffered a setback. He was shot in the heel, but he survived and marched north to continue the Risorgimento, or resurrection, of Italy. In 1991 part of the battle site was turned into a national park, with Gambarie as a ski resort at its edges. The area also boasts the Museo di Garibaldi.

About an hour later the bus stopped at the municipal offices of Santo Stefano, which served as the records office, mayor's office, and police station. The ticket man took my arm. Two women and a tall blond young man got off, too. The ticket man greeted everyone as we walked up the stairs together until we came to the records office. The tall blond man turned out to be a carabiniere from Rome who had been stationed in the Gambarie area for a year. The carabinieri were never from the cities in which they worked, a policy designed to thwart corruption.

A woman with bleached hair rolled into a bun greeted us at the records office. She knew the ticket man, who introduced me, saying, "We are looking for records about Musolino, Giuseppe."

"Giuseppe Musolino?" the woman said. "Why?"

"This gentleman is visiting from New York and wants to know more about him."

"*Va bene.* When was he born?"

The ticket man looked at me.

I shrugged. "Sometime at the end of the nineteenth century?" I didn't remember the exact date.

"Last century," the woman said. "Then we have to look in these files." She opened a closet and pulled out a book two feet wide by three feet high. She opened it and placed it in front of us. Everything was handwritten and documented by family name.

The ticket man, very patient, asked her, "You know who we're talking about, don't you?"

"No," the woman said innocently.

"He's famous, he's a *brigante.*" A brigand.

"Oh, I see, Giuseppe . . . Musolino . . . Brigante . . ."

"No, no," the carabiniere interjected from behind us. "*Dio mio,* he's a brigand—famous!" He looked at me and rolled his eyes.

She pulled out another record. "Oh, here it is! Giuseppe Musolino, born November 21, 1892." I was pleased to hear that it was the same year my grandfather was born.

"Where did he die?" the ticket man asked.

"It doesn't say. In Reggio, maybe?"

"That could be it," the ticket man said.

"I thought the birth date was earlier than that," I said. The carabiniere nodded in agreement.

Time had run out, and the three of us went outside to wait for the bus. As we walked out, a woman walked in. She had dark brown eyes and curly dark brown hair and a gap between her front teeth. She reminded me of a Greek woman I had dated my first year in New York. The carabiniere invited the ticket man and me to stop in the local bar for a drink. Inside, we met three other officers. The carabiniere ordered beer; everyone else had a coffee. The ticket man started up a conversation with the other carabinieri, whom he seemed to know.

"I like American women," the Roman said to me.

"Why is that?"

"They're not shy," he said. "They're fun. Easy to talk to."

"How have you found the women here?" I asked.

"My God, they're afraid to talk to any man."

This I found to be true. I was hardly able to engage any woman in conversation. Even when they were with their husbands or boyfriends, they seemed guarded.

"Here in the south everyone is watching. Everyone will talk about them afterward."

I nodded.

"Anyway, all they want is to get married," the Roman said, "and that's no fun."

A horn blew outside.

"Mi dispiace," the driver said. "Back to work."

We got on the bus, and the ticket man and bus driver traded places.

"So, was it worth it?" the jazz man asked.

"I need to spend more time here one day," I said.

"You should spend time at Gambarie," the jazz man repeated as he opened the change purse strapped to his waist and took out a stack of tickets. "Come in the winter and go skiing. Then, when you're tired, relax on the sunny beaches in Reggio."

I felt a hand on my shoulder. "You should also visit Musolino's grave next time."

I turned to find the dark woman sitting behind me. She smiled and blinked slowly, as if embarrassed to initiate a conversation with me. "His grave is across the street from the commune, just up the hill. But that's when you return."

And I believed I would.

WHERE THEY SPEAK GREEK

AT THE END OF THE STREET I spotted a white Mercedes taxi and the back of a man's head. I walked up to the car and peeked in. A man in his sixties, not the man my age I had been expecting, sat in the driver's seat. As I walked away, I heard the car door open, and the man called out behind me, "Roccaforte?"

I turned around. "Yes," I said. "But I'm waiting for Pino."

The man flashed a bright smile. "Come in. He's my son; he couldn't make it today."

I hesitated, then got in the car.

"Good morning," the man said, and offered his hand. "My name is Mimmo."

I shook his hand, and we were on our way.

"Excuse me, but would you mind if I picked up my niece?" Mimmo asked. He kept covering his mouth when talking to me as if he were afraid he had bad breath or would spit.

"Your niece?" I asked. I hadn't really expected anyone else to ride along.

"Yes, she's very nice," Mimmo implored. "She's poor; she doesn't get out too much."

I thought for a moment.

"She's never been to the Aspromonte," he said.

"That's fine." I relented. I imagined her to be a shy, quiet girl with a bad haircut and bad teeth.

"Thank you," he said. At the next light he reached out the window and removed the taxi light from the top of the car.

"Off duty," he said. Then we slid alongside another car and waited in front of a doorway between an ice-cream store and a shoe shop. He rang up someone on his *telefonino*.

"I'm down here," he almost whispered. "Come quickly." He turned to me and smiled.

A young woman in her late teens with short dark hair and short pants bounced down the stairs of the doorway and hopped into the back seat. She wore plenty of rouge, eyeliner, and lipstick. She looked ready for an adventure.

"*Ciao, Zio!*" she screamed, and gave her uncle a big kiss on the cheek, ruffling his thin hair with her hand.

"Who are you?" she asked, turning to me.

"A visitor," I said.

"From where?"

Mimmo interrupted. "Don't ask him too many questions. He's here to see the sights."

"What sights?" she said, and, without waiting for an answer, reached in between Mimmo and me and turned on the radio. Treacly Italian pop music bounced around the car. Settling back, she brushed my shoulder with her hand. "What's your name?" she yelled over the music.

"Marco," I said.

"Marco?" she said. The next two sentences out of her mouth seemed to end in a question, but were entirely incomprehensible to me, filled with vowels and dead-ended consonants. It sounded like Arabic.

"I'm sorry, I didn't quite understand," I said.

She continued to talk to Mimmo in dialect as we left the city and skirted the coast along the Ionian Sea.

"Francesca," Mimmo said, "speak in Italian."

"In Italian? Why?"

"Because I don't think our friend speaks our dialect."

"Marco, friend, why not?" she said.

"Because I'm from New York."

"New York!" Francesca bellowed. "Zio Mimmo, why didn't you tell me he was from New York?"

"I didn't know," he said.

The Aspromonte Mountains loomed above us. I had left my map at the hotel and had no idea where we were heading or how we were to get there. I was surprised to see that we were following the coast, though. I could have sworn when I last looked at the map that Roccaforte was in the center of the mountains.

Francesca and Mimmo talked, again in dialect, then turned to me and burst into chest-splitting laughs.

"Do you like music?" Francesca asked. She offered me a stick of chewing gum. I declined.

"Some, not all," I answered.

She ignored me and once again reached over to turn up the radio that Mimmo had just turned down. She belted out the words to the song, a lament with a catchy melody and thumping bass. Unfortunately, she was tone-deaf, but she continued to sing, stopping only to ask the occasional question, to which she did not wait for a response.

"Take me to America!" she demanded, with the innocence of a young girl. "Do you live far from Disneyland?"

"Yes, that's across the country, in Calif—"

"Take me! I want to go to . . . what did you say?"

I began to answer.

"Are you married?" she asked, then hummed the next phrase of the song.

After an hour of driving, Mimmo slowed down at the exit for Melito, one of the cities whose name came up whenever "sequestering" or "kidnapping" was mentioned.

"This is the way to Roccaforte?" I asked. I began to feel nervous, silly as it seemed. And I knew I sounded nervous.

"Don't worry," Mimmo said with a smile.

"Yeah, don't worry," Francesca yelled. They turned to each other, laughed, turned to me, then laughed again. Francesca smacked her gum.

Finally, we reached the mountains and quickly climbed the steep roads. Behind us, the sea fell to the distance, and in a matter of minutes we had driven out of range of civilization. Prickly pear cactus grew along the shoulders, dropping their fruit. We wound up and down, tires grasping the sinewy roads, staying tight to the edge.

I could understand how someone could disappear here, never to be found again.

We drove through stands of olive and fig trees. The distant mountains were eerily bare, all brown soil and jagged rock. They seemed uninhabitable.

I realized that the back seat had gone quiet—no gum smacking, no talking, no singing. I turned around to see Francesca hanging her head out the window, her body shuddering each time her stomach released its contents.

"She's never been to the mountains," Mimmo whispered. "It's all the curves."

I remembered Giuseppe's telling me about traveling through these mountains a few years back. It was late afternoon, and he was slowly ascending a mountainside when right before a curve a man stepped out in front of him with a machine gun. He motioned for Giuseppe to pull off the road and cut his engine. Then, with his gun, the man motioned for Giuseppe to get out of the car. In a calm, matter-of-fact voice, he said that Giuseppe couldn't go any farther—and he couldn't go back. He must wait until he was told to continue. The man with the gun then disappeared into the brush. Giuseppe waited two hours, his car parked at a curve on the road so that he couldn't see what was in front of him or behind him. After almost three hours, with no sign of the man, Giuseppe decided to take a chance. He got in his car and drove ahead. There was not a soul in sight. He realized that something had been going on in front of him that the man with the gun didn't want anyone to witness.

We had been winding through the mountains for almost an hour and had seen only two other cars, both heading in the opposite direction. Francesca had curled up and fallen asleep in the back seat. Mimmo was silent, glancing at me from time to time and offering what seemed to be a forced smile. For the first time we passed what might be called a village, five or six adjoining houses built on the uphill side of the road. Across the street were small barns or chicken sheds. Two men and a woman were walking along the road; we slowed down and passed them with just inches to spare. They stared into the car. They didn't return Mimmo's nod.

Mimmo's *telefonino* rang. He answered and spoke softly. He looked at me, then shrugged his shoulders. He continued to talk on his phone, turning his head so that he was talking almost into the window. Just at that moment we passed a white car parked along the side of the road. Mimmo nodded to the two men, one of whom was also on a cell phone.

The white car pulled out behind us. Mimmo hung up. My pulse quickened.

"Who's that?" I said, trying to hide my nervousness.

"Who's who?" Mimmo said, looking perplexed.

"The car behind us?"

Mimmo looked in his rearview mirror, then back at me and said innocently, "Just two guys."

I told myself that it was just a coincidence. But I began to plan my escape, just in case. I could jump out of the car and run. But where? How far to the next village or even the next person? And what would happen when I got there? Who would help this foreigner, especially here, where everyone relied on the mafia? I remembered the expressionless faces of the people we'd passed just minutes ago.

I looked to the right, out of Mimmo's window, and saw that the white car was pulling alongside us. My heart raced. Then the car passed us and disappeared into the distance. I felt foolish.

We stopped to let a shepherd guide his sheep across the road. Mimmo rolled down the window and asked him, "How far to Roccaforte?"

The man said, *"Diesh."*

"*Diesh?*" Mimmo turned to me. "Aah . . . *dieci.*" Ten kilometers. "I can barely understand the language."

We wound around a large curve. Francesca woke up and, like a child, said, "Are we in Roccaforte yet?"

And there it was, in front of us, the village of the Greeks. I had imagined sweetly rustic houses destroyed and rebuilt over centuries of earthquakes. What I saw instead was four tiers of brick houses, without any stucco, the Italian equivalent of wooden shacks in 1950s Appalachia. Only the church and what looked to be the foundation of a Norman castle below it stood out against the rocky gray cliffs and the run-down cinder-block buildings.

"This is Roccaforte?" I asked Mimmo.

"I guess so," he said hesitantly.

Just then we passed a simple white sign with black letters that read ROCCAFORTE.

One of my British guidebooks explained that there was a town that could only be reached by mule from here. I shared this with Mimmo.

"I wouldn't doubt it," Mimmo said. "Although I believe there is a new road that goes to another Greek village, Roghudi."

Three old ladies sat outside their houses, blankly staring at us. Two dark-haired children with Down's syndrome faces regarded us with a bit more curiosity. At the church we parked and walked out to the edge of the Norman wall.

I realized that we had arrived at siesta time; the town felt empty, as if it had been evacuated. So far the only beautiful thing about Roccaforte was the view out above the Aspromonte tree line. In front of us an almost mythical landscape unfolded. The sandy riverbed slithered through jagged peaks and led out to a hazy horizon. I could just make out the trickle of a stream cutting through the bed of the once-powerful Amendolea River. In the distance, where the river reached the Ionian Sea, the sun cut through the clouds and shot down to the water in a blaze.

Francesca, not yet over her nausea, waited in the car. Mimmo and I walked to a doorway covered with beads. I thought that it might be a café, but it turned out to be the entrance to someone's house. An old man approached us. His gray eyes glowed in an un-shaven face.

"Excuse me," Mimmo said. "Is there a place to get something to eat here?"

The man adjusted his head in a way that said he didn't understand.

"Mangiare," Mimmo said. "Is there any place around here to eat?"

The man shook his head, then spouted off something completely incomprehensible to me. Usually I can understand a little bit of dialect, but this language didn't even seem Latinate.

As we walked off, Mimmo said to me, without a hint of irony, "I'm sorry, but it's all Greek to me."

The road to Roghudi was yet another hour. Mimmo said that he could take me there. Perhaps it would be nicer than Roccaforte. Or, if we hurried, we could make it to Scilla, on the other coast, by sunset. I had wanted a chance to see the legendary home of the six-headed sea monster, so we drove just far enough across the village to see Roghudi in the distance, set snugly in the saddle between two mountain peaks. It was smaller than Roccaforte, and its only distinguishing feature was a kind of watchtower or concrete silo poking above the village.

Francesca came to life a couple of hours later, as we returned to civilization. In the village of Chorio, we stopped at a little roadside café. I offered to treat. Mimmo and I each ordered a *panino.*

Francesca gleefully ordered. "I'd like a panino con prosciutto crudo. And a panino con formaggio e piccantino. Oh, yes, a bag of chips. Oh, and can I have an aranciata? And a limonata?"

Mimmo opened his billfold, but I motioned for him not to worry about it. "I'm sorry," he said. "She's very poor, and she doesn't get to go places much. But I have no idea how she can eat so much."

"Musolino was not a thief," Mimmo was saying. "He only took back from the padroni what they took from the peasants." We were talking about how far Musolino's travels took him.

"He went everywhere," Mimmo said. "He would be here in Montebello one day, and the next day someone would say they'd seen him way over on the other side of the mountains in Delianuovo. But he never stole from the peasants. On his travels, whenever he ate something, a fig, for instance, he would leave money, maybe place it by the trunk or hang it on the branches."

Driving along the highway that would take us along the coast to Scilla, Mimmo pointed to a rock formation called Pentedàttilo that looked like a hand with its five fingers joined together, pointing up to the sky. When I looked closely, I saw that there were houses built into the mountains. Mimmo told me that in the 1950s, fearing future earthquakes (and in order not to have to put in plumbing or electricity), the Italian government subsidized the villagers' move to new apartment buildings farther down the mountain. The old village had been virtually abandoned ever since.

Scilla is a dragon's head emerging from the water. I climbed it from behind and looked down, remembering the passage from *The Odyssey*:

> *There was Scylla, and on the other side godly Charybdis*
> *Sucked back terribly the salt water of the sea.*
> *Whenever she disgorged, like a basin in a large fire,*
> *She seethed, all stirred up. And from overhead, foam*
> *Fell down on both sides of the peaks of the crags,*
> *And when she swallowed down the salt water of the sea*
> *She appeared all stirred up within, and the rock roared*
> *Terribly about, and the earth appeared underneath*
> *In dark blue sand. Sallow fear seized the men.*

I was surprised to see the waves docilely lapping the rocks, like a Labrador retriever licking the hand of its master. Looking out toward Sicily, I tried to locate the spot where Charybdis might have been. Believed to have been a series of whirlpools in Homer's time, it would have swirled at the narrowest point between Calabria and Sicily. The sea was glassy calm, reflecting the orange-and-red rays of the setting sun. Perhaps with the shifting of ocean plates and the subsequent volcanic activity, the seafloor and coast have all changed. At any rate, Charybdis, like Odysseus—like the Greeks, Saracens, Normans, and Spanish, and the peasants themselves, emigrating to America—had moved on.

We drove back to Reggio with the setting sun warming the car. My eyes fluttered to a close.

"Sleep, sleep," Mimmo said. "I'll wake you when we get to the hotel."

That evening back at La Bracieria, I told Giuseppe, the waiter, the events of the past two days. He seemed pleased and surprised that I had visited Musolino's grave site—or had at least tried to. He shook his head, though, when I told him that I had gone to Roccaforte.

"You didn't get kidnapped, did you?"

"Not unless you consider Mimmo and Francesca kidnappers."

"Do they really speak Greek there?"

"I couldn't understand them for the life of me."

Giuseppe brought me an antipasto platter even larger than the one he had provided two nights before, with homemade ricotta, still bearing the imprint of the wicker basket, pitted olives and roasted peppers with oregano, eggplant and zucchini fritters, and a selection of *bruschette* topped with tomatoes and *piccante*.

Next, he brought me the house special, stuffed calamari grilled on an open fire. And once again he set in front of me a cordial glass of *bergamotto*.

Sweetly drunk, I stumbled out onto the chilly Corso Garibaldi. Its ornate lampposts and balconies at first reminded me of what New Orleans's Bourbon Street might be like without the tourists. Then I stopped for a moment and looked around. I was transported back to

Tampa, Florida, to La Settima Avenue in the Latin Quarter of Ybor City. Perhaps this was what Ybor City had been like in the 1930s.

I was feeling homesick, but not for Florida and not for New York, although I missed Martha. Knowing that soon my trip was coming to an end, I was homesick for Gimigliano and the people I knew there.

TRAVELING AT NIGHT THROUGH
ROWS OF OLIVE TREES

JUNE OR JULY, and the figs will arrive," Giuseppe said, nodding toward the trees in the distant fields. Red herbs blanketed the ground all around the trees. "Maybe they'll be ripe when you come back for the Festa della Madonna di Porto."

I was already excited about returning in just two months with Martha and my parents; it made going away less difficult.

Giuseppe had two clients back south in Brancaleone, which we had driven through on our trip a couple of weeks earlier, along the roads leading to the Aspromonte Mountains. Compared with his trip to Apulia (which hadn't been quite the business catastrophe Giuseppe had expected), this was just a country drive.

We sped down the coast, the bright blue sea to our left and the dark, forbidding mountains to our right. Giuseppe pointed to a distant city on a hill. "I think that's San Luca, where Corrado Alvaro was from."

Calabria's greatest twentieth-century writer, Alvaro, born in 1895 (three years after my grandfather was born), wrote about peasant struggle in such novels as *Revolt in Aspromonte*, which was published in 1932. Leslie Gardiner, in *South to Calabria*, places Alvaro in the pantheon of Italian writers: "The primitive communities of Trieste produced Svevo; those of Sicily produced Pirandello; from the Abruzzi came Benedetto Croce and from Sardinia, Grazia Deledda; and the poor highlands of southern Calabria contributed Corrado Alvaro to the literary galaxy of the twentieth century." No other Calabrese had written so evocatively about his region. He beautifully depicted the harsh lives of its people and explained their strong code of ethics. Unfortunately, nowadays, Alvaro's star burns less bright.

In Bovalino Marina, one of the reputed sequestering towns, Giuseppe had a hard time finding the store he was looking for. After a few wrong turns we finally arrived, but the store's gates had been lowered.

"*Cullu ruputu e sensa cerasa,*" Giuseppe said, which literally translates from dialect as "Busted ass and no cherries," or "I busted my ass for nothing."

"Why the ass and cherries?" I asked.

Giuseppe explained the story in terms of his own history.

Ten kids would set out to play just outside groves of cherry trees. (Giuseppe proudly noted that the trees in the mountains, where he lived, blossomed first.) While they were playing, five of the kids would run into the fields and climb the cherry trees. Whenever the owner looked out his window or passed by, he'd simply see children playing in his field—no harm in that.

However, it was only a matter of time before the padrone figured out their plan. He would run through the grove with a stick and beat the ass of the first boy he found. Since all the boys had spread out, the others could make away with their cherries. There was always one scapegoat. All the boys would go home with their cherries except for the one boy who would come home with a sore *culo* and no cherries to show for it.

Farther down the coast was Brancaleone. This was one of the few towns that Giuseppe admitted to liking.

At first I couldn't understand the attraction. The buildings that lined the road, all one or two stories high and nicely painted, reminded me of North Miami Beach in the 1970s; charming, but so what?

"It's a small town that has been spending money on making itself attractive to tourists," Giuseppe explained. "And it's been doing it the right way. Slowly, tastefully."

You could see the ocean from the road. I breathed in a lungful of air—the smell of the ocean mixed with orange blossoms, sweet and pungent and soothing.

Giuseppe greeted the store owner, a man roughly my age. They set about talking. A blond woman smiled at me. She was small-boned, with light skin and deep-set blue eyes. When she smiled, her eyeteeth protruded from her gums, but this didn't detract from her beauty. She was soft-spoken and smiled effortlessly.

Her name was Mirella Bala. The name sounded Italian, but she explained that she had moved here from Albania four years ago. She was now twenty-two; she had an Italian boyfriend and said that she had pretty much adapted to Italy.

"Life here is better," she said, "although I miss my family back in Albania. But the Italians have been very nice to me and my parents."

As we left the city, the modern apartments and strip stores struck me as suburban American. One of the last buildings I saw was a Range Rover dealership.

We returned north. At Gioiosa, the northernmost edge of the Aspromonte Mountains, we turned toward the center of Calabria. We passed Mammola, then sped through Calabria's newest *autostrada*, a series of suspended highways and tunnels that had been cut through the granite. Giuseppe kept turning to me as he talked. "Mammola has a decent cultural museum, but the village is nothing to look at."

I looked at the road ahead of us, hoping he would do the same.

Giuseppe looked at me, at the road, then back at me. Did he register my discomfort? "This is one of the most dangerous highways in

Calabria, not for robberies but because this valley acts like a wind tunnel. When it rains, the winds are so strong that you can't see in front of you. On the rare occasion when it snows, forget about it."

Giuseppe was trying to meet a client in a town called Taurianova, which lay in the shadow of the Aspromonte Mountains almost to the other coast. On the way we passed through a town called Cinquefrondi, known for its olive oil.

I couldn't believe how fast we were going or how much land we were covering. It had taken days to travel from one coast to the other in Norman Douglas's time. I was slightly envious of the travelers of that time who would actually have gotten to know each road and path. They had been forced to become intimate with a country in which each village is a country unto itself. I knew that my grandfather had seen more of the United States within the first months of his arrival than he had seen of Calabria in all his life. Traveling in Calabria had been far too dangerous then.

The valley road to Taurianova was lined with mythically proportioned olive trees, the tallest I had ever seen. Some must have been a hundred feet tall. They reached across the road, forming a seemingly endless canopy that blotted out the sky.

"A shortcut," Giuseppe said. He slowed the car and turned onto a small road. Here, next to smaller olive trees, were some of the few freestanding houses I had seen in Calabria. They looked like American ranch houses, complete with driveways. It was as if we had taken a detour from the the Middle Ages straight to wealthy modernity. I thought about Giuseppe and realized that he, too, straddled the time periods. He knew the literal meanings of folksy sayings, and he knew how, and preferred, to make bread the old-fashioned way. He picked herbs and grew vegetables. But he was also an entrepreneur, he was well read, and he knew the ironies of the world around him. While he enjoyed leisurely strolls through the woods scavenging for porcini mushrooms or walking through his garden picking figs, he became annoyed at the people of Calabria who, to him, couldn't look beyond their fields of mushrooms and their own fig trees. The engines of progress had long shifted from steam to gas, but the Calabresi preferred mule carts.

"Look at all the olives, look at them," Giuseppe said. "More olives grow here than anywhere else, with the exception, perhaps, of parts of Spain." He sighed. "And with all these olives, or the oranges or figs or onions or artichokes, for that matter, do you ever hear of anything coming from Calabria? No, no, you don't. And why? Because of Calabrese *pride.*"

"Their pride?" I said. Then I realized that he was being sarcastic.

He looked at me. "Yes, their pride. They don't want anyone else telling them what to do; they want to control their own land, their own manufacturing.

"All these olive trees. The farmers could easily do what they do in Tuscany: form a union, pool their fields together, and produce massive amounts of olive oil—and rich, green olive oil! And they don't. Why? Because they are stuck in the old ways. They refuse to change. *Testa dura!*" he barked, rapping his knuckles on his head.

I couldn't help thinking how in the heavily industrial, conglomerated, mass-produced, pasteurized and homogenized United States, people were yearning for a return to simpler times with mom-and-pop companies. Here in Calabria you bought your olive oil not from stores but from neighbors, or you bartered it for, say, some fragrant, potent miniature strawberries.

Of course, nowadays entrepreneurially minded Calabresi are everywhere, and many of them are trying to use the indigenous agriculture to their advantage. At a time when everyone is looking for organic produce, the lack of large-scale farming has nicely poised Calabria to fill that need; here the farmland has been largely untouched by pesticides (though I did see many private gardens coated with them). More and more in specialty stores in New York, I've been finding food products from Calabria touting their organic origins.

It was almost nine at night by the time we pulled into the village of Rizziconi. The piazza was run-down and completely empty, except for a tiny, clean *tabaccheria*, which we entered just before closing time. The two old ladies behind the counter looked up and, after a moment's pause, called out, "Ah, Pino!" using Giuseppe's nickname.

"We had no idea you were coming," the younger of the women said.

"I've been trying to call since this morning, but no one picked up," he said. "I was worried that you had moved or that something was wrong."

"No, we've been here all day."

"And you didn't hear the phone ring?"

"That's funny, it hasn't rung all day."

For Americans, this would have been bizarre, but for these older women, all was just as it should have been. No one really needs to call a store.

Giuseppe took out his cell phone and dialed the number. "Listen," he said, and held the phone up to the woman's ear. "I'm getting the ringing signal, but it's not ringing here."

"Oh, my gosh, how is that? I wonder what calls we missed," one woman asked, more out of curiosity than concern.

An old man who had been standing by the cash registers looked at the phone. "Maria, could it be the fax machine?"

"Oh, my God. I forgot to switch it back to phone," the older woman said.

"When did you use the fax?"

The two women thought about it, looked at each other, then began giggling.

"We turned it on to receive a fax, but that was the day before yesterday," one woman said, turning to Giuseppe. "Thanks, Giuseppe."

Giuseppe and the two women caught up on what had been happening since they last saw each other—almost a year ago. I was starving, but knowing Giuseppe, I realized it would be at least a half hour before we got out of there.

I walked outside, looking in vain for a pizzeria. The piazza was truly empty. Naked lightbulbs lighted the street in a way that reminded me of the postwar Italian movies set in Rome or Naples. A young man, a teenager perhaps—I couldn't tell—walked out onto the street, sputtering with laughter. He was out for the night. Italians don't keep their disabled children indoors; they aren't embarrassed by them, and in any case, the streets are safe enough.

I looked the other way, and between two buildings I saw a tall shadow limping its way toward me. I focused on the shadow. An old man walked out of the alleyway and passed under the light in front of the church. With the aid of his cane, he hobbled his way home for dinner.

CATANZARO

"THIS PLACE IS LIKE AN ESCHER PAINTING!" Thessy screamed in frustration. "That's it, Catanzaro is Escherville!"

I had come late to the Giallorossa, the soccer sports bar and pizzeria, my first night back in town and had taken a table in the back but with a full view of the TV screen. It was showing the latest Reggio loss, which would kick it back down to Serie B.

I noticed a woman sitting by herself directly under the TV, reading. Her long graying hair was pulled back in a ponytail, and her angular face was rosy white.

The waiter was uncharacteristically brusque for a Calabrese, but he paused a moment when I asked who the mysterious woman was. "I don't know," he said. "But she comes in here from time to time—and always by herself."

"Does she speak Italian?"

"Yes, but she's not Italian." He looked over at her. "She must be English or American."

For some time I had been anxious to speak to someone, anyone, an outsider with whom I could compare notes. Calabria isn't Venice or Florence, where every other person you see is a tourist oohing or aahing or complaining about the rude Italian waiters. I approached the table and I addressed her in Italian. *"Mi scusi, signora, ma ho pensato che, forse, Lei parla l'inglese?"*

She looked up from her book, her blue eyes beautiful but cold. *"A chi vuole conoscere?"* And who wants to know?

"I'm sorry," I said hastily in Italian. "I'm from New York, and for a moment I thought you might be, too." Embarrassed, I walked away.

"Wait," she called out to me in accented English. "You're from New York? So you speak English?" Her voice almost cracked.

"Yes," I said. "But I'm sorry for bothering you."

"Oh, no. My God, please, please join me," she said. "Could you?"

"I'd be thrilled," I said, and I really was.

I had barely sat down before she began talking in English. "I'm sorry to seem so rude. But I thought that perhaps you were some young Italian man who, at night's end, was desperate for a female companion."

I learned that Thessy was Swiss. She and her husband, a painter from New York City, had lived in Florence now for several years. A specialist in historical costume design, she had gone to Urbino a few years before, after an earthquake had cracked open tombs there that dated back to the Middle Ages, in order to study the clothes the corpses were wearing.

Now Thessy was in Catanzaro, far from the Renaissance riches of Urbino and Florence. She had accepted a well-paying job at a newly formed technical design school in Calabria, figuring it might be exciting to teach in this poor southern province. She had negotiated an arrangement to teach three days a week and fly back to Florence to be with her husband on the weekends and had signed a yearlong contract.

But this weekend she was stuck in Catanzaro because of an airline strike that had begun on Friday. Everyone knows of Italian strikes; *sciopero* is one of the first words tourists traveling anywhere in Italy learn. The railroad workers go on strike, the airline workers strike, truckers strike. But an entire industry doesn't strike at the same time. It strikes by division: one day it's the pilots; the next it's the controllers. The strikes are reported in the newspapers a week ahead of time, and no single group can strike more than once in the same month.

I was scheduled to return to New York in five days, but when I read in the papers that yet another segment of the airlines, the food services, was going to strike the day I was supposed to leave (after which was a holiday, then another scheduled strike), I decided to fly out a day earlier rather than stay another week. I needed to get back to work, and I didn't want to impose on my relatives any longer.

I would have enjoyed an extra weekend in Catanzaro, but for Thessy, it was a life sentence, which led her to describe the city as Escherville. The haphazard planning of the city, with its incongruous mix of old and new architecture, did resemble an Escher Möbius strip.

The owner of the restaurant, a man with longish graying hair and a mustache, came to the table and asked us in dialect if we wanted anything else. Thessy ordered another liter of wine. The owner gave us, or rather me, an impressive grin, cocked his head, and said, "Right away."

"Look," Thessy said. "They think they're matchmakers. That they've created a couple."

I asked her about her students. I figured that as a Swiss she was probably underwhelmed by Italian education in general and likely appalled by the schools in the south. But she said the students were better prepared than she had expected.

"They are, after all, somewhat better educated than the Americans I teach.

"Really!" she continued, in response to my dubious look. "The Americans are rich, so sure of themselves, but they have no awareness of anything else around them. They want, want, want."

"And the Italian students?"

"In general, very good." She emptied the liter. "Down here,

though, the girls just want to get married. The boys, they are still boys. But that's all over Italy."

The waiter brought our bill and made an extravagant display of placing it in front of us. We left the money and stood up.

"Oh, my God," Thessy said, "I am drunk."

"That's okay," I said. "Me, too. But don't worry. I'll walk you to your hotel."

"Where are you staying?" Thessy asked.

"Albergo Grand Hotel."

"Ah, that'll be easy then. That's where I'm staying."

I offered her my arm, so she could descend the stairs easily.

"Oh, yes, very good." She giggled. "Let's give them something to talk about tonight."

A cool Ionian breeze from the mountains funneled through Catanzaro's streets.

Rather then walk along the main drag, I suggested we take a couple of side streets, which I hoped might be more scenic.

"Be careful of these potholes, Mark," Thessy warned loudly. "They are the product of poor urban planning. This city is built on a mountain of sand—sand! And below the concrete streets pits have been known to open up. It happens all throughout the south. . . . Just last year in Naples an electrician was doing work on the side of a building, and his ladder and he were instantaneously sucked up by the earth. He was never found!"

It was past eleven. Two young men hanging around in front of a dully lit café nodded as we passed.

"Look at these streets! At one time, beautiful architecture, I'm sure. But now, look at the eyesores that these poor people have put up," she said, indicating a square cinder-block building. "What other city would let something like this be built?"

I could think of many places in Europe and in the United States, even New York, that had at one time allowed ugly, cheap buildings to be constructed.

"They're not so bad," I said.

"You're an American," she said. "You see the good in every-thing."

"You've been living in the north too long," I said. "Calabria has a bad reputation throughout Italy, I know, which makes it easy—acceptable—for everyone to see the ugliness, the dirt."

I did recognize that, compared with other Italian cities, Catanzaro was one ugly, poorly planned mess. But my eyes had chosen to focus on the medieval facades tucked away in side streets or the tiny alleys lined with potted flowers.

We came out on Piazza Indipendenza, directly in front of city hall and our hotel. Thessy stopped. "Look at that monstrosity," she cried. The focal point of the piazza was a concrete staircase leading nowhere. Thessy said, "We should get back to the hotel." She seemed exhausted by so much ugliness.

At the front desk the clerk locked eyes with me, unsmiling. I knew he knew which rooms were ours, but he would not reach for the keys until we asked for them by number. He made a conscious effort not to create a sense of familiarity.

"Do you notice the people who stay here who gather around seven-thirty or so in the morning?" Thessy asked.

"I'm never up that early," I said.

"They are all lawyers," she said. "The clean-cut, boring ones are state lawyers, and the ones with the long hair and jewelry are the ones hired by the mob."

From the outside the five-story building looked like a generic new apartment building anywhere in Italy, but the entire first floor housed the university where Thessy worked. I had agreed to meet her there two days after our dinner. She had told the directors about me, and they were eager to meet me. I stepped into a very modern office, where a secretary greeted me and called the director.

The director was a slim man in his mid-thirties wearing wire-frame glasses. He called me into the office of the university's president and vice-president—his father and mother, respectively. His mother was curious about my name and told me her mother was also a Rotella. The director then gave me a tour of the school. It was modern and spare. The classrooms all had brand-new chairs, desks, and new Apple computers. Thessy had told me that the school received considerable grants from the state and charged its students only a nominal tuition. She had praised the school's progressive thinking and adventurous curriculum, but she had the impression that under-the-table deals enabled the school to continue.

Just before I was to go, the director took me to Thessy's class. Her students, all women, were presenting their final designs. One design was of a brightly colored purse, another of a wedding dress. Thessy had described the prevalent style as "tacky, over the top." Perhaps it was, but of course, Calabria had given birth to Gianni Versace.

Thessy walked me out. She said, "You know, Marco, yesterday was a beautiful day. I walked all over Catanzaro. I found those streets you were talking about, and you know, I finally saw Catanzaro through your eyes—with your American optimism. And there *are* some very attractive—appealing—elements to the city. There is actually some charm here. But I could be feeling that only because I'm leaving today."

That evening in Gimigliano I met Giuseppe at his store in time for the *passeggiata*. Giuseppe's son Domenico, still home from the university on vacation, was watching the store. The three of us walked along Corso America. It was a beautiful spring afternoon. I took off my jacket and breathed in the soft mountain air. Flowers seemed to have bloomed overnight in all the balcony flowerpots.

"Ah," Giuseppe said, "you can practice your Russian." He pointed to a tall blond couple in warm-up suits and white sneakers.

Giuseppe introduced us. Peter and Marlissa were in their early twenties and spoke Italian with heavy Slavic accents. They were from Ukraine and had been living here for a year as paid caretakers of an elderly couple whose sons lived in the north and who had outlived their other relatives.

"It's lonely here," Marlissa said. "It's tough when you don't have family. You say hello to people as you pass, but you never really get to know anyone else."

The money was good, much better than in Ukraine. In another two years they thought they'd have saved enough to go back to Ukraine to buy a house.

"You must miss your family," I said, missing my wife just then.

"Actually, my father died a long time ago, and I am bringing my mother here next month to live with us," Marlissa whispered. "But it's difficult, because we can never leave Gimigliano. We can't go to Catanzaro to meet other people our age."

"So your employers need a lot of care?" I said.

"No, we are here illegally," Marlissa said, again quietly, though not as if she were hiding; in fact, it was impossible to imagine that anyone in Gimigliano did not know. "You see, if we get caught without our papers, they will send us back."

I wondered if this circumspection was the result of years of Communist fear.

"Anyway," Marlissa continued, "when a policeman—or any man here—sees a blond Ukrainian woman traveling by herself, they automatically think she's a whore."

Peter nodded in agreement.

At dinner that evening I told Giuseppe and his family that I had cut my trip short by two days to avoid the strike and would be leaving the day after next. Giuseppe looked hurt, and his wife, Elena, seemed disappointed.

"But what about Longobucco?" Giuseppe said. "You haven't seen Longobucco. It's a long way away, but beautiful. The artisans there are known for their wood carving."

"I'll be back in two months," I reminded them. But as I spoke, two months seemed a long way away.

"*Va bene*, we'll plan a big dinner for you tomorrow night," Giuseppe announced.

"I think I'm going to have dinner with my family tomorrow night," I said. I felt an emptiness in my belly when I saw the look on Giuseppe's face. Giuseppe was the reason that I had found my family, the reason why I continued to return. He and Elena had become family. I didn't know how to express this to them.

"But what about the limoncello we made?" Giuseppe asked.

The *limoncello* was to have been our goodbye drink. I felt selfish. It seemed rude not to have left time for them to send me off, to bid me farewell.

"It'll be warmer when you come back in June," Elena said. Giuseppe looked out the window and said nothing. "And Martha, she's coming with you, yes?"

I assured Elena she was.

Giuseppe quickly turned around and said, "We'll open the bottle when you come back." He seemed to be forcing a smile, a Calabrese smile that let me know nothing was bothering him. But it bothered me.

Elena had prepared *fraguni*, calzones filled with eggs, ricotta, and chopped parsley, followed by a simple pasta with tomato sauce, then fava beans cooked in their shells with bread crumbs and pecorino cheese. It was a meal that made me homesick in advance for Gimigliano. For dessert, she brought out dried figs that had been halved and filled with crushed hazelnuts and chopped mandarin orange rind, then baked to warm softness.

"You and your father," she said, shaking her head. "I always have to have figs around."

MY GRANDMOTHER'S STORY

I WAS WONDERING when you were going to stop by," my aunt Caterina said.

"I know, I'm so sorry," I said. Once again I felt terrible. I had seen Zia Caterina at Zia Angela's house, but I hadn't gotten around to visiting her before. I added feebly, "I have been traveling so much. I knew that you were in Catanzaro visiting your stepdaughter." I didn't mention that because she lived alone, I'd thought she wouldn't want to have to cook for me.

"That was only three days," she said. "You've been here a lot longer than that."

She disappeared into the kitchen, and I looked around the dining room. Pictures of Caterina and her husband, who had died of a heart attack about ten years before, lined the shelves of a dark-brown china cabinet and matching sideboard. A potbellied stove, its black body and gold trim shining, filled one corner.

She returned with a huge pan of lasagna and poured us each a glass of red wine. I took a bite of the lasagna and tasted ground pork and sliced prosciutto.

Of all my relatives in Italy, Caterina most reminds me of my grandmother. She has the same smooth, wrinkle-free skin, and the corners of her eyes turn down when she smiles, making her face seem sad even when she is happy. Caterina was born in 1925 to my grandmother's eldest sister, Francesca. Twelve years Caterina's senior, *my* grandmother, Angelina, had been born in 1912, the second youngest of twelve brothers and sisters. Her father, Francesco Critelli, was a severe man who had had six children with his first wife, who died giving birth to the sixth, then six more with a second wife. The eldest of this set was Francesca, Caterina's mother, and the second to last was Angela, my grandmother, who was called Angelina. She was twelve when her sister gave birth to Caterina in 1925.

"My grandmother must have hated to leave this place," I said. "When I was growing up, she always seemed so sad to have left her family behind."

"We really missed her," Caterina said. "But she was happy to leave here."

"Happy?" I said. "I thought it was an arranged marriage, that she was dragged away from her family."

Caterina took a sip of her wine. "It was arranged; her half brother Tommaso set her up. I can't tell you how excited she was to leave, to have a husband. You see, Angelina's mother had died in 1932, and her father had just died in 1935."

Caterina remembered my great-grandfather, Francesco Critelli, as a strong, quiet man, six feet tall, with blue eyes and leathery skin. He was gone most of the year, working as a quarryman excavating white marble from Carrara, and when he was home, he spoke very little. When he was in his seventies, he broke his hip on the job, and after almost four years of lying in bed, he finally succumbed. When he died, Angelina felt the loneliness of the empty house. Soon afterward Caterina had moved in. "She was more like a sister to me than an aunt," Caterina remembered.

It was an unusually warm day in March when Caterina heard a knock at the door. She opened it to find an older man standing there. He had the same harsh features as Angela's father.

"I've come to see Angelina Critelli," the man said. "My name is

Filippo Rotella." He said he was a friend of Tommaso, Angelina's brother, in Danbury, Connecticut.

Caterina judged by his accent that he was from Gimigliano Superiore.

"She's in the fields. She'll be here this afternoon."

Filippo left an envelope for Angelina. "I'll come back this afternoon."

In her heart, Caterina knew that this man had come to take Angelina away.

At age twenty-four, Angelina was the only child in her family yet to marry. In Calabrese families at that time, the responsibility of taking care of aging parents often fell to the last unmarried daughter. Now that Angelina's parents had died, she was free to get married, free to leave. When Angelina came home that afternoon, Caterina was angry at her.

"An old man came by this afternoon," Caterina said. "He was so old and ugly!"

Caterina paused in the middle of her story to duck into the kitchen. She reappeared with a platter of turkey breast sautéed in garlic and oil, a dish of *baccalà*, salt cod, baked with oil and lemon, and, as if she hadn't brought out enough, a bowl of piping hot peas and garlic. Then she resumed her story.

Filippo Rotella and Angelina Critelli were married almost two months later, at the Santa Maria Assunta in Gimigliano Inferiore. Then Filippo went back to Connecticut to earn money for my grandmother's passage to join him. My grandmother's brothers Giuseppe and Tommaso were living there, so she would have family, a husband, and with luck a family of her own. Within a month after Filippo's return to the United States, however, Angelina got word that Giuseppe had died, so she would have one fewer family member in America.

My grandmother boarded the SS *Conte di Savoia* in Naples on November 5, 1936. Two weeks later, Filippo met her in New York City with the news that Tommaso, too, had died. So now she had left a place where everyone knew everyone to go where she knew no one and no one knew her.

A year almost to the day after she arrived, my grandmother gave birth to my father, Giuseppe, named after Filippo's father, followed by Francesco, Tommaso, Rosa, and Saveria. Although my grandmother never learned English during the sixty years she lived in Connecticut, she had given her children American names: Joseph, Frank, Tom, and Rose; only the youngest daughter, Saveria, received an Italian name.

My family knew her as a sad woman, never content with anything, always wanting more for her family. But Caterina recalled her differently. "I remember," she said, "your grandmother always, always smiled."

Caterina offered to take me to see Zio Giuseppe, the widower of Grandma's sister, also named Caterina. My aunt guided me along Via Assunta and stopped in front of a plain-looking house, one of the least charming in the alley. It had almost no ornamentation, not even flowers in the windows, but in the afternoon the front windows got sunlight at least.

"This was where your grandmother was born, where that old, ugly man appeared one day," Caterina said. "But like so many of the houses here, it's abandoned."

"Who owns it?" I asked

"It's still owned by the Critelli family."

A couple of alleys beyond was Zio Giuseppe's house. Inside, he sat in a wheelchair, wearing a knit cap and two heavy sweaters. Two five-year-old boys babbled next to him. He could do very little but smile. Nearing one hundred, he'd outlived almost everyone.

"Are those two boys his great-grandsons?" I asked

"No." Caterina sighed. "They are the children of the couple hired to care for him."

"Doesn't he have anyone else?"

Caterina shook her head and puckered her mouth. "It's a shame. No, his children live in the north, and they have hired this family to care for him."

My father and grandma had stayed here when they visited the

village forty years ago. Zio Giuseppe had been away in Canada, so my father never got to meet him. But he and his mother stayed with Grandma's sister, Zio Giuseppe's wife.

My father had told me how on the morning of the Festa della Madonna di Porto he decided to lie out in the sun on the patio and drink his coffee and eat his brioche. He heard women's voices scolding and young girls giggling below him. He looked down over the railings at the tiny piazza below, where about twenty older women, all in the Gimiglianese black skirts and vests and white lacy blouses, formed a circle around just as many teenage girls by raising their skirts and joining hands with the women on either side. The young girls, giggling more from excitement than embarrassment, stood in the middle of the older women and stripped off their daily clothing to change into their festival costumes.

My father, who was twenty-two years old and just out of the navy, decided to put to use his brand-new palm-size 16-millimeter camera. He lay down flat on the deck behind a row of potted plants, held the camera just over the balcony, and began filming away.

"*Che cosa?* What's that sound?" a woman said. The camera clicked away. Another woman noticed. Then the talking stopped, and my father lifted his finger from the button. The talking resumed, then the singing, and my father filmed the singing and the undressing. After a few more minutes he stopped filming and went back inside, wondering how he would ever get the film developed. When he set the camera down, he saw a roll of film on the table. He had forgotten to load the camera.

Zio Giuseppe looked at me with delighted consternation.

"*Zio Giuseppe, quest' u figliu di Angelina,*" Caterina said to him. "*Ricordu Angelina?*"

The old man nodded his head. He remembered my grandmother. Then he said something in dialect and pointed to the wall.

"He says that this is your grandmother's father," Caterina said in Italian. She pointed to a photograph on the wall, framed in oval rosewood. I had seen this picture in my grandparents' house. The man in the photo stared into the room, his clear eyes seeming to sear through the photo, an impression heightened by strong cheekbones and a handlebar mustache. Then I noticed something else. I looked closely, thinking maybe it was only a hole in the faded photo.

"Is that an earring he's wearing?" I asked Aunt Caterina.

She squinted at the photo again and smiled. "Ah, yes," she said. "He always wore an earring."

"Why, was it fashionable then?"

"Well, some men did wear them, but it was to help his hearing."

"How did it help his hearing?"

"Well, it was thought—this was before there were doctors here—it was thought that the gold ring would attract sound to the ear."

During my father's visit in 1962, he had developed a boil on his right forearm. It grew larger each day until his uncle took him to the local doctor, who was playing *scopa*, a card game, in a bar connected to his office. The doctor, who had just dealt, told my father to wait in his office. My father sat in a stiff-backed chair. On a tray on the table next to him was a metal trough that held a couple of scalpels and other metal tools, all of which were beginning to show signs of rust.

About fifteen minutes later the doctor walked in, cigar in mouth, reeking of wine. He examined my father's arm, then picked up one of the rusty scalpels. My father yanked his arm away. "You're using that?"

"What else do you want me to do?"

My father thanked the doctor and walked out of the office. Over the next few days the boil swelled to the size of a golf ball, and my father developed a fever. There was talk of taking him to Catanzaro. Then one evening my grandmother brought in three old women—the local witches, my father called them.

They began reciting the Ave Maria, then broke into some chants in a dialect my father didn't recognize. In Calabria, Catholicism had long since assimilated the older pagan beliefs and rituals. And in the absence of good doctors, the Calabresi trusted these wisewomen more than any professional.

Then one of the women slathered a mudlike substance on my father's arm. The next day another of the women brought a bowl of wild herbs. She stuck a wad of them into her toothless mouth and gummed them down to a wet, fibrous mass, which she pressed to my father's forearm. It was warm and gooey. She repeated this for three nights. On the fourth day, just before lunch, my father felt an ooze down his arm. The boil had finally burst, leaving an inch-long scar that he has to this day.

Caterina and I were about to leave Zio Giuseppe's when another photo caught my eye. It was of a good-looking young man in a three-button suit with wide lapels, standing against a stone structure. He had a pencil-thin mustache and was holding a walking stick. Tucked into the bottom of the frame were photos of three other men.

"These men are all your grandmother's brothers," Caterina said. She explained that they were memorial photos.

"And who's that?" I asked, mesmerized by the larger photo.

"That's your grandmother's youngest brother, Salvatore." Caterina crossed herself. "He died in Africa in 1942 in an English prisoner of war camp. His death affected your grandmother more than anyone's."

I know that my grandmother had asked for me, her eldest grandson, to be named Salvatore when I was born in 1967. But she probably knew that, by this time, my father wanted nothing more than to be fully American. And my mother, who came from Montreal when she was ten years old and whose first language was French, probably wanted the same. In the end, my parents gave me as American a name as they could find, down to the hard *k*.

I kissed Zio Giuseppe on both cheeks and said goodbye. The kids followed us out.

"I remembered when your grandmother died," Caterina said. "She died in February, but I didn't hear until August. I suspected, because I didn't hear from her. I telephoned and left a message, but no one called back, or there was no one there to return my call. It was awful. I felt like I should have been there with her."

———

When I told Zia Angela, Zio Mimmo, and my cousins that I'd be leaving a couple of days early, they seemed hurt. "On your last night we were all going to take you back to Il Semaforo after the beach," Luisa said. The weather had finally gotten warm enough, and the day before my scheduled departure was May Day, a holiday.

Instead, on my last night Sabrina and Masimo invited to dinner everyone who had been together during the *Pasquetta* in the Sila. Sabrina served another amazing meal, and Masino brought out jugs of his father's wine.

They raised their glasses to send me off, wishing me a good flight and a speedy return.

Masino turned to me and shook his head. *"Cazzo americano!"*

You American dickhead.

Part V

GIMIGLIANO

AN ITALIAN-AMERICAN

I AM HALF FRENCH-CANADIAN, but you wouldn't know it by talking to me. I look Italian, I'm gregarious and friendly, and I gesture a lot with my hands—just like my father. And you wouldn't guess it about my sister, Michelle, either. She speaks with a hint of a Southern accent, but her dark hair and flawless olive skin betray her Italian genes, and just about the only food she and her husband eat (he happens to be of Sicilian descent) is Italian. It's hard to guess even about my Montreal-born mother, Murielle Marie La Fontaine—that is, until you hear her talk to my Acadian grandmother in French. (I grew up thinking that everyone's grandparents spoke with foreign accents.)

Our family has been overrun by all things Italian. It's not because my father has ruled the family with an Italian fist. Also, ours was not the stereotypical *famiglia* who entertained masses of relatives every Sunday dinner. But something in me longed for that sprawling Italian family.

My father, the eldest of his siblings, left the Calabrese enclave of Danbury for work down south in Florida by way of Atlanta, Georgia. Like his father before him, he moved away from family to find better work, and each time he moved, he seemed to slide further away from the culture of his parents.

But Italian identity runs strong, even if not always apparent. Our family ate Italian food almost exclusively (though my mother did futilely try to introduce us to other cuisines, including her own). My parents ate at local Italian restaurants and shopped at Fante's, an Italian deli in downtown St. Petersburg. My father kept track of famous people of Italian lineage, even when their names had been anglicized: Lou Costello of Abbott and Costello, Anne Bancroft, Dion and Fabian, Alan Alda, Ernest Borgnine, Bernadette Peters, Perry Como, Bobby Darin, Jim Croce. He'd even heard somewhere that Bruce Springsteen had Italian in him, and he insisted that Joe Namath must be part Italian.

Though my father doesn't recall living amid much prejudice in Danbury, he remembers being beaten to the point of tears by Irish nuns on the first day of grade school because, having spoken only Italian at home, he could not understand a word they said to him. When as a teenager he ate at the home of his best friend, Marty Keane (who became my godfather), Marty's Irish father would refuse to sit at the table with an Italian. And when he moved to the South, many people feared him as a mafioso or an FBI agent.

For me, growing up in the South, my dark skin and dark hair, as well as the vowel at the end of my last name, always gave away my heritage. (It could also have been the Virgin Mary pendant and gold Italian horn that I wore around my neck.) Once the Southern Baptist father of a girl I was dating greeted me at the door, showed me his gun collection, and said, "Ro-tella. That's Eye-talian, idn't it? Ya'll are good family people, aintcha?" But being recognized as Italian was never unpleasant for me the way it sometimes was for my father's generation, although my father won't admit that prejudice shaped him in any way.

Nor will he admit that our travels made him feel any more Calabrese than he already did. But we speak Italian to each other more; we seek out new Italian food, revel in a dish of fried zucchini flowers or tomatoes and fresh mozzarella even as we laugh at the price; we share with each other any mention of Calabria in the news; he tells me more stories of his childhood. (Martha always jokes that when she and I have kids, they will only be a quarter Italian, but they will think they are 100 percent.)

As my father and I waited for the train to take us from Catanzaro back to Perugia on that first trip, we waited in a relaxed, thoughtful silence. I went downstairs to the bathroom, and when I came back up, I said, "So, Pa, what's been your favorite part of the trip so far?" I knew he was thinking about our trip together. I wanted to hear him say it.

"That five minutes you just spent in the bathroom," he said, without missing a beat.

He wouldn't give in then, and he won't give in now. It must be that Calabrese *testa dura* of his. And yet . . . I notice that he will no longer let slide even the most innocuous-sounding comment if it denigrates southern Italians. When overhearing someone describe Tuscany's beauty and civility in contrast with southern Italy's, for example, he asks just what the speaker means—and then shoots him a firm look that says, "I'm sure you don't really think that." He will likely take offense at some of the descriptions of Calabria in this book.

As for me, my father was right: I am a romantic. With each trip back to Calabria, I've felt myself becoming not only more Calabrese but more Italian. I've struggled with my triple identities, as Italian, Calabrese, and Italian-American, and at one time or another I've believed myself more one than another. But as I returned to Italy again and again, I realized that it wasn't just my response to the Colosseum, the paintings of Michelangelo, the voice of Pavarotti, the poetry of Dante that made me Italian; it was also how I was perceived by my fellow Americans.

It took a trip back to my homeland to discover it, but for me, much of my Italian identity is defined by Italian-American red-sauce restaurants, the local Italian deli, Frank Sinatra, Tony Bennett, Gay Talese, Mario Cuomo. My identity is shaped by the Italian stonemasons who built downtown New York City and constructed churches all over the Northeast; by men and women who can cook mouth-watering *'scarole* and beans. Even Italians who have spent a relatively short time in the States, a year or two, return to Italy a little less Italian than they were before. Back in Italy, anywhere in Italy, a returned son is referred to, often affectionately, as *l'american'*. Whether he wanted to or not, my grandfather shed a thin layer of his Calabrese identity the moment he stepped off the boat. In short, I'm only as Italian as my father is.

I shared these thoughts with my father. He smiled, "What did you expect? Do you think I'm any more Italian than you are?"

CALABRIA, FULL CIRCLE

THE STREETS OF CATANZARO were as empty as I had ever seen them. Not a car passed us along the usually busy Corso Mazzini; not a single one of the city's population of one hundred thousand lingered outside. It was a hot, sunny Sunday in June, the first day of the four-day Festa della Madonna di Porto, and it was siesta time.

Two months had passed, and I was back in Calabria, this time with Martha and my parents. I felt like a century-old bridge, connecting my Old World and New World families.

We'd begun our trip with a few days of Swiss orderliness in Como, an idyllic, though touristy, lake village. The first day there we bought tickets for a ferry across Lake Como; when my father, who presented his passport, asked in Calabrese dialect how much a senior citizen discount would be, the attendant whined an annoying "What?"

It's in the north that I am sometimes aware of my southern heritage, and it's often when I'm with my father, listening to him try to communicate as people strain to understand him, that the feeling becomes acute. While very few people are actually rude, there are instances that make me angry and, sadly, sometimes embarrassed.

After Como we traveled to Milan, where we finally managed to see my aunt Saveria and uncle Cecco, who for the past couple of decades had been dividing their time between Milan, where they worked in a restaurant, and Gimigliano, where they spent two months in the summer. Now their children, Monica and Angelo, both in their early thirties, had careers in Milan, so although Cecco and Saveria were recently retired, they continued to split their time between the two places. Monica was now an architect and, with Angelo, owned a hip Futurist-themed restaurant called Lacerba—a sibling effort inasmuch as Monica had designed the smartly colored, sharp-angled interior, Angelo served as maître d', and a number of their Calabrese friends worked as waiters and cooks.

Almost every night we ate dinner with Monica and her fiancé, Marco, who was, like her, Calabria-born but Milan-educated. The fast-paced lives of Marco, Monica, and Angelo in Milan reminded me of Martha's and mine in New York; like us, they had shed any hint of a regional accent or other clue to their backgrounds—except, that is, for an affinity for Calabrese food.

The day before we left Milan, Aunt Saveria had joined us all for a shopping trip along Corso Vercelli, a central shopping area. She alternately linked arms with me and with my father, with whom she got along as if forty years had not separated them. At one point she stopped and faced him, saying, "Giuseppe, after all these years, why did you finally come back?"

My dad looked at me. "It's him. He wanted to see where the family was from."

She reached out and took my hand. "So if your Marco didn't make you come, would you ever have visited again?"

"No," he said.

There were no hard feelings; no one was upset. That's just how it was, how the world worked. It was enough to be happy that events had brought us together.

When I'd called the Albergo Grand Hotel in Catanzaro to confirm our reservation, the voice on the other end of the line, that of the morning clerk, said, "Of course you're confirmed, Signore Rotella. Don't you remember? You made the reservation with me." The familiar tone in his voice made me eager to go back.

So here we were, in the eerily deserted Corso Mazzini. Everyone was hungry, and the prospect of all the restaurants' being closed made our stomachs feel all the more empty—and me feel all the more responsible for filling them.

I led my family off the *corso* and onto an arched alley, where they waited while I went to check if my old standby Da Salvatore was open. My heart sank when I saw that the sign was down and leaning against the building. Still, I reached for the door. It swung open, and voices burst forth, waiters rushed around, and in the back room a group of children sat at a table festooned with helium balloons.

The maître d', Massimo, came out of the kitchen bearing a stack of plates. *"Signore Rotella, mangia solo oggi?"*

"No, today I've brought my family," I said excitedly. "Do you have a table for four?"

Massimo called to one of the junior waiters, "Table for Signore Rotella and his family—quickly." I stepped out and waved to my wife and parents, who quickly walked down the path just as a half dozen boys and girls, dressed in their Sunday best, emerged and began singing religious songs. They were celebrating their First Holy Communions.

We opted for the day's specials, which arrived at the table with classic Calabrese pacing, meaning just enough time between courses to allow the appetite to reassert itself. After an antipasto of *soppressata*, freshly smoked ricotta, mozzarella, and peppers, a most typical Calabrese dish appeared before us: penne with sautéed tomatoes and spicy sausage, topped with a fresh grating of parmigiano. Then Massimo set down a plate of braciole—thinly sliced veal, rolled around bread crumbs, ground pork, and parmigiano cheese, covered with fresh tomato sauce. Alongside was a layered dish of thinly sliced zucchini, eggplant, mozzarella, and *soppressata*.

Full as we were, my father wanted to know what was for dessert.

"After what you all ate today, signore," the waiter said, "I recommend only fruit—something to help the digestion."

We finished the meal with an espresso and headed back to the hotel to rest. The streets were still desolate, and it was still dry, hot, and windy.

"This feels like a *Star Trek* episode," Martha said.

Just as she spoke, a tour bus stopped in front of Catanzaro's Museum of Modern Art and disgorged a load of what seemed to be Italian pensioners on a field trip. A heavy dark-haired woman, probably in her early thirties, raced to the head of the group, hardly seeming to notice one of the older women clinging to her arm, her feet practically levitating off the ground as she struggled to keep up.

At first mostly Italian was spoken. Then a large man stopped in front of us and bellowed in a thick New York accent, "Ah, geez, more frickin' stairs."

In my several years visiting Calabria, I had never run into a single American tourist, and now, at the sleepiest time of one of the sleepiest days of the year, a busload of New Yorkers seemed to be invading the city.

We followed them to the main lobby, where a Calabrese stamp show was in progress. I introduced myself to the heavy woman, who seemed to be the tour leader. Sure enough, she represented a New York agency that took Italians back to southern Italy. They were mostly second- and third-generation Italians who had never been here before, although some, like the old woman still hanging on to the guide's arm, had been born and raised in Calabria, had even, like my grandmother, kept Calabria so close to them that they had never learned to speak English.

Just as we were approaching the hotel, we heard a series of rhythmic booms coming from another part of the city. Then, a bit closer, we heard the honking of a car horn, followed by another, then several others. Cheers erupted in between the horn blasts.

Like an invading army, cars and *motorini* filed into Corso Mazzini, their drivers and passengers waving flags. Above the cheers, people blew trumpets from scooters that held as many as three strapping Italian teens.

It was a sea of yellow and red. Fathers and sons paraded together or drove by, jammed into cars. One man drove by on a *motorino*, his pubescent daughter clinging to his back with one hand and waving a rippling Catanzaro team flag—the *giallo-rosso*—with the other.

Back at the hotel, the desk clerk was staring out the window as the parade wound around and around the square.

"Sounds like we won," I said with a local's pride.

The manager turned to me and with an uncharacteristic smile said, "We tied."

LIMONCELLO WITH GIUSEPPE

THE TWO-CAR DIESEL TRAIN slowed going into the Gimigliano station. In the parking lot, I saw Giuseppe's car, but no sign of Giuseppe. When the train stopped, we stepped onto the platform and, once again, looked up at Gimigliano Superiore to see the pale yellow houses with red terra-cotta roofs, just as we remembered them. Then we turned to the station to see Giuseppe poking his head out of the station-master's office, his head cocked to the side in his characteristic understated way, his arms open as if to say, "Ah, you've finally arrived."

The sun was bright, and the air dry and crisp. After an exchange of kisses and hugs, Giuseppe drove us up to his house, where Elena greeted us with more kisses and hugs. The house was filled with the warm, welcoming aroma of tomato sauce and *maccheroni*.

Alessio ran past everyone and grabbed my arm. "Marco, Marco," he called, "come look at my new computer game."

"Alessio," Elena said, not really scolding, "say hello to Martha and to Marco's parents."

"Ciao, ciao, ciao," Alessio said, barely pausing to extend his hand. "Marco, *tutto* okay. Let's go see my game now."

Elena brought out meats and cheeses and eggplant that Giuseppe had pickled. We all sat down, and my father and Giuseppe began a conversation in dialect. I managed to discern that they were talking about me. Giuseppe paused for a moment to note, "In Italian, they say *figlio*; in dialect, we say *higliu*, like your father." My father had been referring to "his son."

I marveled at the ease with which my father communicated with Giuseppe and remembered with chagrin the embarrassment I'd felt when he spoke dialect in the north and was misunderstood or treated like just another poor southerner.

Elena brought to the table a large dish of lasagna. Giuseppe poured everyone wine. My father and I drank two glasses for every one of Giuseppe's. Elena brought out dishes of vegetables and more wine for my father and me. A couple of hours passed in talk of food and the growing seasons, punctuated by Giuseppe's narrative of our trips together.

Then Giuseppe stood and announced that it was time for *limoncello*. He brought out the liter bottle of smooth yellow liqueur, which had begun to frost at the bottom. My mother and father oohed with pleasure. Giuseppe opened the bottle and fished out the bits of lemon peel that floated to the top.

"Marco and I made this," he said. "It took a lot longer than usual because your son is slow at peeling the lemons." He described the process, then went on to explain how the procession to Madonna di Porto would play out the next day.

"You will see nothing but people," he said.

"How many people can there be?" my mother asked.

Giuseppe paused. "Usually, on average, twenty thousand."

I tried to picture that many people in the streets of Gimigliano but gave up when I realized that it was more than could fit in Madison Square Garden.

Elena began clearing the dishes, and my mom jumped up to help. I heard them at the sink, Elena speaking slow Italian to my mother, my mother responding in her native French at the same pace. At one point, my mother called me over to help translate something for her. "Mark, please tell her that I would love the recipe for the lasagna."

As I translated, Elena's face became red, and she seemed to stifle a giggle. Finally she burst out laughing. "Marco, I don't think your mother needs it; she already has one."

I was nonplussed.

Elena laughed again, then said, pointing to her breasts, "Marco, you keep asking for a nipple, not a *ricetta*, a recipe." While my father was speaking perfect dialect, I was tripping over my Italian.

After the meal we stopped off at my aunt Angela and uncle Mimmo's house to see Luisa, Sabrina, Tommaso, and Masino, whom we were supposed to accompany to the festivities in Superiore. But when we arrived, they had just been told that Mimmo's brother was in the hospital. They offered us biscotti and coffee, and we tried to console them. Then we saw them off to Catanzaro to the hospital and stopped in on Zia Caterina, who served us more biscotti and gelato and told us a story about the expensive haircut my father got in Naples when he first visited Italy. Apparently, just off the boat and not quite used to the lire, he paid three times the going rate. But the funniest story was about how my father came to Italy thinking he spoke Italian and was amazed when no one north of Naples understood him!

We kissed Caterina goodbye and went up to Gimigliano Superiore for the beginning of the festival. Martha and I peeked inside the Chiesa di San Salvatore. The *festa* was one of the few times when men participated in the work of the church. Men, and only men, were meticulously placing lilies around the feet of the statues at the base of the painting of the Madonna.

Then we joined the flow of villagers in the evening's *passeggiata*. In the piazza, tech crews set up the stage where folk music would be played the next night, followed by a rock band. The techies all wore black T-shirts.

Martha stopped and pulled at my arm. "Mark, look over there." A teenage boy was wearing a tan T-shirt that read "Critelli's Auto Body, Danbury, Conn."

We sat on the church steps and watched everyone walk past. Elena waved to us from the store, and Giuseppe stood outside smiling and greeting people as they walked by, shaking hands with the older men, and pulling down the caps of the children who passed. I felt at home.

From the far end of the *passeggiata*, a sound I remembered only from the movies—the bright notes of clarinets and booming brass behind them—echoed between the stone buildings, becoming louder as it approached. Giacomino stopped right in front of me and opened his arms. Vincenzo appeared next, along with Francesca and a few others. My friends from Gimigliano were welcoming me back to the village.

The band approached around a corner. They stopped in front of the church, and all of Gimigliano Superiore seemed to be gathered around them. They were wearing caps and navy blue uniforms, the pockets of their jackets trimmed with dull yellow piping and gold buttons. Mimmo Morante, the high school music instructor who frequented Maria's bar, led the band, playing one of eight clarinets, followed by three trombones, one of them Tonino Ventura, whom I'd met the first day on the plane to Calabria; there were two French horn players, including Stefano, the high school student who wanted to live in Toronto; six trumpet players; two saxophones; and two sousaphones. Keeping the slow, mournful pace were the four percussion instruments—a bass drum, two snares, and a crashing cymbal. On each of the two sousaphones, black letters encircled the curve of the bell, forming the words "Gimigliano, Italy." The minor notes hit me in the heart, and the clarinet wails reminded me of *The Godfather*. Mimmo Morante noticed us sitting on the steps, and with a nod and a widening of his eyes, he seemed to say hello.

The band took a break, and Mimmo came up the steps to greet us. Martha asked why it said "Italy" and not "Italia" on the sousaphones. Mimmo explained that the band sometimes traveled to Toronto to play for the festival of the Madonna di Porto there. He showed Martha the music, four-by-six-inch sheets attached to the instruments themselves, handwritten by a sheet music company down the Ionian coast in Soverato. Stefano came up, as did Tonino. He introduced us to his wife, who invited us over for dinner.

Mimmo went back to the head of the band, and the group fell into formation. The sky darkened to a deep blue as the sun dropped below the distant mountains. Tall arches of tightly wound bright yellow and red lights had been hung especially for the festival. They lighted the piazza and spidered out, leading through alleys, along roads, and down the mountain path to Gimigliano Inferiore.

LA FESTA DELLA MADONNA DI PORTO

A T SEVEN-THIRTY IN THE MORNING, all five cars of the train were packed. We wound along the mountain tracks, swaying with the curves. A soft breeze blew through the open windows; the smell of dew still hung in the air. Within half an hour we were at Gimigliano, where about half the passengers, including Martha and me, got off. We had decided to walk the procession from Gimigliano to the Madonna di Porto. The rest, including my parents, stayed on the train to the Porto, where they would await the Madonna.

By the time we got to the Chiesa S.S. Salvatore, a large crowd had already gathered. We lost hope of getting any closer, let alone going inside. There was a reverent calm in the piazza, punctuated by the squeal of children playing. Over the balconies, villagers had hung handmade blankets woven in the typical Gimiglianese herringbone pattern, some red and yellow, some white and red, others black, with red and green.

After about twenty minutes, the church doors were flung open, and the people in the piazza gasped in unison, then burst into claps and cheers. The procession sang the Ave Maria as the five-foot-high

Archiropita made its way outside and down the stairs. I could barely see the men supporting it, so Mary looked as if she were floating.

Fireworks erupted all around us, and the brass band struck up something joyfully bombastic in a major key. From the balconies, old men and women threw buckets of confetti. The young and middle-aged women cheered; the older ones cried and prayed.

Martha nudged me. "Mark, the band is playing Sousa. Wait, that's 'Stars and Stripes Forever.' "

She was right. And from that point on, the band played Sousa marches exclusively as it led the procession through the alleys of Gimigliano. Martha and I fell in at the rear. Confetti descended on our heads as we funneled through the narrow passageways. I was amazed at how many people I recognized in the crowd. I spotted Tonino's family along with a few friends of my cousins who had joined us at the restaurant in the Sila for *Pasquetta*. I waved to Maria, who owned the bar in Inferiore, and to her husband, Cecco.

"Marco, Marta!" I heard someone call out. I looked through the crowd and saw Giuseppe standing on his toes in front of his store.

Elena joined us in the procession. She pointed down in front of us. Many of the older women, and some young ones, walked the three miles to the church barefoot to demonstrate their devotion. Others compromised by wearing socks.

"I used to do that, too," Elena said.

"What made you stop?" Martha asked

"It wasn't very comfortable." Elena laughed.

The procession circled back to the piazza, and before it continued, the Madonna stopped and turned to face the crowd. Once again everyone gasped in unison; many people approached to pin hundred-thousand-lire notes to the Virgin's frame, about fifty dollars, more than a small family might spend on groceries for a week. Martha and I made our way just behind the band as the procession continued even farther above Gimigliano Superiore, to the houses of the wealthy. Soon the road turned to the left and cut through green, lush woods of chestnut and red-leafed cherry. The band played "Semper Fidelis." We passed through a tunnel of cheering people.

The band paused to catch their breath and let the Virgin and the rest of the procession catch up.

The sun rose high, and a cool wind rustled through the trees. Gimigliano fell away from us as we continued up the mountain road, passing through intense sun and patches of breezy green shade. I turned to look at the procession behind us. Older women sang; young mothers and fathers pushed baby carriages; old men casually strolled with their hands clasped behind their backs as if they were walking the *passeggiata*.

Mimmo Morante announced the next piece, another Sousa favorite, "The Washington Post March." He winked and started up the band just as the procession joined us. Behind us, the pilgrims closest to Mary were singing the Ave Maria once again. The bright brass brand at first overwhelmed the slower, unaccompanied singing, but as the mass of voices began to build, the dissonance blended pleasingly.

The road curved ahead of us, and I looked down through the chestnut trees at the valley and church. The fairground in front of the church pulsed with people circulating among rows and rows of stalls. It seemed as if tens of thousands of pilgrims had made the trip. The surrounding fields were covered with picnic blankets. I wondered how I would ever find my parents.

The band led the descent, once again at a smart clip. At a pause Mimmo joined us.

"The music last night was all Italian. Why is there so much Sousa today?" I asked.

"Sousa's music is more celebratory."

"Isn't there any upbeat music by Italian composers?"

"You need it for your book, don't you?" Mimmo said, grinning.

"It would help," I said.

Mimmo corralled the band, directed them to flip a few pages ahead, and started them playing. He walked back to me and pointed to the music, a march from Verdi's opera *Ernani*.

"*Italiano!*" he exclaimed, and ran back to the front of the band.

Martha and I had wanted a closer view of the *confruntu*, when

Joseph, who lives in the church of the Madonna di Porto year-round, greets the Virgin at the church steps. We slipped away from the procession and snaked through the endless aisles of vendors. It took us at least twenty minutes to get through.

Directly in front of the church, a man sold cards printed with reproductions of the painting, as well as rosaries, fans, and floatable key chains. There was no sign of my parents. We made our way to the front of the steps. Being taller than the old men and women who had gathered early for an optimal view, we could see over everyone. Again I looked for my parents, but every Calabrese man looked like my father: dark-skinned with sunglasses, a polo shirt, and a full head of graying hair.

The crowd parted in a wave. The Virgin Mary floated to the steps of the church. The doors behind us swung open; more confetti floated from the sky. A statue of Joseph and the child Jesus emerged from the doorway. The entire crowd of people sighed, and many held their hands to their chests.

We parted to let the statues move into position at the top of the steps. The Virgin wove her way through the crowd as Joseph and Jesus descended the steps to greet her. The three figures stopped within fifty feet of one another.

The band stopped. Chatter rumbled through the crowd of pilgrims. Then, in a single motion, Joseph and Jesus lowered themselves and, in a swift jog, swooped up to greet Mary. The crowd screamed. I thought of my grandmother participating in this same ritual forty years earlier, and for a moment I felt that she was with me. The hair on my arms rose. I looked at Martha. She was crying.

Jesus and Joseph and Mary began to circle one another in a mystical dance. The crowd let loose, an almost mournful wailing quickly giving way to elated cries. The three figures turned to face the church. Confetti poured down, the band played Sousa, and everyone joined in song as Joseph and Jesus escorted Mary to their house.

I spotted my mother standing proudly in front, a white tissue at her eyes. Beneath a chestnut tree just behind her my father alternately clicked away with his camera and wiped his own eyes with his forearm. For me, the reunion of Joseph, Jesus, and Mary was the reunion of my own family.

That evening a mile-long, candlelit parade escorted the Virgin back to Gimigliano. Fireworks lit the sky all the way across the peninsula.

The next day Giuseppe saw us off at the Gimigliano train station.

"When will we see you again?" he asked.

At that moment I didn't want to say goodbye to Giuseppe. How could I possibly have thanked him for sharing his world with me?

"Soon" was all I could say. "Probably next year or the year after."

"Yes, you tend to come every two years," Giuseppe said. *"Como l'ulivo."* Just like the olive, which bears its fruit every other year. "This year we were lucky," Giuseppe said. "You arrived like the fig—twice in the same year."

BIBLIOGRAPHY

Acton, Harold. *The Bourbons of Naples*. London: Prion, 1998.

Alarco, Mario. *Sull'identità meridionale: Forme di una cultura mediterranea*. Turin: Bollati Borenghieri, 2000.

Alvaro, Corrado. *Revolt in Aspromonte*. Translated by Frances Frenaye. New York: New Directions, 1962.

Barzini, Luigi. *The Italians*. New York: Atheneum, 1983.

Blanchard, Paul. *Blue Guide: Southern Italy*. New York: Norton, 1990, rev. 2000.

Calabria: Dal Pollino all'Aspromonte le spiagge dei due mari le città, I borghi arroccati. Milan: Touring Club Italiano, 1999.

Calogero, Alessandro. *Riflessioni su Gimigliano*. Soveria Mannelli: Calabria Letteraria Editrice, 2000.

Calvino, Italo. *Italian Folktales*. New York: Harcourt, Inc., 1980.

Cornelisen, Ann. *Women of the Shadows: Wives and Mothers of Southern Italy*. South Royalton, Vt.: Steerforth Press, 2001.

Croce, Benedetto. *History of the Kingdom of Naples*. Translated by Frances Frenaye. Chicago: University of Chicago Press, 1965.

Curci, Vincenzo. *Prodotti tipici della terra di Calabria*. Castrovillari: Edizioni Prometeo, 2000.

Donzelli, Claudio. *Magna Grecia di Calabria*. Rome: Meridiana Libri, 1997.

Douglas, Norman. *Old Calabria*. Marlboro, Vt.: Marlboro Press, 1993.

Duggan, Christopher. *A Concise History of Italy*. Cambridge: Cambridge University Press, 1994.

Facaros, Dana, and Michael Pauls. *Bay of Naples & Southern Italy*. London: Cadogan, 1999.

Finley, Milton. *The Most Monstrous of Wars: The Napoleonic Guerrilla War of Southern Italy, 1806–1811*. Columbia: University of South Carolina Press, 1994.

Gabaccia, Donna R. *Italy's Many Diasporas*. Seattle: University of Washington Press, 2000.

Gardiner, Leslie. *South to Calabria*. London: William Blackwood, 1968.

Gissing, George. *By the Ionian Sea: Notes of a Ramble in Southern Italy*. Evanston, Ill.: Marlboro Press, 1996.

Harrison, Barbara Grizzuti. *Italian Days*. New York: Atlantic Monthly Press, 1989.

Hinton, Amanda. *Visitor's Guide: Southern Italy*. Edison, N.J.: Hunter, 1993.

Holmes, George. *The Oxford History of Italy*. Oxford: Oxford University Press, 1997.

Homer. *The Odyssey*. Translated by Albert Cook. New York: Norton, 1974.

Lamannis, Domenico. *Gimigliano*. Catanzaro Lido: Vincenzo Ursini Editore, 2000.

Laruffa, Domenico. *Incontro con la Calabria*. Reggio Calabria: Laruffa Editore, 1996.

Laurino, Maria. *Were You Always an Italian?* New York: Norton, 2000.

Levi, Carlo. *Christ Stopped at Eboli*. Translated by Frances Frenaye. New York: Farrar, Straus & Giroux/Noonday, 1996.

Lonely Planet. *Italy*. Victoria, Australia: Lonely Planet, 2000.

Mangione, Jerre, and Ben Morreale. *La Storia*. New York: HarperCollins, 1992.

Mazza, Antonino. *The Way I Remember It*. Edited by Antonio D'Alfonso. Montreal: Guernica Editions Inc., 1992.

Morton, H. V. *A Traveller in Southern Italy*. New York: Dodd, Mead & Co., 1987.

Palmer, Mary Amabile. *Cucina di Calabria*. Boston: Faber & Faber, 1997.

Placanica, Augusto. *Storia della Calabria*. Rome: Donzelli Editore, 1999.

Ramage, Craufurd Tait. *Ramage in Italy*. Edited by Edith Clay. Chicago: Academy Publishers, 1987.

Root, Waverley. *The Food of Italy*. New York: Vintage Books, 1992.

Spezzano, Francesco. *Proverbi Calabresi*. Florence: Giunti Gruppo Editoriale, 1998.

Talese, Gay. *Unto the Sons*. New York: Knopf, 1992.

Vecoli, Rudolph J. "The Italian Diaspora, 1876–1976." In *The Cambridge Survey of World Migration*. Cambridge: Cambridge University Press, 1995.

Virgil. *The Aeneid*. Translated by Robert Fitzgerald. New York: Vintage, 1990.

Walston, James. *The Mafia and Clientelism: Roads to Rome in Post-war Calabria*. London: Routledge Press, 1988.

ACKNOWLEDGMENTS

When I first traveled to Calabria, I couldn't have guessed that the stories my father told me about the place and our family there would ever be committed to paper, much less that I would soon have Calabrese stories of my own to tell. That I now do is owing especially to the generosity of the Calabresi, who made my journey a soulful adventure. To all of them, *tante grazie*, with a warm thank-you to the people who have been, so to speak, my traveling companions:

To the Critellis and Rotellas in Gimigliano and Milan for their welcoming embrace, and to the Rotellas in Danbury for their love.

To Giuseppe Chiarella and his family, who, while not blood, took me in as if I were, and showed me a Calabria I would never have found on my own.

To my sister, Michelle, who, while home with her children, was with us in spirit; to my mother, for her sense of adventure; and to my father, for his pride and his bounty of stories, and for letting himself be cajoled into returning to our ancestral home in the first place.

To Maria Massie, who first encouraged me to write about Calabria, and to Alexis Hurley, for her help and enthusiasm along the way.

Many thanks go to Paul Elie for his thoughtful guidance, critical eye, and friendship; and to Becky Saletan, an indispensable guide on the last leg of the journey.

To Susan Mitchell and Abby Kagan, for their artistic grasp of things Calabrese, to fellow Calabrese Steven Arcella for his map of our region, to Elisabeth Calamari for her professional *vivacità*, and to Cecily Parks for always knowing the answer.

To my colleagues at *Publishers Weekly* and *Library Journal*, with particular thanks to Jeff Zaleski.

To Natalie Danford for her time and advice, and to Rebecca Miller, Stephen Morrow, Carl Zimmer, and the poker gang for lending their ears to my stories.

Most of all, I thank my wife, Martha, without whose eye for detail and endless love and encouragement I would never have been able to write this book. A Calabrese in spirit, Martha helped me to see the subtle beauty of the region I can now call home.